IMPOSSIBLE
my story

IMPOSSIBLE
my story

STAN WALKER

with Margie Thomson

HarperCollins*Publishers*

HarperCollins*Publishers*
Australia • Brazil • Canada • France • Germany • Holland • Hungary
India • Italy • Japan • Mexico • New Zealand • Poland • Spain • Sweden
Switzerland • United Kingdom • United States of America

First published in 2020
by HarperCollins*Publishers* (New Zealand) Limited
Unit D1, 63 Apollo Drive, Rosedale, Auckland 0632, New Zealand
harpercollins.co.nz

A catalogue record for this book is available from the National Library of New Zealand.

ISBN 978 1 7755 4147 9 (pbk)
ISBN 978 1 7754 9178 1 (ebook)

Cover design by Mark Campbell, HarperCollins Design Studio
Front cover image by Raf Wetere
Back cover image by Damien Nikora
Typeset in Adobe Garamond Pro by Kirby Jones
Printed and bound in Australia by McPherson's Printing Group
The papers used by HarperCollins in the manufacture of this book are a natural, recyclable
product made from wood grown in sustainable plantation forests. The fibre source and
manufacturing processes meet recognised international environmental standards, and carry
certification.

Akiaki te tī o te tangata

Nurture the indescribable light in a person

CONTENTS

I am the mountain

Ko au tō maunga, tū tonu
Ko te moana pari mai koe
Ko koe te awa i taku remu, ko tāua anō tāua
Nō te one i Kurawaka, hei tiaki i te whenua nei
I am the mountain, you are the sea flowing toward me
You are the river that runs through me, I am her, she is me
Created from dust and sand, born to lead this land

— 'Aotearoa'

I AM EIGHT YEARS OLD, ALL SKINNY AND WILD, DRESSED in yesterday's clothes. My body bruised, my feet bare. It's early morning and I'm by myself on the top of my mountain, Mangatawa, the hill that rises behind my home at Tamapahore Marae in Tauranga Moana. From where I stand, I see all of this sacred land spreading below me. I see across the blue of Te Tāhuna o Rangataua, the blue that fills up the whole world. I know that down there in the early morning haze are the other nearby marae I'm also connected to — Matapihi, Maungatapu, Te Whetū o te Rangi — and I can see right across it all to the distant, rounded cone of Mauao.

I've dreamed of this place, this moment, ever since my whānau left to live in Australia four years earlier. Four years, half my lifetime.

I've missed this hill. I've missed breathing this air. I've missed my home. I dream of it constantly. Away from it, I feel empty and lost and out of place.

It's early winter and the grass is chilly, wet with dew, and my feet feel this ground in the same way that the trees around me put their roots down into it. My people have lived here for hundreds of years, and my spirit knows it. There I am, just a little kid, reconnecting with home, my tūrangawaewae, my standing ground. Smelling, breathing, dreaming.

I remember that morning so well. I woke up really early, went outside and stood in the middle of the narrow gravel road that runs between our house and the marae, looking up at that hill. No one else up yet, the marae itself peaceful — deserted and yet filled with the presence of the world that's beyond our senses. It was all right there, as it had been in my dreams.

I easily made my way up past the wharekai, dining area, past the old club building, round towards the urupā, the burial ground, so peaceful, overlooked by the hill and the trees. It's a place I always feel very safe; us kids love to play in there, lying on sun-warmed graves and talking to our beloved dead. But this morning, I didn't go in. I jumped over the fence and walked straight up the hill.

I always had this yearning for home, just to smell it and breathe it and be in it. It's hard to articulate and explain what it is for indigenous people, for tangata whenua, the people of the land — this ultimate connection. Maybe it's like when babies smell their mother's milk and they know where they come from. They've been connected for nine months and they ain't going to just disconnect. They know their source.

It's like that for me this morning. Nothing has changed. In this moment, at the top of the hill, I delete Australia from my mind. Even the burden I've told no one about but which is waiting for me like a snake for when I get back there, and which I'll carry as a dark, disgusting self-loathing for years to come — in this moment it vanishes into the early morning air. All the other usual stuff — the violence that means my body is always a palette of bruises, new purple ones, old yellow ones, the fear that soaks into every aspect of my life

— is nothing to worry about now. Those things are lost in the birdsong, in the familiar trees still standing where I last saw them, in the taste of the feijoas that I pick and eat as I walk, in my little-boy dreams that I dream as I wander along.

I am alive.

I look around at the enormous world expanding on all sides, and my head fills with the thought that I am on a stage. The world is green and blue and grey, only a few cows chomping nearby, but in my mind there are thousands of people, a massive stage. The spotlight is on me. And I sing. Sing my heart out. It's like freedom. It's the expression of everything that's in me. And in my imagination, the crowd roars out my name and cheers and claps.

That little eight-year-old kid. Me. My daydream, nobody else's and nobody can touch it. Nobody can take it.

On my way back down the hill, I find me a cool stick to have an adventure with, whacking at bushes and trees, pretending it's a gun, maybe a taiaha, a spear. When I get home, my dad takes the stick and says he'll use it on me later. I know that he will. But he can't take my dream.

In reality, the chances of anything good happening in my life are virtually nil. I am already a statistic. What is the likely outcome for a kid whose parents have both been in jail? My world from my earliest being has been filled with drugs and violence and sex — things no kid should even know about. Our kitchen cupboards never have enough in them. My chances in life are not pointing in the direction of any hope at all.

But I am the impossible made possible.

My whānau is the impossible made possible.

I'm ready to tell my story.

CHAPTER ONE

Black box

There's a little black box, yeah
Somewhere in the ocean
Holding all the truth about us
It's a little black box
A record of emotion
Everything that ever was

— 'Black Box'

'AND THE WINNER ... OF *AUSTRALIAN IDOL* ... IS ...'

'It's you,' I mouthed to the other finalist, Hayley Warner. 'It's you,' she mouthed back at me. We were clinging to each other as the wait went on and on — nearly ten seconds. A lifetime.

I was waiting for Hayley's name to be called out.

'Stan Walker!'

My name. It was me! The programme host Andrew Günsberg actually said my name. I was stunned. I can see it when I watch the video footage — I jolted as if I'd been zapped with electricity. Everyone else was screaming and jumping, but I stood there in a daze.

'This is it, Stan,' Andrew kept saying. 'This is it!'

We were on a huge stage set up outside the Sydney Opera House on a sticky-hot night, the sky shifting from pink to purple to dark. The Opera House and the Sydney Harbour Bridge were silhouetted behind us, and in front of us were 6000 people, just like I'd imagined all those years before when I was singing on my hill. Filling the air was the high-pitched screaming and cheering of our supporters — those who wanted me to win, and those who wanted the prize to go to the other finalist, the awesome Hayley Warner. From the stage, I could just see — caught in the lights, arms raised, hands waving — signs that said my name over and over, and I could hear that people were yelling my name.

How can you go in the space of just a few weeks from being a nobody — a guy who left school at sixteen and who worked part-time in a men's clothing store — to being someone more than a million people are watching and screaming for?

My whānau was there, my parents — yes, even my dad — seated in honour near the front. Three hundred other family members had travelled from all around Australia and New Zealand to support me.

It was the beginning of everything. It was *the* moment, as Andrew keep saying. *It.* The big pivotal moment in my life. There was before, and there is after, but it all hinged on that moment when the doors opened for me. I entered the music industry, like going through the wardrobe into Narnia, or through the looking glass into Wonderland, and everything changed.

Get ready, I want to say to that boy now. *Get ready. Arm yourself.*

Look at me then. I was so young. So little. I don't even look like me. For most of the competition, I was eighteen years old, but I had turned nineteen less than a month before that final night. I was a little bit chubby. For the first few auditions, I even had a rat's tail. It used to be really long but I bleached it until a lot of it broke off. It was my pride and joy, but everyone on the programme thought it was disgusting so in the end I had to cut it off. It was a fashion statement, or maybe a cultural statement, that whispered of a different kind of life, the life I had come from. It was totally out of place in the world that was now embracing me.

When I look back now, that me seems very clean and fresh. Innocent. Because I had become a Christian just a few months before Idol, I had left a lot of my self-disgust and hatred behind me, and so at that time I felt … pure. I wouldn't mind feeling that fresh again. Now I've been in the industry for ten years — feels like twenty, even thirty, because so much happens and everything is magnified — I've changed hard-out. I'm definitely more cynical and sceptical now, but I've learned heaps and I've found how to be the Stan Walker I want to be.

When Andrew G. shouted my name, my family out there in the audience broke into a haka, all 300 of them, causing a real commotion. I wanted to just stop and be there for them as they did that for me, but at the same time Andrew was pushing on, telling me I was now signed to Sony Music.

'You're signed to Sony Music, Stan.' He had to say it twice. I hardly heard him. All I could think of was my whānau, my family, and what this meant for all of us, but the industry was already dragging me into its own orbit.

Before the haka was even done, the beginning of 'Black Box' started and that was it — the sky behind me exploded in pyrotechnic colour and the next season of my life had begun.

* * *

Little kids want to fly, they want to explore to the bottom of the ocean, they want to go to the moon. For me, I wanted to sing like I saw Guy Sebastian sing on *Australian Idol* back in 2002, when I was twelve years old.

Getting on Idol was my dream ever since then. We were living in Hamilton, New Zealand, by that stage, and the whole family would watch — my mum April, my papa Ross, my two older brothers Mike and Russ, my little brother Noah and my baby sister Mary-Grace, and whoever else was living with us at the time — all sitting in the lounge together, rooting for our favourites, yelling at the TV.

This is what I'm gonna do. Right there, it became my dream, the day when I would be the one getting accolades, dreaming that people would love my voice, dreaming of meeting all my idols like Adeaze, Che Fu, Dave Dobbyn, Beyoncé and JoJo. Dreaming of using my voice to save my people, having money, buying my own clothes, my own furniture, my own house. This is what Idol was to kids like me. I came from poverty. I was the kid who stole other kids' lunches out of their schoolbags. I'd been suspended from every school I'd ever been to. So, Idol was a jumping board for dreams. The hope that life could be different, that anything was possible.

Where we grew up, we had to be *given* an opportunity because we didn't know how to get it otherwise. That's what Idol was for me.

Ever since I was a little kid I loved to sing. It was my comfort, the thing I did when I was by myself, when I was sad, when I was happy, when I was silly. When I was a child, and even a teenager, when times were the toughest and life seemed hopeless, I got comfort from singing myself to sleep. I *found* myself in singing.

But I didn't have any understanding about how I could make it my life. I'd never had a singing lesson. I didn't know anything about success. I didn't have any understanding of that word 'career' and how to achieve one. It was all a complete mystery to me.

In the ad breaks, and after the show, I'd get up and sing. I'd leave the room, then come back in like I was walking on stage, and I'd say, 'Kia ora, my name is Stan and this is the song I'm going to sing. And you're going to listen!' And my family would listen, cracking up, going, 'Oh, yo!' Cheering like it was the real thing. We had a lot of hard times, but we had some really cool times, too, like that, when we would laugh a lot.

In the lounge at home, I sang 'Circle of Life', from the movie *Lion King* — my favourite song ever, from my favourite movie of all time. That song carried me all through my childhood, from when I was really little watching the movie every day, first on video and later on DVD. That movie's got it all — redemption, forgiveness, aroha, friendship, whanaungatanga. Way back then, at just twelve, I decided I'd sing 'Circle of Life' for my Idol audition, and I practised it from then on.

The other one I knew right away that I wanted to sing at my Idol audition was Metallica's 'Nothing Else Matters'. It's such a close song to me, a song with a lot of pain in it, like it was a song about me, my life.

I had it all planned, way back then, and I never changed my plan. Six years later, those were the exact songs I sang for my audition. I was prepared. I'd got myself prepared, not really understanding what I was preparing myself for. Man, it was such a crazy thing.

Night after night, Guy made it through the eliminations and I watched, so excited, thinking: *One day I'm gonna be there.*

* * *

At the end of that Idol final night, the cover of my first album popped up on screen. *Introducing Stan Walker.* A huge image of me: Stan Walker, me and not me, me but more than me. It was exciting, trippy, and a bit confusing.

I had been Stan Walker my whole life, but now I was 'Stan Walker' — a product of other people's imagination, an image created by an industry.

That night, I sang what was to be my first single — a song called 'Black Box'. It had been chosen for me by the show's producers, not something I had much of a say in. I just went with it, although it wasn't a song I would have chosen for myself. I didn't feel it really made the most of my voice. But at the same time, right then, it was so exciting. *This is the first song coming out that's going to be mine. It's going to be on the radio.*

And, in fact, it went on to sell 15,000 copies in its first week.

Despite my feelings about it, it was my beginning, my first industry success. And the words do actually have some resonance with my life.

Some weeks before the final, when there were still nine of us left in the competition, I had sung Prince's 'Purple Rain', a song that's all about music as a redemptive force, and it made me think a lot about me and my mum, and the relationships within my family. After I'd sung, judge Ian Dickson said that even though I was a 'giggle monster' backstage, I made singing that song seem so easy.

'I think it's because you hardwire your heart to every song that you sing,' he said.

I didn't contradict him at the time, but it's not really true. It's true that when I sing it's the most articulate expression of me. It feels like freedom. It feels beautiful to sing — if I don't crack! But when I sing, my heart doesn't have to feel those feelings at that moment for my voice to carry pain, or love, or any other feeling within the song. My voice is the instrument. It holds the record of everything.

My voice is like my own little black box that carries all my memories. My voice takes all the things that have happened to me and finds a purpose for it all. It spins my straw into gold. That's been our life story — not just me, but my mum and dad and our whole family.

It's been over ten years since that moment and I've worked hard to build my career — I've written so many songs, released five albums and acted in five movies … but I'll always be the guy who won *Australian Idol*, and I was blessed to get that opportunity. Winning that show back in 2009, just ten years on from being that little kid with the impossible dream singing to the cows on Mangatawa, was the moment I became this new Stan Walker.

When Michael Bublé came on and met the Idol contestants, one of the things he said to us was: 'Never forget where you came from. Never forget who you were before this.'

I will never forget.

* * *

'Boys,' I remember my mum saying to me and my cousin Kaha when we were about ten and had been fighting, 'don't you ever forget, blood will always be thicker than water.'

Blood *is* thicker than water. My whānau is at my very core. There's no danger of me forgetting that. It gives me everything that's important to me in my identity. It's where I look for love, for belonging, for meaning. Yet it was the biggest part of the chaos and pain in my early years. Most of the shocking stuff that happened to me when I was a little kid happened within my whānau.

Some parts of my story seem confusing, I know. Things that are totally contradictory live right up alongside each other. Bad moments live right up against good moments. Poverty lives right up against riches. Violence lives right up against love. Sexual abuse lives right up against incredible togetherness.

I can't make sense of it all. I just accept that that's how it is. Maybe that's why I've managed to survive in the music industry for so long, because it too is full of contradictions: the highest of highs, the lowest of lows. But the bad stuff doesn't cancel out the good stuff, and the good stuff doesn't mean the bad stuff never happened.

When I won Idol, my whole family won. It's just incredible to see how far we've come.

CHAPTER TWO

I am a seed, born of greatness

He kākano āhau
I ruia mai i Rangiātea
And I can never be lost
I am a seed, born of greatness
Descended from a line of chiefs,
He kākano āhau

— 'He Kākano Āhau'

THE SOUNDS OF MY CHILDHOOD. ENDLESS MUSIC. Always singing. Whether it was the voices of my aunties, or the sound of all our voices together; whether it was the hymns of the Rātana Church, the traditional karanga, kapa haka, 'Whakaaria Mai' or a song by Renée Geyer, there was always music, and always someone with a guitar.

It's part of Māori culture. Any occasion, whether it's formal or informal, there's a song. If there's a speech, there's a song. If there's food, there's singing. If there's a funeral, there's singing. Birthdays, weddings — any kind of party, there's singing.

I was always fascinated by the sound of our language. Maybe because things were so difficult in my home, from my very earliest times I used to always hang with the nannies up on the marae and that's where the sound of our language was thick in the air. My great-grandmother Ngawaiwera was the kaikaranga for our marae, the woman who called visitors on to the marae at the start of the pōwhiri, the formal welcome. I loved the sound of her voice singing the karanga, and I have a memory from when I must have been nearly three, of standing next to her, right next to her legs, at the top of the steps leading to the wharenui, the meeting house. She was dressed all in black, with her black scarf on her head, and I copied her with a tea towel or a colourful shirt to cover my hair, singing in my little child's voice, trying to follow her lead. I wasn't meant to do that, and probably some people thought it was wrong, but most people would have just thought it was funny.

The female elders, or kuia, would wail in their beautiful, eerie way, and then as soon as they finished they did their harirū, all going around to greet each other, and next thing they're laughing and eating their mints; then all of a sudden they're popping their gums and they've got no teeth! Next we go and have a kaputī, and these little old kuia, all in black, some of them not so little, would be dipping their bread in the tea and eating.

From my very earliest existence, I have heard our language and it made me feel special. I watched the kaumātua as they spoke Māori together. They never spoke English. They would always be laughing. I still love it.

The reo, the language, and the music are the two things that were like the air that I breathed in since forever.

Man, those parties. There was a club next to the marae that would open up on Thursdays and Fridays, and the grown-ups would sit in there, having their ciggies, big brown bottles of beer on the tables, guitars playing and their voices singing together. Us kids could hear it from outside. We'd be hanging around, trying to scab money off them, or get them to buy us chocolate bars — Caramel Chews or Peanut Slabs. Those drunk koros were good for getting stuff off.

'Can I have two dollars, Koko?'

'Here you go, boy.'

And then you'd ask the next one, 'Oh, Uncle Tahi, can I have two dollars?'

Or there'd be parties at someone's house — our house, often, a rage we used to call them, back in the day, with all the aunties and uncles and cousins. Same thing — the crates of big brown bottles, and I'd just be running around being a little mischief, little kid, playing with my cousins, doing whatever we did. They'd be singing party songs. Renée Geyer. I thought she was black, but then I found out she was this white Australian woman. She just resonated: those songs, her voice, her tone. It sounded like *us*. *It only happens when I look at you* ... Every single Māori person, I guarantee you, will know that song. It was an anthem for us.

Do you know that scene in *Once Were Warriors* when Jake and Beth are partying and singing? That's just like it was for us, guitar out, everyone good-drunk and happy. In the movie, their daughter Grace goes, 'I love it when they're like this.' Because that was beautiful. It was really beautiful. You just saw people happy and you would hope that it would stay like that.

It never stayed like that.

People would end up getting wasted. It would always end bad for my mum. My dad would end up in a fight, and by the end of the night she'd be getting a hiding, getting crashed and smashed around the house, us kids right in the middle of it, quite likely getting smashed too. If we didn't get smashed then, say I'd gone to stay at my koko's like I often did, I would probably get a hiding the next day for doing something stupid that was really nothing.

This is the way it was for us. The two sides of our lives. The beauty and the violence; the richness and the poverty; the love and the hate. Everything, but nothing.

18

After the parties there would be photos of all the laughs, all the good times. But there wouldn't be any photos of the hidings. Everyone knew about it but those things have a way of being secret. People pull their curtains and pretend it's not happening.

* * *

I grew up at Tamapahore Marae in Tauranga, on the lower slopes of Mangatawa. Even though I was born in Melbourne, where my parents had gone in search of a new beginning, we came back almost immediately and stayed till I was four. Then we came back again when I was nine and stayed for another couple of years. In between, we were in Australia. But when I was eight, we came back for a brief visit because Koko — my grandfather, my mother's father — was dying, and that was the time I wrote about at the very beginning of this book. Mangatawa is where my story begins, but it has its own history, too, and its history is mine, so really my story began long before I was born.

The story of Mangatawa is this. Long ago, a whale and her baby came into the harbour and swam up past Te Pāpā and Matapihi toward Maungatapu. Finding the water becoming too shallow, they tried to return to deeper water but instead turned into the Rangataua arm of the harbour, between Matapihi and Maungatapu. They could hear the ocean waves pounding on the beach at Ōmanu and Pāpāmoa, but as they struggled over the mudflats towards the open sea, they stopped, exhausted, at Karikari on the eastern shore of Rangataua. There they drank from a magic spring whose water transformed the mother whale into Mangatawa, gazing northward out to sea; her baby, nestled in beside her, became the smaller hill beside Mangatawa, on the Pāpāmoa side.

The father whale followed them into Tauranga Moana, looking for them. He also drank at the spring at Karikari and was transformed into the high rounded hill south of Mangatawa that's called Kopukairoa.

And yes, through all the centuries up until the 1950s, Mangatawa really did look like a whale gazing out to sea. Unfortunately, Mangatawa looks much less like a whale now because the northern end, Maungamana, the eye of the whale, was taken by the Ministry of Works and Development in 1946 and turned into a quarry.

The hill that was quarried was the site of an ancient pā, an ancient Māori village, where Kahungunu lived before he emigrated to the East Coast and founded his tribe down there. The bones of those buried over past centuries were within that land, exposed by the quarrying. Some were removed with dignity, but we believe the bones of the oldest ancestors were quarried along with the rock and now lie within the highways and bridges that criss-cross Tauranga today.

The blasting from the quarry could be easily felt at the marae. Rocks often landed in the paddocks we farmed around the quarry. This is well within living memory and I have often heard the story of the quarry, and felt the sadness of the land my whole life.

When the Tauranga Harbour Bridge was opened in 1988, built from the rock and bones dug out of our land, we, along with everyone else, had to pay tolls to use the bridge.

Grievance and sadness lingers in our hearts and minds. It's the icing on the cake, the final insult after everything that went before. To see our land desecrated is quite literally soul-destroying. I feel the land is mamae, so sad, and if our tūpuna, our ancestors, were here I know they would be sad, too.

Even today, visiting Tamapahore, I feel like I'm coming home. The blue of Tauranga is a welcome-home kind of blue for me — warming, calming. I go there to visit my Nanny Maybelle, who lives literally a stone's throw from the house I grew up in. There is still nothing more beautiful to me than looking at my hill from my nan's house on a summer's day, on a hot day when there's no clouds. Just like that little eight-year-old kid, I still love standing at the top of the hill. My favourite time is in the afternoon before the sun goes down, and it's still, and I can see Mount Maunganui across the harbour, and I feel tau. I feel still.

The older I get, the more I appreciate nature, views, the ocean, the land. As a kid you don't have the words for it all, but I always knew, *I love this, this is my hill, my home.*

If I walk around near Nanny Maybelle's house, I can see the driveway leading from what was Koko's house, down to the house we lived in. I see my old bedroom window that I used to climb out of — pretty much as soon as I could walk, whenever I got a hiding or got sent to my room, which was every day, I'd be out that window, fingers hanging onto the ledge, knees banging against the weatherboards, then dropping to the ground below. Then I'd run as fast as I could, straight to Koko's house and he'd always take me in. He'd say, in his gentle, playful voice, 'Oh, come in. Come in, you little tit,' and either tuck me up in bed if it was late, or make me some food like porridge or cornflakes — he'd pour milk on the cornflakes and put it in the microwave. Hot cornflakes. It was yum as.

Growing up on the marae was growing up in a village. All our next-door neighbours, every house was our family. Everyone is descended from the three brothers who had the first houses up there. My mum comes from one, my dad comes from another. Their grandfathers were brothers, so my mum and dad are second cousins. They lived in the village together. We mock them about that. I say to my mum, 'How the hell?'

She goes, 'I hated your father. We all hated him. But one night, we were drunk, he looked good ...'

And I'm like, 'Yuck, Mum!'

First, my dad's side. His father came from Tauranga and also from Ruatōria on the East Coast, and was one of fifteen siblings. The woman he married, my grandmother, was one of twenty-three siblings; she came from Rūātoki in the Urewera. So on Pāpā's side I am Ngāi Te Rangi, Ngāti Porou, Ngāi Tūhoe. My great-great-grandmother on that side — that is, my grandmother's grandmother, Ngapera Black (Taahu) — was one of the last kuia moko in Tūhoe, that is, one of the last to receive the ancient tradition of female facial tattooing. She was just an incredible woman who right into her eighties rode her horse from Rūātoki to Tauranga. She was a nurse for her community; so was her daughter, who managed to work as well as having twenty-three kids. Ngapera passed away at the age of ninety-six in 1982, just two weeks after receiving a Queen's Service Medal for her community work. She was a founding member of the Māori Women's Welfare League in Rūātoki. I am very proud of her. I wore her korowai, a type of cloak, when I MC'd the Vodafone New Zealand Music Awards in 2018. When I stay with my whānau in Rūātoki, I stay in a house adjacent to the big old family home that she lived in most of her life, and her marae, Ōhutu, is my marae in Rūātoki.

My dad's side is very big. He's got over 150 first cousins. I sometimes feel like I'm related to everyone.

However, my dad was the only child his mother had, although I've heard that she lost eight babies. But before he was born, they had already adopted my Uncle Stan, who was actually her nephew. The concept of whāngai is normal in our culture — that's where a child is brought up by someone other than his or her birth parents, usually someone in the extended family.

There was a lot of violence in that house as my grandfather was a vicious and brutal man. He was the reason why my nan lost so many babies. As tough as my childhood was, my dad's was much worse. Anything that happened to me was a by-product of a by-product — a history of violence that we in this generation have the chance to end.

Then on my mum's side, she's one of five. Her dad was Rangimarie McLeod, my koko, the one who lived next door to us at Tamapahore and was my special person, my safe place, when I was a child.

All my grandparents are Māori but my mother's mother, Raewyn, was not brought up in Māori culture. Her father was a Punjabi Indian, her mother Māori but very English in the way she lived, so my grandmother only knew the Pākehā world. But then she met my grandfather and got pregnant at fifteen; by the age of sixteen she was married and had given birth to her first child, who was my mother. Raewyn struggled to adapt to life on the marae. Also, my mum was born with a cleft lip, so for the first six months my grandmother had to feed her with breastmilk using a teaspoon. She had two more kids a year apart and the pressure got too much for her, and she ran away.

My mum didn't see her again for many years, and instead she was brought up by her grandmother — Ngawaiwera, who I would later help do the karanga, and who was nicer to me than she was to my mum. In fact, Ngawaiwera was very hard on my poor mum because Mum looked very like Raewyn, who Ngawaiwera resented for having run away.

It wasn't until 1999, when we were living in Australia, that Raewyn finally made contact with Mum. On my ninth birthday, in Surfers Paradise, we went to see her for the first time, and she asked my mum's forgiveness. Mum had become a Christian by then, so she did forgive her, and since then Nan's been back in our lives. I still remember to this day how shocked I was looking at them side by side and seeing how similar they looked and sounded — even their mannerisms were so in sync, despite the disconnect.

I don't blame Raewyn. I feel sorry for her because she was put in this position and she didn't know what to do. She was a young girl, married with three kids. She was overwhelmed.

I once asked her: 'Nan, do you forgive yourself?'

She goes, 'No, I never can, for what I did to your mother.'

'But Nan, we forgive you.'

'But I can't forgive myself.'

Not being able to forgive yourself, or forgive others, is more toxic than smoking or alcohol, I reckon, and it seeps down through the generations just as destructively. I recognise it on people's faces — a tired, bitter look. Nan looks so much older than she is; her looks are a result of her life and how she feels about herself. When you have forgiveness, when you've forgiven people and you've forgiven yourself, you can see it in the way a person presents themselves to the world — or I can see it, anyway. It's a spiritual thing, but it also changes the way someone looks, physically. It lifts their sadness and their tiredness.

My mum has encouraged others in the family to forgive Nan, too. My mum, she holds us all together. That's what mums do. They're the pillars of the home, and she's definitely the pillar that's holding us all up.

It's interesting for me to see things in Nan that are so like my mum and me, even though we didn't grow up with her. I see so much of her in me. We're rebellious — she was the young woman, remember, who never did the things that were expected of her, for better or worse. If somebody says don't do something, we're going to do it. If somebody says do something, we're not going to do it.

I've been able to do the whakapapa for her side of the family. On one side, she's Ngāpuhi and on the other Ngāi Tahu. Her tupuna was a woman named Meri Pakinui, from Waikouaiti, whose father was a Native American sailor, William Elisha Apes, a Pequot from Massachusetts — so that's in the mix as well. I was buzzing out when I discovered that. Meri Pakinui was, among other things in her long life, one of the two midwives at the birth of what was to be the first Plunket baby, and she worked closely with Sir Truby King, the founder of the Plunket Society, so our tupuna was right at the core of the organisation that did so much for the health of mothers and babies in Aotearoa.

I'm proud of *all* that I am and who I come from, which is a melting pot of different peoples. I have Scottish, Indian and Native American ancestry, and my DNA links me all the way back to Rapa Nui (Easter Island), from where my ancestors set forth in their mighty waka hundreds of years ago.

But I am a hearty Māori. I'm a marae boy. It's all I've known and for a long time I was anti everything else. Since I've learned more about my whakapapa, I've come to be proud of all the bits of me. My whakapapa from all sides is full of fighters. Ngā mōrehu, the survivors. They always strove to take control of their own fate. They have shown great wisdom and strength.

My marae, Tamapahore, is named after our ancestor who, in the eighteenth century, led his people and the descendants of his half-brother, Te Rangihouhiri, from Matatā into Tauranga Moana. We are Ngā Pōtiki a Tamapahore, which is a subtribe of the Ngāi Te Rangi iwi, stemming from that migration more than 300 years ago.

I am descended from Tūtahi and from Nuka Taipari, two chiefs who signed the Treaty of Waitangi. I am descended from two Ngāi Te Rangi chiefs — Hone Taipari McLeod and Taiaho Hōri Ngātai — who fought and won against the British forces at Gate Pā in 1864, a famous and incredible victory, being outnumbered almost ten to one. The battle was fought where the city of Tauranga stands today, and is especially remembered for the sophistication of Māori trench warfare, and the humane treatment given to British wounded.

I am descended from Hone Taipari McLeod on both my mother's and my father's sides. Taipari's father was Scottish but he was brought up by his Māori mother. We have the McLeod crest at our marae. Scottish are like Māori — they, and the Irish, were chucked off their land, had to fight.

Taipari was an awesome warrior. *The Boy's Own* magazine of 1865 described him like this:

> We were particularly struck with the appearance of …
> a half-caste of the name of Macleod *[sic]*. His symmetry
> was as perfect as that of a Greek statue, and yet he was
> an unmitigated savage. His father, one of those roving
> Scotchmen who are to be found in every country, had
> perished in a small trading schooner, his own property,
> which had been wrecked on the coast, leaving his son
> to be brought up by his mother's tribe. It was only in
> complexion, features, and physical proportions that he
> differed from them, in everything else he was a Maori.

Following the battle of Gate Pā, Taipari continued to be influential all his long life, and was a member of the Tauranga Māori Council for many years, before he died in 1916.

The other ancestor from Gate Pā was Taiaho Hōri Ngātai, son of Tūtahi. Ngātai married one of Taipari's daughters, and my dad is descended from that marriage. My mum is also descended from Taipari, but the line is different.

Ngātai worked all his life to promote understanding between Māori and Pākehā. He is quoted with the saying:

'Let there be peace in the land.' He was a spokesman for his people, a man of peace who worked tirelessly to preserve his people's ancestral rights in the face of government legislation and local government actions that undermined the holdings and mana of Māori. About fishing rights, he told the Minister of Native Affairs John Ballance in 1885:

> I … look upon the land below high-water mark as
> being part of my own garden … . My mana over
> these places has never been taken away … . But now,
> in consequence of the word of the Europeans that
> all the land below high-water mark belongs to the
> Queen, people have trampled upon our ancient Maori
> customs.

Such beautiful language. It's like poetry. He was pre-empting the Foreshore and Seabed Act by more than 100 years. I'm proud that my tūpuna were so strong and intelligent and strategic. Nothing has been given up without a struggle. We fought long and hard against the establishment of the quarry on our land and, although we failed to prevent it, we got a better deal than had been originally offered. When the local council used the existence of the quarry to then put, first, a rubbish dump, then a reservoir, and then sewerage ponds on or right by our land, we still did everything we could to prevent such things happening. Many of my kaumātua were a part of the Ngā Tamatoa activist group in the 1970s, fighting for te reo Māori, the Māori language, to be taught in schools, and for recognition and recompense for things that had been taken from us.

I'm so lucky and blessed to have sat with all my nannies, listening to their stories of those old and more recent struggles, and asking questions. And now that older generation is dying. Both my nannies have died. And when they die they take that knowledge with them, gone forever. So many take our old people for granted. We need to sit with them and love them and learn from them. People are going on Google and reading books when we've got *actual people* from the past still living among us — people who had experiences, who saw things, who lived it, and who carry the stories of even earlier times. I'm the question-master when it comes to old people. I love to know.

* * *

Karikari, where the three whales drank from the magic spring, was a special place for our whānau. There is still a spring there called Te Waiū o te Tohorā, the milk of the whale, and sometimes the water flowing from it is actually white, as if it's the milk from the whale. But that land is special in my memory for a couple of other reasons.

Right on the shore, between the base of Mangatawa and the Rangataua estuary, there's a broad strip of flat land where we'd all go to camp in the summer. My nan, my dad's mother, would stay down there in her caravan all summer, and everybody else would come and go, pitching their tents, sleeping in cars and vans. My mum was too busy to come, and my dad wouldn't come down, so I'd go with my Uncle Stan and Aunty Leonie, and we'd all sleep together in their van. We'd put the nets out for mullet when the tide went right out, us kids helping the grown-ups, and that's how we learned. We'd go floundering, dragging the net around and spearing the fish, or looking for cockles. Or we'd go whitebaiting in the streams and put out the hīnaki to get eels. Then we'd bring it all in and everything would be cooked at the campfire. Maybe there'd be a guitar down there, and us kids would just play our games, living this outside life, running around in the dusk like little lambs.

My Koro Whetu, along with the help of my uncles and cousins, eventually built a bach down there for my nan and that's where she lived before she died, living off the land, only having a long drop, no electricity. She grew her own veggies, put her nets out for fish. She had everything she needed. We all wanted to pamper her but she'd be like, 'I don't need anything.' That was her. I would have done anything for her but she had everything she wanted.

That area is where the old Tamapahore Marae used to be, before it was moved to its current location in 1957. The old marae was very historic. It's where Tamapahore himself used to live, and there was a fully carved meeting house there — carvings from it are now in the Tauranga Heritage Collection. In the nineteenth century, the marae at Karikari was often visited by the Māori kings, and large and important gatherings were held there. It's hard to imagine now — there's no trace of that old meeting house. In the last few years it's got overgrown, big clumps of kikuyu grass and gorse and regenerating cabbage trees, as if it's been forgotten.

The nearby urupā, much older than the one near our current marae, is one of the most peaceful places you can imagine. No one's been buried there since the early 1950s and it feels like time itself has stopped — very different even from when I was a kid camping down there. Nothing but birdsong, the lapping of the water in the estuary, the breeze in the trees and that stillness that comes in special places like that.

Those summers of camping seem so long ago now. A different time. Everything's changed. People have changed. Everybody's grown up. Many of the people we used to camp with have died.

Sometimes I miss those carefree days.

That estuary, Rangataua, is the waterway that connects all our marae throughout the area. At low tide, you can walk to Mangatapu, Matapihi, even to Tauranga — it's a long walk, but you can if you want to. When we were kids we felt like the estuary was the street that we all lived on.

Being a kid at Tamapahore was to be always in a gang — a moving crowd of cousins. In the summer, there could be thirty or forty of us kids. We'd collect up our cardboard boxes and take them up the hill and slide down, seeing who could go fastest. Just the smell of that dry grass; you'd fall off and get burns, then get up and do it all again. You rumble and tumble and mock each other about who's got the best cardboard. You laugh the whole time and next time there's five of you on the same cardboard and you all crash down.

Or we'd be trying different ways to fly down with umbrellas, using them like wings, wearing the umbrella like a skirt.

Just looking around at all your cousins. I can hardly believe it when people tell me they only have three or four cousins. I only know the multitudes of family that you can just go do anything with, live with. All our cousins, we are brothers and sisters. First, second, third cousins — we didn't know the distinctions, or care about them. Blood is blood. If you have even one drop of shared blood, you are family. I've got cousins who are black as the night and cousins who are white as the day, with blue eyes and everything in between, and there's no difference. They were our best friends, they were our enemies, they were everything. They're the gang that's got your back for life.

Back then, on the hill with our cousins, we actually had no cares in the world. Even though there might have been stuff back in the village, getting hidings, seeing adult things we should never have been exposed to, up there on the hill we were just kids. We were kids being kids.

We spent most of our days climbing avocado trees, building huts in the orchards, having wars. We chased the calves and tackled them, and tried to ride them because they weren't fast enough to get away from us yet. You'd stay on as long as you could hold on and then you'd fall off, crashing to the ground. They were still little, and so were we. We played hide and seek in the corn maize. Imagine what it looked like: all these native kids running around the hill every which way. We'd pack our little backpacks and go walking over the hill on a journey, down the back to the estuary, two or four or ten of us.

We almost knew every inch of that hill. The curves, the bumps, where to go, where not to go. That whole hill was our playground.

Or we'd run through the orchard and into the urupā and dare each other to touch the electric fence, and some would be crying, but even that, we loved it. And if we were feeling lazy we'd lie around on the graves and talk to our whānau who were resting there. We knew who everybody was, even from when we were little kids. Oh, that's our aunty and uncle, that's our great grandmother … for us it's never been a scary thing. It's very different to those grey, gothic graveyards that are haunting and old school. This is a warm place, on our own land, with our hill rising up behind it, and we were just saying hello to our family.

And the thing is, that urupā has grown so much, even in my lifetime. We are a family that has known so much death, so much cancer because of a hereditary mutated gene; more than twenty-five from that alone in my lifetime, and so much tragedy — suicides, car accidents. The fences around the urupā have been pushed out, the number of graves increases too quickly. Maybe that's why I am not afraid of death or the urupā — it's full of people who I remember or heard stories about. It's like another room in our house.

Whenever there was a funeral all the kids would just run straight to what we called the bed — it's a big, flat grave, stony but nice and warm. It belongs to Tautoko McLeod, my grandmother's little brother. He was the youngest in the family to die of cancer, at just 16, way back in 1972. He's been lying here quietly ever since, with the trees whispering, the birds singing to him, hearing the sound of children's voices above him. He is not forgotten. He is known still.

When I die, I want to be buried here. I want to be buried right on top of the hill with a huge, big-as monument. Huge. Here I am. Here I lay. I. Layeth. Here!

In those days of childhood, of feeling the grass under my feet as I explored the bounds of our land, if I looked out from Mangatawa to the east, towards the ocean at Pāpāmoa Beach, I'd just see more of the same — green paddocks, our trees and animals, all the way to the sea. Now, there's a four-lane motorway and overpasses, and when you turn off the motorway at Pāpāmoa, if you're driving to Tamapahore, all you see is endless grey — the sprawl of roofs and suburban development that now lies between us and the sea. But back in the day, when I was little, that was still our land, our farm, and we'd all pile onto my koro's ride-on mower, maybe ten of us kids all clinging on, and we'd cross the rickety bridge at the bottom of the village, cross the quiet two-lane road, then paddocks all the way to the beach.

Tamapahore was a working farm, and many of our aunties and uncles were employed on it, in the large nursery or in the orchards. We grew avocados, kiwifruit, corn maize, chestnuts, feijoas, grapefruit, oranges, tangelos … even us little kids helped when we were needed to pick things. We'd crowd into the back of the ute after school, standing up, and that was the best bit, going all together round the back to where the chestnut trees are, bumping and rolling into each other. Who fell off? Bianca? We would all be laughing. That's the thing, we'd just laugh — laugh at everybody's demises!

We picked chestnuts every day after school. I remember that I only got paid $26, for the whole week.

We knew about working, we knew about farming, we knew about the veggies and what seasons the fruits come in. We'd have fights over the feijoas: *Don't touch them! You took one! Nah, you took it! You got to wait for them to get soft!*

That kind of life creates an incredible bond. It's whānau.

Whānau for me is everything. It's my core, it's my identity as a son, a brother, a boy, a man. That life — we had our house and then right by us, with no fences in between, we had my great-grandmother's house, my koko's house, my other great-grandmother's house, my aunty, my other nan's house.

They say it takes a village to raise a child. We were raised by all our grandparents, all our aunties and uncles. We were raised in this community, in this village very much like it still is in the islands. It's the communal everything. Everybody looks after everybody and you don't have much, but you have everything. I could just go into anybody's house and they'd be like, 'You want a jam on toast, boy?' I'd eat there and then go to the next house, or if we needed flour or milk or sugar we could just go and get it off someone. I took it for granted.

We moved in big units, never by ourselves, never isolated. There were always three, four families that moved together. Our house was always full of whānau. It was never just me and my mum and dad and my siblings. We'd have cousins and nephews and nieces, aunties and uncles.

There'd be a whole family living in the shed. For a while, my brothers and my cousin lived in a tent while the shed was getting built. They lived in the caravan, they lived in the shed.

So I always feel weird when I'm in a place where it's not a home. I'd rather stay on the couch at my mate's house than stay in a big flash hotel. I'm used to being in clutter and chaos and loudness. I have learned, though, to love the quiet sometimes. That's something that's different for me now, compared to when I first entered adulthood and this crazy industry. Sometimes now I choose to be alone, to go to my apartment and just be me. I've learned to love it. But that's not how I began, and it still ain't my natural setting.

Life is changing, and not just for me. I was talking to some of my nannies and koros and they explain it like this. They say, 'You know, back in the day, we were all siblings, all first cousins. That's why when my cousin dies, that's my brother who died, my sister who died.' And they were saying, 'You know, you fallas are changing, you're not like that anymore. You stay away from home, you don't come back as much. Everybody's fighting, doing their own things or some people are too cool for each other. But we were all siblings. We lived on each other. We could all sleep together and know that we were safe with each other. If anybody tried to come in, all the boys would beat them up.'

It makes me feel sad that life isn't like that anymore. And now we live in big cities, live in different countries, hardly come home. Our kids don't even know our other nephews and nieces. That's sad for me. Because we had the luxury of that, and I didn't realise that other Māori weren't brought up like me. I thought every Māori person was exactly the same.

CHAPTER THREE

We lived in those dark places

Mā te mārie a te Atua
Tātou katoa e tiaki
Māna anō e whakaū
O tātou ngākau ki te pai
The peace of God
Keep us all
He will confirm our
hearts in goodness

— 'Mā Te Mārie'

ON AN OVERCAST, CHILLY DAY IN MID-2018, WRAPPED in a korowai from my mother's side of the family, te whānau Ohia, I took my place before a microphone in Te Whetū o te Rangi Marae, a stone's throw from Tamapahore and one of the marae in our rohe, our tribal area. I was there to record the lovely Rātana hīmene 'Mā Te Mārie' for The Offering Project, an initiative in support of The Salvation Army, where twelve artists each chose and recorded a gospel hymn. I sang a cappella but accompanied by a choir of my whānau. As the singers were warming up, the project's producers said they were getting goosebumps, the hairs on their arms rising, because the singers sounded like angels in the Sistine Chapel.

'Mā Te Mārie' is one of the most famous hymns of the Rātana Church, and one of the first songs I ever learnt to sing. It is truly a song of my childhood. I can't hear it without remembering the voices of my aunties and nannies singing it — especially my Aunty Connie, the voice of voices, and one of the reasons I started singing myself. She led the Tauranga Takutai Moana Choir, singing all the Rātana hymns from the blue songbook, accompanying the āpotoro, or apostles, who give the sermons at church services. I grew up with those hymns. We'd go down every year to the big celebrations at Rātana near Whanganui, where we listened to the brass bands and the choirs. I didn't understand anything about the religion, but I always loved the music.

If you visit our urupā you'll notice that many of the graves bear the symbol of the Rātana Church — the white crescent moon and the five-pointed star. Our family was a part of the Rātana Church since my great-grandparents joined many decades ago; many of my whānau are still Rātana, although my immediate family turned to the Assemblies of God in the 1990s.

Just three weeks before I made that recording, I'd been at the same marae singing the same lovely song, 'Mā Te Mārie', at the funeral of one of my nannies. Two of my nannies were laid to rest within a week of each other and so, for me, the song became imbued with new meaning. As I sang it again, I pictured both of my nans sitting there with us — little old ladies holding my hands. It felt like a completion, me, coming home, singing in my own language, in an event that shared all our richness with the world. My heart was very full that day.

Singing 'Mā Te Mārie' for The Salvation Army was part of the feeling of completion. I had already written a couple of songs for Salvation Army campaigns in Australia, because I have so much respect for the work they do. They are all about service, the kind of people who are there in the pits and dark alleyways, places where people are found at their worst. The places where everyone else goes 'yuck' or 'I feel sorry for them' yet still walk past. The Salvation Army are the selfless ones who actually get stuck in. They may look like a bunch of nice old people, but trust me, they are actually total gangstas! They deal with things most people aren't ready for.

And that means a lot to me because in my family we lived in those pits, those dark places, and I will never forget what that feels like.

* * *

I am scared of a lot of things. I'm scared of the dark, scared of dogs, scared of spiders, scared of birds. I've never been scared of dead bodies. Even as a little kid, I was used to them. I was always curious. I was always comfortable with the dead; death seemed very natural to me. Because we lived on the marae, I often used to go and lie with the bodies, or sit there and touch them.

Often it would be a person I had known — a nanny or a koro, but even if I didn't know them, if they were aunties and uncles I didn't know, I would sit by their coffin all the time.

My great-grandmother, Ngawaiwera, the one I'd sung the karanga with, died when I was three, and hers is the first funeral, the first death, I remember vividly. I recall her being on a bed in my koko's lounge — she was his mother — and looking very sick. I remember staring at her and I felt that she stared back at me. I don't know what that feeling was exactly.

When she died, I knew she was lying up at the marae and I wanted to go and be with her. Mum was out, and I knew she wasn't with Nan. She hated all that, she hated to stay at the marae; she was always wanting to get off the marae, get off the hill and go to the city. She only stays with the body on the last night. I'd been told to stay home with my brothers, but I didn't want to. So I did what I always did and climbed out my bedroom window; but instead of running to Koko's house, I took off across the road and into the marae. There must have been people in the wharekai, hanging out or preparing food, but there wasn't anyone else there at that moment keeping my nan company, so I went straight to her and lay down and quickly fell asleep on the coffin.

Next thing, mum's yelling at me — 'What do you think you're doing?!'

But the dead have always been a comfort to me.

* * *

I'm standing in the kitchen at home. I'm three years old. I've just had a hiding. I've been screaming and crying, out of control, and my face is exhausted. I am exhausted. I am sore. I am tender. And now I've got to do all the dishes, all by myself, like I'm a teenager. There is nobody else there and no one to help me. If I don't do them, I know what will happen.

I want to die. I don't want to be here. I want to kill myself. I want an end. I know exactly what I am thinking and feeling. I pick up a knife and I begin stabbing myself in the side, in the stomach. I haven't chosen a sharp enough knife. It hurts but it doesn't cut me.

Deep inside myself, in the place where my core self lives, in the place that the knife is trying, trying to get to, there is something wrong with me. There was always something wrong with me. I hate myself. But even more than that, I hate my father. More than anything, I wish he would die.

That was the first time I had the conscious thought that I wanted to die. I don't know how I could have even thought that or understood what that was, but I knew exactly what I wanted. And I can tell you: kids, even little kids, know those feelings and have those thoughts. I look at my nephews and nieces now and it would break my heart to think they knew that kind of feeling or those thoughts. But believe me, if a kid is being abused, is being beaten, that kid will know the feeling of despair.

That was when I was three and from then on that feeling was there all the time.

I remember looking out my bedroom window. A police car was parked in the drive, sending its red and blue lights flashing over our house, over Koko's house, making the hill invisible in the darkness. There was shouting. I could see Dad struggling with the officers trying to get him into the car. Then they were gone.

I don't know who would have called the cops. Mum maybe, if she could've, or Koko, who must have often heard the screams and crashes. It's hard to think of any one specific time but I just remember watching out the window as Pāpā got taken away. It happened lots of times.

He always came back. Mum always wanted him back. She'd get a bit of strength back and then it would be, 'I don't know what else to do. I'll go back to him.' He would say he's sorry. He'd say he wouldn't do it again. Then boom.

My poor, poor mama. 'Don't go. Don't go, hun.' She's begging my dad, trying to stop him from leaving. He's chucking her against the wall. He's chucking her on the floor. I'm crying. I'm so little. 'Māmā, Māmā.' Just a little kid, trying to hold on to Mum.

They must have been so young back then.

She didn't know anything else. I'll never know what it's like to be a mother being abused. But for her, that's the version of love she knew, and she was scared: if he left, if she left, she wasn't going to be loved, nobody would want her. So she just stayed in it.

People so often judge these women: 'You should just leave.' We think we have all the answers for people in that situation but it's so much harder than that.

Women like my mum was back then have been so damaged and conditioned. That's their normal and they think that's all they're going to get. I'm just explaining it like my mum explained it to me, but I will never actually know the emotional, physical, spiritual hold that my dad had over her.

When I was older and watched movies about slavery in America, it struck me how sometimes, even if they got the chance, they wouldn't escape because it was all they knew. 'I'm a slave, I'm nothing else.' Their spirit was beaten. I felt like I understood: my dad was the master, my mum was the slave.

I just feel so sorry for my mum, that she was still so desperate, that she didn't know anything else but to have him there, that she was begging for him to stay.

When I was really little, I don't remember thinking, having the brain to even think, *I want you to leave*. It was only later that I thought: *I hope he goes*.

But I did wish he would die. I was always scared. Always.

I think about my unformed brain at that time, my developing little child brain, taking on these adult things that I should never have had to take on, and trying to survive in that. Man, I don't want that for anyone.

* * *

I have this memory of riding in the back of my dad's ute, this big ute. We'd be in the back, no seats, no seat belts, just little kids bouncing around, not having any control over ourselves, not able to stay sitting up. That's exactly what our lives were like.

Mum was the worker of the family. She did her best for us, but we were very poor and there never seemed to be enough of anything. But she always worked and always managed to put food on the table for us. She used to work night shifts. I hated it when she had to go to work because then we had to stay home with our dad.

She did night packing at Countdown. She worked at a café. She worked at a sandwich bar. At other times she worked late shift at Caltex, or at a deli in town. If we didn't have enough money for food she would ask my aunty who worked at the food bank. That happened quite often, and I never thought of it as a shame thing. I loved it! To me it was like Chrisco — it just seemed like they had everything there, made to order. Oh my God. We'd get home and there'd be all these packages and we'd be like: Wow, we've got heaps of new food! Most things were in half-pack — a half-pack of milk powder, half of rice, flour, milk powder, pasta, all in these little bags with a rubber band wrapped around each. Some things would be brand new and untouched and in their original packaging. It was like a lucky dip.

If you'd opened our cupboards, you'd see all the budget brands of bread, milk powder, pastas, rice, porridge, noodles. White bread. Budget sausages. Heaps of budget-brand baked beans and spaghetti. We lived off baked beans in cans. We always had Weet-Bix but rarely had real milk. When we got it, it went really quick, and when it was gone, it was gone. Once, I sneaked out to the kitchen at two o'clock in the morning and drank the real milk that was in the fridge. Far out, it was amazing. Got a hiding for that, of course.

But we were lucky, we were fortunate enough to live on the farm. In our village, we had the avocado orchards, kiwifruit and all the rest of it. So we always had fruit because of the trees outside.

When we were at Tamapahore, being poor didn't bother me. We were all the same, and I didn't have any way of comparing what we had with people who had more. I didn't like the food mum would cook us, meals made using cheap meat and canned stuff — fatty, basic food that was easy to make. I went to someone's place once and they had dessert; I could hardly believe it — dessert, like on TV. We didn't have stuff like that. All the fancy stuff like ice cream, McDonald's, KFC — we couldn't afford that. Fish and chips, yes. Fish and chips is always going to be good forever.

As I got older and realised how other people lived, I was dissatisfied with what we had. Same all the time. No options.

You only see your own poverty when you get to school and you're with people who've got more — nice cars, pay TV, DVDs and fancy lunches. Things that didn't exist in our world, like LeSnaks, Dunkaroos, Roll-Ups, Tiny Teddies … we didn't have that stuff and I wanted it so badly.

I will never forget this one particular moment. It was lunchtime at school and I had a meatloaf sandwich I was embarrassed to take out because kids were like, 'What's that?'

and it smelled yuck. But my mate, he had fancy bread and he had lettuce, tomato, cheese and ham. To me, it looked amazing. The kind of sandwich I'd never had in my life. He goes, 'Do you want to swap?' I'll never forget that. But the main problem was, I just never had enough to eat.

I used to steal people's lunches. I'd make an excuse to leave the class and I'd go into the bag bay. I knew who had the best lunches. I'd take those fancy lunches out of their bags and stuff them into my bag, or eat them as quick as I could. Or I'd pretend I was sick because I knew the sick bay had sandwiches in the freezer that they'd defrost for me. Or I'd be the kid scabbing money at the canteen so I could get something to eat. 'Can I borrow twenty cents?' Borrowing. But you'll never get it back.

There was just never enough. I would notice all the nice things around me, and I would dream of having them for myself. Which is why, when I got to the Idol house and they asked me what food I wanted on the shopping list for our chef to cook, I couldn't believe what I was hearing. I was like, 'What do you mean?'

'Like, for food. What do you want to eat? You can have anything.'

'Anything? I can put *anything* on that list?' My first thoughts were of all that stuff I'd wanted when I was a little kid. So on that fancy shopping list at the Idol mansion I put LeSnaks, Dunkaroos, Nutella, Coco Pops, Nutri-Grain, Shapes. Everything that I never had as a kid.

Poverty in our world is the thing that sets you apart from the mainstream. For instance, when I got old enough to wear a uniform to school, I always had the wrong uniform.

I always had the second-hand one, but the uniform would have changed completely, so everyone knew that you were one of the poor kids because you still had the old uniform. It was shame at school.

That poverty lifestyle was my life every day. But, back at Tamapahore, in my very young days, I didn't really know about that. I think I always understood, though, that my life had this massive contradiction in it. I had the stuff going on at home — being scared, getting beaten, being frightened for my mum, being frightened of my dad. That was ugly. But everything else was beautiful. It was the best and the worst possible. Complete polar opposites.

* * *

Often it is those who deserve the most blame who also deserve the most compassion.

Oh, my poor papa. I didn't understand him until I was much older. He was just the end result of the things that had happened to him, and what had happened to him was way worse than what we went through. I say that because even at the worst times for me, I still knew that I belonged to my whānau. I never doubted that, and so I had an identity, even though that was often confusing for me. But Dad fitted nowhere.

His father, my grandfather, was a very abusive man. He used to beat my nan, really smash her, and I believe that was the reason for her losing so many babies. He was vicious to her. When she got pregnant with my dad, which was a miracle after everything that had happened to her, she said to my koroua that this baby wasn't his. She hadn't thought that he was going to take it out on my dad for the rest of his life. He would smash my dad every day. And if my Uncle Stan, who was a whāngai to my grandparents, did something wrong, my dad would get the bash for that, too.

He never experienced love; he never got love from his dad, and he was estranged from his mother. He was ugly to her, took everything out on her until she turned against him, too. So he never received love and he didn't know how to give it. Even as a very small child, I definitely never heard my dad say, 'I love you.' I don't remember him ever hugging me, I don't remember him holding my hand as we walked somewhere. Anger, violence, and the expression of *those* feelings, was all he knew.

My dad used to eat out of the bins at school. He was mocked and beaten up by everybody. Because he came out much whiter than his parents, everyone used to call him a ghost. When he got bigger, he became evil. Monkey see, monkey do. That's what happens when you've got nobody else to help you or there's no way out.

They used to call him 'Hypo' because he was just like this little crazy, always looking for a fight. He used to go to league games just to stand on the side of the field and get into a fight. He'd swear at people just so he could fight.

It got worse as he got older. On his eighteenth birthday, he thought he was a big man. He took a knife and tried to stab my grandmother, his mother. She turned the knife back on him and ended up cutting his finger off. It was like Mum said: everyone seemed to hate him, even his own mother. And he hated everyone in return — with the exception of his Aunty Hira, his mother's sister, and his first cousin Mary. They had a soft spot for him and were the only ones who gave him the time of day. Aunty Hira especially had seen him go through everything and understood why he was the way he was. Aunty Hira was always special to my dad and still is to this day, and because of my father, she was always special to us.

But still, he had nothing to lose. He was out to destroy.

He got into the drug world, growing it and selling it, and using. By the time I came along, he'd been in and out of jail lots of times, including a nine-month stint when he was twenty, for fire-bombing someone's house. He was a drug addict and an alcoholic, and that was another cause of his crazy violence — using it, needing it, recovering from it. The drugs he used were low-level. Peasant drugs, bottom shelf. Dope, of course, but then it was petrol, glue, gas — absolutely everything and anything he could get his hands on. He's done it all. Getting access to more expensive Class A drugs was harder, so that only happened if he was in the right crowds, or he managed to steal it somehow. He'd just do whatever he could get, and the side effects of that are well known, and include violence and even brain damage.

He wanted to be tough, he wanted to smash everybody. He was a rip-off artist who stole other people's drugs and got into wars. My older brothers had to harvest his dope for him, and him and my brother both had a price on their heads, after my dad got caught stealing drugs from the wrong people.

A lot of guys in our world get into gangs — one of my grandfathers was a founding member of the Greasy Dogs, and they've got their pad on our land. We've got uncles and cousins from different gangs: Black Power, Mongrel Mob. It's just normal for us. We grew up around it. The Greasy Dogs' pad was a safe place for Mum back in the day — it was just the whānau.

But not my papa. He was a lone wolf. He was like Jake the Muss from *Once Were Warriors* — he'd take on everybody, take on the world. He didn't care. That movie came out when I was three, and Mum tells me how she bawled her eyes out when she watched it the first time. She knew it was her life.

But in other ways my papa was not like Jake the Muss. He was way worse. He needed no provocation. He didn't have to be emotionally charged to give my mum a hiding. He was on all the time. It wasn't like: oh, you caught him on a bad day, or you did something to make him angry. There didn't have to be an argument or any answering back. There was just: you moved wrong, you looked wrong, you ate your food wrong, you looked at somebody. He was hunting for the opportunity. He wanted it. He was sniffing for it.

He'd be sitting there, on the couch or at the table, always watching my mum, always watching us, always a ticking time bomb. He was ready. And when he hurt you, he wanted to make you bleed. We had to be on our toes. Even as a really little kid, I knew: be on your toes.

We couldn't do anything right. *You're going to get it. Someone's going to get it. We're all going to get it.*

I was always scared. Scared to do anything.

There's a lot of cases you hear about where the husband beats the wife up, but away from the kids. Maybe they hear it from their bedrooms. Pāpā didn't care. We saw it. We were there, part of it, watching our mum get a hiding right in front of us. Often, we were the reason she would get smashed. He'd be giving me a hiding, or me and my brother, and she would jump in to defend us, and then she'd get a hiding. It would make him even worse. She put her body on the line to protect us, and ... that was the hardest thing. It was harder watching her get beaten up than it was to get beaten up ourselves. It was hard as a little kid to see the person you love the most get wasted. Your mum.

This one hiding she got, it was in broad daylight outside of Koko's house. Koko was there, and my mum's brother, and me, Māmā and Pāpā. Pāpā was arguing with my mum and Koko, and then he started bashing her up, and Koko was trying to get him off Mum, going, 'Just F off, Ross. Just F off.' But my dad was out of control. He started smashing my mum's head into the house, chucked her on the ground, put her head in the dog's bowl, stomping her head, and he just couldn't be stopped. I remember crying, and my koko and Uncle Whiti were trying to get him off. That was sad. My mum, who I cry for, who sends me to sleep, who is my everything, and I'm watching her getting smashed by my dad.

Oh, Koko hated Pāpā in those days. But he couldn't do anything.

So, it happened in public, and yet not in public. I don't know if people just didn't want to see it or they ignored it. People choose not to see things. I feel like there was a lot of that, because that has happened in our family and in our communities for years: sweep everything under the carpet. You know who's the rapist. You know who got raped. You know who's getting beaten up, but you don't say anything. Ssshh. That's not our problem. Don't say nothing.

To say something is to expose the truth. Maybe they don't want to cause any dramas. Maybe they're in denial, so they don't have to do anything about it. But it's happening. And it was happening.

It was so much the reality of our everyday lives that I had never thought about whether it happened to anybody else. I had no big picture for domestic violence, and no words for it. But one day when we were staying with my aunty and uncle and cousins, I saw down the hallway and I saw that my uncle had put my aunty on a seat like she was a little kid, and he was yelling at her — 'What did I tell you?!' — then boom, in her face. It reminded me of my mum and dad and I felt so sad for my aunty. I had never seen other people go through that. Years later, I saw my aunty and I said, 'Do you remember?'

And she was like, 'Yeah, I know, boy.'

* * *

I was always a mummy's boy. I always wanted her. I always wanted my mum's love. I smothered her and she couldn't stand it. I was just too overbearing for her. I wanted too much and she didn't have anything left to give. She was like, 'Nah, get away from me.' Didn't want to give me a kiss, didn't want to hug me, and that made me want it more. Those feelings of rejection became a big part of the pain I carried around with me, and I used to get angry and frustrated at her. I would answer her back and we'd get into arguments, and then she'd shut me in my room or give me hidings — not just a smack, either. She could give mean hidings, too.

She's a scrapper from way back. She's been in prison herself a couple of times, before I was born, and she told me she had a fight with the top dog in jail, this big Dutch lady, and beat her up. My mum was little and skinny but she apparently got her in a chokehold and was just elbowing her head. So she's a fighter, and when it came to her kids, back then, she wasn't just going to give light smacks. She'd give me smacks, screw my ears and give me the belt.

The funniest was when she used to give me the belt; I'd pull my hand back and she'd miss. Then she'd be like, 'Argh, you little shit!' But she gave us hidings like it was discipline, not like she was out of control. The only time she went overboard was once when she was on top of me, and she was punching me, saying, '*This* is how you make me feel. You make me feel like *shit*,' and she went *pfft*, and she spat on my face. '*That's* how you make me feel.'

I was so shocked, I'm thinking, 'Did you just ...' I couldn't believe it. She kept punching me but I didn't really feel anything, because I was like, *You spat on me.*

That's how much I stressed her out, and that's how out of control we all were. My mum just couldn't handle me.

But there were some lovely times. I remember when I was a little kid, maybe two and three, she used to sing this song to me when she would put me to sleep. *Moe moe pēpē, moe moe rā. Hoki mai a Māmā, āpōpō. Hoki mai a Māmā, āpōpō* ... There's nothing more beautiful than a mother singing a lullaby to a child — it's a quiet, peaceful moment among all the crazy, and I craved for that.

I don't know whether this was an actual physical problem, or a psychological effect, but I used to have bad stomach pains and bad knees, and it's weird because those are happy memories, too. My knees would be aching and I would be screaming that I couldn't walk, and I'd have to drag myself to her room, going 'Oh, Māmā … Mum …' I was so dramatic. And then I'd jump in bed with her and she would rub my knees until I fell asleep.

Other times, I'd be crying and screaming about my stomach pains, and she would always get me a cup of boiled water. After she got converted to Christianity, she would say, 'Just imagine Jesus on the cross. Jesus will take the pain away from you. Look at Jesus on the cross, boy. He's taken all that pain for you, He's already taken it.' And I would be drinking this boiled water, and actually trying to think of Jesus taking my pain away. And she would stay with me, and eventually I'd get better.

It must have been hard for her, me wanting her so much. But after the beatings from my dad, she didn't care how battered she was herself; she would protect us and guard us and she would be the one comforting us. Even though she needed comforting herself, she would be there for us. 'It's all right, it's all right …' She used to call me her 'little bulldozer', because when I was really young I was a little fat thing, a little chubby thing. *My little bulldozer.* And I would feel safe again with her.

I have so much empathy, understanding and compassion for my mum, because I can remember vividly her face at those times. I could see she was trying her hardest.

Sometimes we would run away. I remember we ran away to my Aunty Maria's and Uncle Andrew's in Auckland, and another time to Aunty Ronnie's house in Tauranga. She must have felt so much fear then, knowing Pāpā was looking for us. I remember him saying, 'I'll catch you and I'll kill you.'

She always tried her hardest. She did everything for us. She came to all my brother's league games, my league games. She was my brother's coach. She was the rugby coach, too. She taught us how to play rugby because she played rugby. She was sporty. She was the one who was the driver behind any of our success, even today. No one in my family except for my baby sister ever finished school but, in those early years at Tamapahore, Mum even did a course at polytech. Even though she never finished high school, she's proven over the years that she is smart and ambitious.

With what she's had to deal with, and what she was given with my father back then, she's done so amazingly. When it comes to us kids, man, she'll do anything. She'd die for us, and she did. She died for us so many times in so many different ways.

I feel like I understand her, even though I can't understand everything she went through. I don't think she was, in her actual nature, a violent person back then. I'm the only one who ever got punched up by my Mum because I drove her to the very edge. She just couldn't handle me. I definitely feel like I was the biggest pain in her life.

Now that I'm older and understand things better, I see that there might have been reasons for my behaviour. But she didn't understand, she just thought that I was like my dad: he was a hypo and so was I. She used to even tell me: 'You're just like your father.' I never expected her to understand everything. She tried the best she could with the cards she was dealt.

One of my best memories ever of my early life was a time when it was just me, my mum and two older brothers at home together. We used to have a chip-maker — you know, you put the spud in and it slices it into chips, and then you put them in a pot with the hot oil. We did that and then we put all the chips on this one plate between us, and we sat there and we ate those chips and watched TV. It was just us. Pāpā wasn't there, so we were all relaxed. I just remember it being such a perfect moment. *Whoa, we're eating hot chips for dinner.*

Usually, dinner times were very strict. We hardly ever watched TV while we were eating. Mum was pretty hardline with us — 'You better eat that food' — and if we didn't comply she would smack us, bring out the strap, but it was about discipline. Totally different to what we got from Pāpā. If he was there, you had to finish absolutely everything — grind all the fat off the bones. If I didn't finish all the food on my plate, or complained about anything, he would shove it into me, ramming it in with the fork, right down my throat.

I'd be sitting there crying. Tears, snot, dinner, pain. And then he'd smack my head into the table and give me a hiding. Punch me or kick me down to my room. And that's where I'd have to stay.

We got hit with everything. The belt, of course. But we got hit with vacuum-cleaner pipes, the belt buckle, iron cord, the iron, the tennis racquet, the horse whip, the racing cane. We got hit with sticks. With the power-plug end of the kettle cord. With a golf club. But the one that stung the most was the metal coat hanger.

I used to be fascinated looking at all my bruises and the big welts, like, *Oh, how big is this one now?*

The best thing was getting hidings with my brother, because we were in it together. We literally would be in the corner, like, 'No. No. No, Pāpā,' you know, screaming, crying, but also secretly, 'Yes! At least I've got somebody with me,' because when you were by yourself, and there was nobody around to rescue you, that's when he was really evil.

Sometimes he would do it quietly, even when other people came over to the house. One time, I was with my older brother and a cousin. They were on the PlayStation and I was being a pain, 'Why don't I get a turn?' My dad came in and heard me.

'Stan,' he said, in his calm voice, 'come here. Come in the room for a second.' I didn't suspect anything. I got up and went into my bedroom and he was waiting for me. It took me completely by surprise when he grabbed my head and smashed it against the wall. 'You want to make a scene, eh?' I'd fallen with my head stuck in the corner, and he began stomping it. He kept saying, 'You want to make a scene, eh? You gonna do that again?' He picked me up and put my head between his legs, smacking me in the head and face. I was so scared. Mum wasn't there. If she was, she might have come and saved me. She might have yelled at him. But she wasn't there, and I knew that if I screamed, it would have made things worse. I had to just be quiet. It went on until he stopped, and I was left to cry and hate, cry and hate. Hating him, hating myself.

I know I'm lucky I didn't get brain damage. I've got scars all over me, including a lot of little ones around my mouth. You can't really see them unless you come up close. That's from him hooking his hand in my mouth and dragging me around on the ground. All because I answered him the wrong way or had the wrong look on my face.

I was in pain a lot of the time, especially sitting down when there were bruises all up my legs and back. I often had big-as bumps on my head. But the thing is, we were all used to pain. We were used to going through injuries. We never went to the doctor and hardly ever to the hospital. It was too hard because we had to lie. We went once when Pāpā put my oldest brother's head through the wall. He had a bad cut and had to get stitches, and Mum had to lie, and we listened to her lying and we just stared at the floor and waited until the doctor accepted her story and got on with sewing up my brother. But, usually, we had to hide our injuries.

I was good at hiding them. But one day, when I was probably nine or ten, a teacher at Arataki Primary School did see a bit of my back when my shirt rose up, and she asked how it had got so bruised. If she'd taken a proper look, she would have seen I was bruised all the way from my legs to my bum, and all the way up my back, all purple. Up the whole thing, like I had been run over by a car. But she didn't look.

I just said what I always said: 'I fell down the stairs.' We didn't even have any stairs.

'Are you sure?' she asked.

'Yeah,' I said. 'I fell down the stairs.'

I guess it seems incredible that so much damage can be done to a child and nobody really picks up on it, but when you've lived a whole life like that you get good at hiding it for your own shame. Your shame. The shame at being the one who gets hidings. The shame of coming from a home like that. I didn't want to look like that. I wanted to look like everything was good. I always acted confident at school. I told lies about how good things were, our awesome house, our awesome lives. I didn't want to show anything about that life at home.

I know that in some situations like this, kids get taken away from their families, but that would have been terrible for me. I reckon if I'd been taken away from my family, I would have gone crazy. I would have felt abandoned. I would have felt rejected. All I would have known is that my whānau didn't want me. *Do they not want me? Do they not want me?*

I know that's how it would have been for me. My whānau was everything to me, good and bad. I wouldn't have known who I was if I got taken away. I would have been nothing, separated from everything I knew. I was completely trapped.

Love is a really complicated thing. I was terrified of Pāpā. I hated him. But we were whānau.

* * *

I couldn't always hide my injuries.

I got home from school one day and it was just him there. I walked in the door and immediately he goes, 'Get the clothes off the line.' I was tired and I made a little fed-up noise, like 'ugh'.

It was just what he was looking for. 'What did you say?' He went and grabbed the tennis racquet. I ran. Big mistake. You should never run. It just made him more angry and more crazy. He chased me outside the house into the shed. He had me cornered. He went to go smash my face and I put my arm up to protect myself. He started smashing my arm. Smashing it, as hard as he could, with the rim of the racquet. I heard a crack inside my elbow and an agonising pain that joined all the rest of the pain in my body. He was smashing my legs, smashing my whole body with that racquet. 'Get out there and do it. Get out there and do it!' Shouting. But to get to the washing line I had to get past him, and he wouldn't stop hitting. I got past and he was still saying, 'You're going to get another one. You're going to get another few.'

I made it to the clothesline. My elbow was almost making me faint, but I had to somehow get those clothes down, get the washing folded, him watching me, wanting me to fail. My memory from then on, through the next few weeks, is a bit hazy, but it was a terrible time. I couldn't show my mum what had happened because she would have got angry with my dad, and that would have led to another beating. I was terrified of that. I was already in too much pain. So when I was home I made sure I did everything to avoid that. I did everything I was told, crossed my t's, dotted my i's. My elbow had swollen up humungously, and I couldn't even raise my hand to my mouth but I had to try to appear normal so no one would know. And when I went to school, I protected it with a sling I made out of a pillowcase. At school, everyone, even the teachers, asked what had happened and I said, 'I fell down the stairs.' The kids laughed at me for having a sling made out of a pillowcase.

I wore that sling every day, I don't remember for how long. I couldn't do PE, I couldn't do anything for ages, and I had to hide it from my dad. I just dealt with it by myself. It was never x-rayed or seen by a doctor. But I am sure it was broken, or at least cracked.

I've got over all of this a long time ago. Talking about it now is next to nothing. We laugh about this — me, my dad, my brothers. But my mum can't laugh about this stuff at all.

* * *

You're just like your father.

I had the same kind of energy as my father. I was always laughing my fake laugh so no one would know how I was feeling, smiling my fake smile, but I was a little bit evil, too. If anybody hurt me, I would chase them around with knives and forks. I would chase my brother around and chuck forks at him, and knives, and try to stab him — I *wanted* to stick him with that knife. Pāpā was like that. He used to chase people with knives and try to stab them. Like anytime, man, I would use weapons, I would do anything to hurt the person who hurt me. *I'll get you back.* Maybe that's the DNA I carried from my father. We're just always, *I'll get you back.*

I say 'evil' because I knew what I was doing, even though I didn't know why I was doing it. I remember the feeling, *I'm never going to let anybody make me cry.* From a young age, if I was bullied, I was like, *Nobody's ever going to make me cry like my dad does. Nobody's ever going to hurt me like my dad.* I would always be tough. I would never cry in front of anybody. When I was really little, obviously I did, but I would always get them back.

Monkey see, monkey do. This is why I say our family was the impossible. It wasn't just that I was getting hidings form my dad. I got them from my brothers as well, because they got them from Pāpā. In the case of my oldest brother, he got them as bad, if not worse than I did. Mike was so much older that he was both my protector and my attacker. He made a decision when he was little that he was going to look after us and protect us from my dad. But he couldn't control himself in those days. He's the only person who's ever knocked me out cold. It was one New Year's Eve. He was a teenager and he'd been told to stay home and look after me and Russ. I woke up crying in the middle of the night, and I just kept saying, 'Where's Mum? Where's Mum?' and he lost it. I just remember *boom*. When I woke up on the ground, he'd locked me in my bedroom. He used to take it out on me because I was a little shit. I was this little weasel who kept coming back and would never let up. But he tried his best to look after us.

Monkey see, monkey do.

That hiding Pāpā gave me when I wanted to play on the PlayStation, I gave my little brother the exact same hiding when I was about fifteen or sixteen, and I didn't even notice till later how I'd just copied my dad. My little brother's always been this big-mouth screamer, and I was like, 'Shut up, man.' Suddenly I couldn't handle it, and I switched. I was doing the same things my dad did. Holding his mouth to shut him up, holding his head between my legs and smacking his face, chucking him against the wall, stomping him.

It's a dark place. You see nothing and all you have is your anger. It just goes blank. I can't explain it. There was so much rage and anger that I just wanted to inflict pain.

I don't think I would have turned into a violent abuser, but maybe I would have. Who really knows? When you're a kid, you look at your parents, you look at your surroundings, and you think that's it. It's all you know. You are trapped.

I am so sick of these cycles of violence. Of the by-products of by-products of by-products. It's a real issue for our people. Our people, Māori men, are the most incarcerated in the country. Violence and drugs lead to our children being taken away. Our men are killing themselves. Families are destroyed, and so it goes on. I come from that life. Many of my family are in gangs. We have had many suicides. That outcome could easily have been me.

* * *

In November 2016, there was a social media storm when I agreed to headline a Man Up conference at Brian Tamaki's Destiny Church. Man Up is an organisation dedicated to helping men become better fathers and husbands, and to get away from their dysfunctional way of being. It's controversial because Brian Tamaki is controversial. Just a couple of weeks before the conference he'd said that sexual perversion and homosexuality were to blame for natural disasters and there was, rightfully, an uproar about that. What he said, I don't agree with that. It was disgusting and very harmful, and I told him what I thought. I had no qualms telling him that. But it didn't make my decision to go to the Man Up conference any harder. It was still an easy decision for me. Real easy.

I wasn't going there for Brian Tamaki. I was going there for the kaupapa, for the purpose.

People said *I* was disgusting and I should be boycotted. I was like, boycott me! I don't care. I'm here for my people. For me, that kaupapa is one of the most important things. What are your solutions for getting our men out of prison? I don't know if you've ever seen a Black Power and a Mongrel Mob run into each other on the street, but if they do, they're going to kill each other. I've seen so many fights between our men, fists in the face and dogs in their face — but now I've seen these same fallas hugging each other saying, 'I love you, brother.' Those fallas ain't never said that word before.

I went on stage at that conference with my dad and my brother Mike, in front of 1000 men, and we talked openly about how things had been for us. We all remember how things were back then. Back in those days, none of us even thought it was possible for things to be different.

We were there to inspire those men. To have them think, 'Wow, Stan Walker, his dad and his brother, they're just like us. We can get out of this, too.'

There were fresh gangsters there, and fallas who were in jail with my dad, and they were coming up to talk to us. One falla was like, 'Ross, my bro! We were in the same cell together!' That stuff is inspiring, and my job on this earth is to inspire my people, and to change the hearts of these men.

So it was never, *I should watch out for my career. My followers will stop following me.* I already knew what I was going to get. I got told it would be no good for my career. But I do what I do for my people, so that what happened to me doesn't happen to others.

CHAPTER FOUR

Like the movie but without the humour

Can't see you in the dark
I'm trying to find your light
I can't move through the dust
Getting lost in the night

— 'Find You'

IN MANY WAYS, OUR WHĀNAU IS A MICROCOSM OF Māori experience. As I've said, the old people, my great-grandparents, all spoke Māori. They'd be sitting together on the marae speaking te reo among themselves. I watched them do the karanga, speaking on the paepae, and of course we always sang together in Māori at any gathering of people. But the generation after them didn't use the language so much. I think my koko had a bit of reo but I didn't hear him use it much; then my parents came along, and they spoke next to no Māori at all. Partly it was because people would be punished for using it — there were many years throughout the twentieth century when Maori kids were brutally punished just for using their own language at school — but mostly it was the belief that it wouldn't get you anywhere. 'Don't speak Māori. That'll make you look dumb. Speak like a Pākehā.' The language was shunned.

But in the 1980s and 1990s, people began fighting to save the language. Kōhanga reo, Māori early childhood centres, were a part of that — the idea that kids could learn the reo from their elders, just by being immersed in the language every day.

When I was three, a kōhanga reo was set up on our marae, and I began to go to that.

My koko took me shopping for my first-ever school bag — red, yellow and green — and a soft toy of Barney the Dinosaur, which I loved on TV at the time. He wrote my name inside the bag — Stan McLeod, which was my mother's last name, and his of course — and then on my first morning and then every morning he would hold my hand and we'd walk together across the road and onto the marae, across the lawn to where the kōhanga was, alongside the wharenui.

I loved kōhanga. It was fun all the time.

It was full of aunties and uncles and nannies and cousins, of course. Aunty Hanihani, Aunty Rachel, who used to always be bubbly and took us with her for treats and stuff like that. Aunty Tweeny.

When Taika Waititi's movie *Boy* came out in 2010, me and my brother laughed and laughed — it was our life. A lot of our life was just like that but without the humour, but all the other stuff — the aunty who pops up everywhere, driving the bus, running the dairy, coaching the rugby team — that was us. All those aunties and koros had ten different hats that they wore throughout the day, and throughout the week.

There was Koro Pahu who lived in a caravan right on site beside the kōhanga. He drove the kōhanga van, he was one of our teachers, he was the āpotoro, or apostle of the Rātana Church, so he would always be on the marae speaking, and he was the caretaker for the grounds around the kōhanga.

Nanny Maybelle was the nurse and the cook and, later on, she got the responsibility of identifying bodies at the morgue. Aunty Hanihani was one of our teachers but she also used to run the accounts — her office was full of papers, adult stuff that we weren't interested in.

Most of my cousins lived down the road and they got to ride in the van to school with Koro Pahu. I was the only one who lived so close that I could just walk across. I was gutted to miss out on the van, so one day after kōhanga I hid inside the van and popped up suddenly when we were halfway down the road. We laughed!

My whole life was on that marae and I lived there, right in the middle of it. It wasn't just the marae itself, but everything that happened around it. Our village. We had the netball courts, the tennis courts and the league fields behind the marae. We were the base for the oldest Māori league team in the country, the Whalers, the first Māori team to tour Australia.

The club was such a mean place for kids. When it opened on Thursday and Friday afternoons, we were allowed in there till 5 p.m., and they had spacies, pool tables, table tennis. We'd go to Koko's house just across the road. 'Can I have two dollars, Koko?' That would be enough to play a game of pool or spacies and get a Peanut Slab or a Jolly drink, those fizzy drinks that come in bright colours like red, green, yellow. There was a chef who worked in the club making burgers, and the sweat would drip off his face onto the hotplate — *tssssss* — I remember the sound of it.

A few months after I turned four, Mum told us we were moving back to Australia. I didn't want to go. But Pāpā had already gone there and Mum said we had to join him. I suppose for them it was supposed to be a new beginning. They were always trying at a new beginning.

I didn't want to leave Tamapahore. I didn't want to leave Koko. I've got a photo of me hugging Koko — I've got my arms around his waist because I'm so little, that's all I could reach, and I've got a massive smile on my face. I loved him. But I didn't have a choice. And on our last day, he was saying to me, 'Come here, come here,' but I wouldn't say goodbye to him, because I was just … I didn't want to go. And then we were on the plane and I was crying: *I miss him!*

It was summer when we left New Zealand for Australia that time. In Tauranga, me and my cousins had been slipping and sliding at the local swimming pool and lying around on the hot concrete enjoying the heat, but when we landed on the Gold Coast the heat was a whole other thing. It was so hot it shocked us when we got off the plane. And there was Pāpā, and we had our new beginning. But, of course, we didn't. You can't just move somewhere else and expect the problem to change. You're the problem, and you take it with you wherever you go. Be a drug dealer and a rip-off and an abuser in New Zealand, you'll just be exactly the same in Australia. It was all exactly the same, and the cops started coming round to get my dad, just like they did back home.

My nan, my dad's mother, had moved across to Australia for a while, too, and she was living in a three-bedroom house at Ocean Shores, near Byron Bay with my aunty, uncle and cousin. To begin with, we stayed with them. We all slept in one room. It took my parents quite a while to find work. When they did eventually find work we got our own one-bedroom apartment, and Nan joined us in the same building.

The apartment building had a swimming pool — dark and old and ugly, with bush at the back where we used to see lizards and goannas and snakes. Pāpā decided he was going to teach me to swim.

He chucked me in the pool and then wouldn't let me out. He walked around the edge like a sergeant major, and wherever I tried to get out he was there ready to kick me back in. When I started to panic, he yelled at me to go down to the bottom, push off the ground with my feet, and come back up, again and again, until I covered the distance to the side. I was four. I hated it. I cried and cried — but I learned how to swim.

He was mean, but I guess, in his little mind, back then, the idea was to teach me something. He taught me how to swim, and I learnt to be tough. I was tough because of my dad. Little, but tough. Not the kind of tough that I could beat somebody up, but mentally tough. The type of tough that meant nobody could really hurt me.

Once I knew how to swim, he could leave me there by myself, knowing I wouldn't drown. If I ever panicked, I'd do what he'd shown me. I'd go back under and keep jumping up, up, up, up until I got to the side.

Even after I could swim properly, sometimes I would do that. Even as an adult. It's almost like going into a trance: go down, push up, go down, push up, go down, push up. I just got so used to doing it that I guess it became kind of therapeutic, in and out of the water. I became a little water baby.

Nan liked to forage and live off the land almost as much in Australia as she did back at Tamapahore. She took me fishing off a bridge, just using little handlines, like a stick with string, and whatever we caught we'd take home to cook, no matter how small. I remember catching these little, tiny fish that most people would use for bait. And she was like, 'Oh, we can make fritters out of those.'

Nan used to let me make bread, just out of flour and water, then bake it in the oven and eat it. My favourite thing to eat with her, though, was cans of cold spaghetti, straight out of the tin.

Our first place in Australia was in Ocean Shores, Byron Bay, but we moved around a lot, often because we were running away from Pāpā. He would say, 'I'll find yous and I'll kill yous.' We stayed with an aunty, then we ran to Doonan to stay with my mum's gay friend, and that was weird because I slept in the lounge and I could see down the hallway, and his partner came out naked. That was the first time I'd seen a naked man. Another time we stayed with an uncle on the same road as my dad was living. Once, when I was crossing the road, I saw him, and he saw me. We looked at each other, and I ran. I was scared. We escaped to a few different places but those are the ones I remember most clearly. We've got a big whānau so we had a lot of places to run.

But Mum would always go back. Or Pāpā would find us and she would end up going back. And then it would be all good, and the next minute someone's getting smashed up again, head through a wall or something. Oh, my poor mummy.

I have a fractured memory of my fifth birthday. October 1995. I didn't even know it was my birthday. Can it be true that no one had told me? But we were at a cousin's house and there was a big rage going on. There was a cake and someone told me it was mine, and I hadn't known.

It wasn't long after that, in November, that we went to church for the first time. That is, a Christian church that wasn't a Rātana church. We went with one of my aunties.

Mum was in her going-out dress, had a choker on, all dressed up. We were sitting in the church, this big-industrial-shed kind of place, and the pastor was talking about adult things, the things people go through in life. I was too young to understand but I realised Mum was getting agitated. She was sweating a lot. I could see it on her face; I could feel it through her dress where I was pressed up against her. She kept saying to my aunty, like she was angry, 'Did you tell him about me?' She felt like the pastor was speaking to her directly, and so she thought aunty had told the pastor about her. Aunty was saying, 'No, dear …'

Then, at the end, when they told people they could come up the front and be prayed for, she walked up, not even knowing why she did. She felt the pull. My mum first met Jesus that day, and it was the beginning of change for her. On that first day, I had no idea that this place, this huge church that was so different to the familiar wooden Rātana churches back home, was going to be so significant. What I mainly remember is that, while Mum was getting prayed for, I got to go to their Sunday school, and they had snacks.

They had little bread triangles covered in hundreds and thousands. I'd always wanted them, and I'd seen them at other kids' birthday parties. I was like, *Really?* I couldn't believe I was allowed to eat them! And then, to top it off, I got a cookie as well.

Mum found church to be a good place, with good people there, and over the next few months she was sussing it out, going along, keeping her options open. She wanted change in her life but she had things she had to give up. She used to party a lot, so it took her a while to stop drinking and doing drugs and getting into fights with these different ladies.

It was March the following year, 1996, that she fully committed herself to Jesus. She was done with her old life. 'No more am I going to take any of my old life,' she said. 'I'm done.' That was at the Christian City Church, or C3, in Byron Bay, and it turned out to be the church that Mum and Pāpā grew up in as Christians. But Pāpā was not yet on this path. Nowhere near it.

Pāpā wanted her back. He didn't want to go to church. He'd say, 'Nah, not for us.' I remember he did go once, early on, and he was just like a little devil, 'Get me the fuck out of here.' He was still busy in his usual life of dealing drugs, using drugs, getting drunk, hating everybody. But it turned out he'd do anything to get Mum back, and he eventually started going along to church. Not because he really thought anything of it, he was just trying to impress Mum. I guess he'd always been able to get her back and he thought this was no different, and before you know it we were back living with him in a big, five-bedroom house in Ocean Shores.

* * *

There's a photo we've got, taken in 1998, just after my little brother Noah was born, and nearly three years after mum began her journey with Jesus. We're standing up the front of the church. Mum is holding Noah in her arms. Pāpā is standing behind me and he has his hands resting on my shoulders and kind of pulling me in towards him. You can see how well built he is, but he looks clean and neat, his

T-shirt ironed, head shaved, beard like a trucker's. I'm seven, nearly eight, and I look skinny and awkward, the way any kid would look if he is up the front of the church. The pastor is talking into a microphone and he also has his hand on me, on my head. It is a happy family photo, a photo that says 'it's over now' — a happy ending to the chaos and violence. A new baby, a new beginning. A peaceful family. A church family.

Noah wasn't part of that old life. He was the new life.

It looks good.

But the photo doesn't tell the full story.

When I won Idol, the narrative in the media was all about my troubled childhood but with the light at the end of the tunnel — how my family found Jesus when I was five, and how we'd been a peaceful home ever since. It wasn't the truth. The truth was a lot more complicated, and a lot less like a fairy tale.

The truth is, change is a long, hard process with many failures along the way.

Pāpā had been coming along to church for a few months, hoping to get Mum back, when one day the impossible happened. He went up the front to be prayed for, and as the pastor prayed over him, he lost consciousness and fell to the floor. He was out for five hours. Church had finished, most people had gone home, but he was still lying there. It looked like he was wasted, but he wasn't drunk, he wasn't on drugs. I was thinking, *What the hell is happening?* He was completely knocked out, fully experiencing God. In that experience, Jesus became real to him. It was like God was really giving him a spring clean, cleaning out every crevice of his dark little soul. When he came to, I remember him saying, 'This is better than any drug I've ever had in my life. This is the highest high I've ever had. This is what it's all about.'

From that moment, his life changed. He stopped taking drugs, stopped drinking, stopped smoking, stopped dealing. He — mostly — stopped beating Mum. He found work — legal work that paid legal money. It was definitely a miracle.

And the same thing happened every time he got prayed over. Every time, he would be out and down for ages, like he was an actual drunk. It was such a weird thing. Well, I thought it was weird to begin with and then it just got boring. I'd be playing down the back of the church thinking, *Oh, hurry up. Here we go again.*

Every time he got prayed for, Mum was like, 'Here we go, we're going to be here for ages.' It's so funny — it used to be, 'Your father's going to drink, we're going to be here for ages. Be careful.' But now it was like, 'Here he goes, he's down again, we're going to be here for ages ...'

In many ways, our situation as a family dramatically changed when Pāpā stopped doing the things that had fuelled him before. But his biggest demons were still his anger and his violence. They turned out to be bigger demons than drugs or alcohol. He just couldn't handle his temper.

He beat Mum up one more time. Mum took us kids and we ran. She said, 'I'm not doing this no more,' and she meant it. She was not going back to him ever. Where did we go? We were kind of everywhere. We were staying with different people, moving around to whoever could take us, and it was me, my two brothers and my mum. For us kids, it probably didn't make that much difference — we'd been moving around a lot before that, and we always lived with aunties, uncles and cousins anyway. I don't remember one single time that we didn't. Whether we were living in a tiny unit or a big, five-bedroom house, or out in the country on farms, there were always other people coming and going all the time. I always shared a bedroom.

My dad ended up in that big house by himself. Then the church pastor got involved. He wasn't scared to confront Dad.

'Ross,' he said, 'what are you doing in this big house while your wife and children are hopping from house to house?' He arranged for Pāpā to go and live with an old couple from the church, and we moved back into our home.

So Pāpā moved in with Tom and Beverley Jackson. He has said himself that at the end of that last beating, he knew that was it. That something had to change. That *he* had to change.

Meanwhile, Mum prayed for a new husband, someone who would take care of us and protect us. Someone rich, handsome, and who would treat her like a queen. She'd had it with Pāpā, converted or not converted.

Tom Jackson was in his eighties when we met him, this old American from Arkansas, and Beverley was this little hippy Australian lady. He was tall and she was short, and they were always going on at each other in a funny, good-natured way — she'd be nagging away at him, and he'd say, 'Oh, you're always moaning, Beverley. Beverley, you're always moaning.' Yet they were the kindest people. They took my dad in to live with them. Tom had breathing difficulties and was on an oxygen machine, but he just had this grace about him. He was firm with my dad, so stern, but he also taught him how to be a dad. Tom and Beverley became like our nan and koro over there, and for years we'd go there for Christmas, New Year's, everything. Tom would always say, 'I've got something for you,' and he'd give me all his loose change. Tom was my dad's greatest mentor.

It wasn't long after Pāpā went to live there, when I must have been six, that something really strange happened. In hindsight, despite everything that was still to happen, it was probably a sign that he really was changing.

Pāpā came over to our house and asked my mum, 'Can I take Stan?'

'Māmā, no!' I was terrified and confused that he was asking for me. 'Māmā, no, I don't want to go with Pāpā …' But my begging was no good. I had to go.

We got in the car and drove off, and before we'd even left my neighbourhood, as we were stopped in front of the dairy down the road, my oldest brother walked in front of the car. There were problems between Pāpā and Mike, who would have been around fourteen at the time. Mike smashed his fist on the bonnet of Pāpā's car as he walked past. All I could think was they were going to have a scrap. *Pāpā's going to smash him.* Pāpā opened his door and got out. And I was like, *Pāpā, don't, Pāpā* … There was no question what was going to happen, right there on the street. It had happened hundreds of times before. *Pāpā, Pāpā.* But then the miracle: Pāpā was muttering and he was mad, but he jumped back in the car, shut his door and we kept going. And I was like, *Far out.* That was the first time I'd seen him consciously decide not to hurt my brother.

At Tom and Beverley's, everything was quiet and awkward. Pāpā didn't know how to talk to me, and I was just being really quiet. He would say, 'You all right?' It was weird, it was like I'd met my dad for the first time in my life and we didn't know what to say to each other.

The next morning, I watched cartoons on *Cheez TV* and he made me cereal. It was Fruit Loops, which I never usually ate, so that seemed special. I remember it was my favourite cartoon, kids riding dragons and fighting an evil dragon, and the cereal was yum, and Pāpā was still asking, 'You all right?' I had the feeling, *This is okay, I like this.* Then he took me to school.

I had never, ever experienced that. I didn't know how to take it. I didn't know how to take this man, what he was doing; but I remember him so vividly trying. 'You all right?' I'd honestly never heard him say that before.

I'd never seen him be soft before. There were other quiet moments — even when he and my mum would see each other and they'd be laughing together, I'd never seen that. The weight had been lifted off his shoulders. He was just a different person. It was weird, hard to understand.

I was still waiting. I still had that constant dread of him snapping. It was my first experience of him being a dad. For the very first time in my life, I saw what he could be.

That was the only time I stayed with him. But for the time that he stayed with Tom and Beverley, which was a few months, there were no hidings.

* * *

Mum prayed for a new husband. But it turned out that wasn't what God had in mind for her. She was about to get her old husband back instead.

She went round to Tom and Beverley's one day, after Pāpā had been there a few months, and Tom said to her, 'April, Ross wants to move back.'

Mum was shocked, adamant it wasn't going to happen. 'Nah.' She was saying, 'Nah, no way.'

'April,' Tom repeated, 'Ross wants to come home.'

'Nah.'

He said it one more time and this weird thing happened to my mum. She just got this peace of God come over her and her mind changed, and she heard herself say, 'Okay then.' Then she was like, 'What the hell did I just say?' But it was too late. Quick as a flash, my dad packed his bags and was like, 'Come on then, let's go.' He was so excited.

Up until then, my mum had believed she didn't love him anymore. She used to say, 'I've never actually loved him.' But that night, the first night of their new life, they lay next to each other and just hugged. The first time in their whole relationship. And Mum's since told me, 'That's when I first fell in love with him.' Honestly, when my mum makes up her mind, that's it. And she felt the peace come over her.

I can't remember how I felt about him coming home. I think he was all right for a little bit and then, you know ... it didn't go back to normal, but it went back to a new kind of normal.

I have one other good memory of my dad from around that time. It was after he was living with us again, and he used to wake up me and my brother Russ at three in the morning to watch Benny Hinn, an American televangelist who had a TV programme called *This is Your Day*. He was a preacher and a faith healer, and we would sit there together in the lounge with the world all dark outside, watching him do healings, watching people collapse on the ground as Benny prayed over them, and we'd be like, 'Wow.'

And then we'd go straight onto WWF, wrestling, on the next channel, the three of us just quiet, a bit sleepy. It was nice.

* * *

But it never stayed like that.

I was six when Pāpā began his relationship with Jesus; I was sixteen when he gave me my final hiding. That's how long the process of change actually took.

In many ways, I could see he had changed, and things about our lives had definitely changed — no drugs and alcohol, no more smashing my mum — but he still gave me massive hidings. So for me, the fear was still there, and I still hated him almost all the time. It was almost worse after a nice time, like the Benny Hinn nights, because of the disappointment and betrayal when the next attack happened. I know hate's a strong word but I actually hated him. I used to fantasise about him dying. I used to look forward to his tangi and how I wouldn't cry.

His anger was a beast that needed to be constantly tamed. It snatched him like a predator with prey, just like he in turn had always tried to hurt us. When he finally came to Jesus, he had so much to learn. He had to learn how to be a husband, a father to three kids and, soon, to two more. He had to learn how to be a man. He had to learn how to control that anger. It wasn't too late, because nothing is ever too late; but in another sense, it *was* too late, because so much had to be undone and redone. He had to start his whole life again.

* * *

It took years for my parents to be able to stop channelling everything through anger. Anger was like the go-to emotion for almost everything.

I had an accident one day when I was playing with my friend at the next-door neighbour's house. We climbed up onto his roof, up the ladder, but he ran down quick and took the ladder away. He left me stuck up on the roof and I couldn't climb down the tree, because red bull ants lived in it.

I looked down at what my options were. I saw a little tin storage shed. I went to jump onto it and somehow I leaned forward, fell headfirst, straight through the shed's roof and onto the concrete floor. Somehow, as I crashed through everything, a screw got pushed into my head.

I got knocked out for a bit and then I came to, screaming and crying. My head was bleeding and I reached up and felt the screw and pulled it out, then I was screaming for my brother. 'Russ!' It was just me and my brothers at home so they wrapped my head in toilet paper. When Mum came in, she was like, 'What the hell happened?'

'Stan fell through the roof!'

'Oh, you little shits!' So she gave me a hiding.

And then because we had to pay for the roof, I got another hiding. But that was normal. It was so normal. They didn't know anything else. They got so scared, they smacked me for getting myself hurt. I understand that, because they used to get frustrated with me.

* * *

I was challenging to my parents, I was always the kid who would answer back. The more I get boxed in, the more I want to break out. The more I'm told no, the more I want to do it. 'Don't touch that hot stove. Don't push that red button.' I've always been that kid who went ahead and did it anyway. I think this was a mixture of my natural personality, because I'm still like that now, but also me rebelling against the way I was treated and reacting to the situation I was in. There was the violence, which didn't stop, and there was also the strictness — both my parents were very strict, and Dad in particular was very controlling. I was always getting grounded, getting sent to my room. Maybe I was always a little hypo kid, but the years of fear, violence and rejection had probably added an extra dimension to my behaviour and attitude.

Pāpā no longer endlessly hunted for an excuse to give me a hiding. That aspect had changed. But if I did anything wrong, like answering back, he would … switch. He still had the same anger and he still hit the same hits. So I still lived with the same fear, the same old habit of watching the signs, watching for the next time, and still feeling the same hate.

I read my dad like a book. I had to or I would never have survived. His eyes. He's got hazel eyes but when he's angry they turn yellow. His voice, when his switch is thrown, is like hatred itself — that's the old Ross, that voice. It's worse than getting smashed in the face fifty times. It put more fear in me than getting hit ever did. It was that voice that said: 'Get back here. I'm going to kill you. I'm going to fucking kill you, you fucking little cunt.' It was a voice that meant every word.

When he was in that state, it was like he'd been bodysnatched. He levelled up, like Super Saiyan from 'Dragon Ball Z', and he went to a whole other place. Ultimate rage. It's amazing he didn't kill someone.

He had found God. He was trying to change. But like us all, he tried and failed, tried and failed. He failed many times.

If I screamed during the hiding, he'd get angrier. If I cried, he'd get angrier. If he thought about whatever I'd done wrong, he'd just keep going and going. And then it would just … stop. He'd leave me. Walk out of the room. Leave me there. But the difference was, after every time now, he would come back an hour or so later and he'd say, 'I'm sorry.' He'd hug me. He would be so disappointed in himself that he had lost control, so disappointed to have once again been in the red zone. 'I'm sorry, boy. Can you forgive me? I'm sorry.' As the years went on, he would even say, 'I love you.' I can't recall how I would respond, but I think I just kind of muttered, 'I love you, too.' But I only said it because I had to.

Maybe during the hidings, or after, he would say, 'This hurts me more than it hurts you.' Now, as an adult, I can see the truth of that, how much it has hurt him that he did that. Even then, I could see how gutted he was afterwards, after the hiding, after he'd lost control. 'I failed you as a father. Can you forgive me?'

It is a big thing to ask forgiveness when you've done wrong to someone. But for me, as a kid, I couldn't forgive him. *You're sorry, but you still smash me.*

I was filled with hate and a fear that would not go away. My face swollen from crying and screaming, my body sore but worse than that, my whole entire being filled with hate for him and for me. Staring at myself in the mirror afterwards, hating myself so much that I, too, wanted to kill me, and hating him the same. *Stuff your sorry, I hope you die. You still haven't changed.*

Sticks and stones will break my bones but words will never hurt me. That's the biggest lie. I know sticks and stones can break my bones. I can show you the scars. But just one word has the power to kill you inside, and those scars can't ever be seen. I remember every word that was spoken to me, and each stuffed me up far more than sticks and stones. *You're nothing, you're gay, little faggot, you're useless. Useless. Useless. You're nothing.*

Now that I'm older, I have more understanding about the process of change. It wasn't true to say that he *hadn't* changed, but he hadn't changed one hundred per cent, and that wasn't good enough for me. The ugliness was still inside him, and that was all I could see.

My poor papa has to live with himself and the knowledge of what he used to be. I can hardly imagine what that's like for him. Because the thing about him is that he now holds everything. He holds everything that he's ever done, all the times he wasn't there for us, the things he did to us, and he struggles with this. Even all these years later, he might still say to me, 'Can you forgive me, please, son, for everything I did to you?' I say, 'Of course. I forgave you a long time ago.'

But my forgiveness didn't come for a long time, and that was part of my own long journey. Back then, with Mum and Pāpā setting out on their new life as Christians, I was far, far from forgiving, and my troubles were far from over.

* * *

My troubles came at me even when I was asleep.

Right from when I was a little kid, I got the most terrible nightmares. They were so bad that Mum and my brothers would tell me I'd been running up and down the hall screaming and yelling, or running around in circles screaming, although I could never remember doing that. I was saved twice, by my brother Russ, from trying to kill myself when I was asleep. I was tormented in those nightmares. I would wake up terrified and confused, screaming, freaking out, and find I was no longer in my bed but outside somewhere, or under the car, or on the kitchen floor. The worst was waking up under my bed and not knowing where I was.

There were three different dreams, always the same ones. I had them often. To me, they seemed non-stop.

In one nightmare, a double of my mum and dad were trying to steal me. They were the same as my mum and dad, but just a little bit off and I knew they were evil. In the second one, I was right next to my mum and I had to watch as she got her head chopped off. And then the third one was the actual presence of claustrophobia. You know how you breathe in air but you can't see it? And how you can't see things like claustrophobia and depression and anxiety, but you just feel them? In my dream, I could actually see those feelings and it was this dark spirit, like smoke, and it was consuming me. Sometimes, the dark spirit was raping me, and its eyes had a darkness that was darker than black. Ultimate evil and fear. And the worst thing was that in my dreams, I was awake. These things felt as if they were really happening to me, night after night.

One night, Russ, who I shared a room with, was in his usual deep sleep, dead to the world, when he heard a voice in his dream: 'Wake up.' It came again: 'Wake up.' And he woke up, and there I was just about to jump out the window of our second-floor bedroom. He hadn't heard me wake up or open the window, but there I was stepping out, and he grabbed me just in time and pulled me in. If he hadn't, I would have smashed onto the concrete below.

Another time, my brother woke up just in time to catch me as I dived from the top bunk, head first to the ground. He caught me in the air.

I don't remember those times because it all happened when I was asleep. But the dreams obviously haunted and terrified me. They felt like spiritual attacks, like the devil had a mark on me.

The dreams eventually stopped being an every-night thing as I grew out of childhood, but even up till just a few years ago, whenever I was tired and down, if I ever forgot to ask for help or support and I was just relying on myself — when my spirit was weary — I would still get one of those nightmares.

The nightmares were one more thing I hated about myself. I always had something wrong with me: sore stomach, sore knees, getting hidings, going through stuff. Always one thing after another, just non-stop. I hated it. I was exhausted by it all. I was exhausted from fear, from pain, and from hating.

* * *

Now that he was a Christian, Pāpā was around more often. Before his conversion, he had been too selfish and preoccupied to work and my mum had to earn money; when they became Christians, it was him who worked. Some months after his conversion, when I was seven, he found work on a pig farm at Newrybar, still in Byron Bay. The piggery job came with a farmhouse and so once again we lived in the country. We had horses to get around the farm — I learned to ride there. We had chickens, cows. Once, when a calf got abandoned by its mother, I reared it for two weeks in the fenced-off area in the yard, feeding it with my little brother's bottle. It used to follow me around.

I had a Shetland pony named Snowy who was thirteen at the time and grumpy. She didn't like to be ridden but I'd take her on these adventures all by myself. I climbed trees, ran everywhere, explored, in my own world.

All through my childhood, through all the horrible stuff and the different kinds of violence, the places we actually lived in were a dream. We never lived in a city. Even when we lived in suburban landscapes, they were always old hippy towns, hardly any houses, big spaces between each other, no curbs, just grass then the road. For us, as always, it was the amazing and the terrible, the normal and the not-normal, all mixed up together.

Now I was always with my dad. To begin with, I was the youngest child, with two older brothers who were often doing their own thing. Then I became the middle child, with two younger siblings who were so much younger than me that our daily worlds were very different. Too young to be with the older kids; too young to be with the young ones. Maybe that's one of the reasons I so often ended up being ordered to go with Pāpā. Even before the piggery, he had me working with him on his first job, which was picking macadamia nuts. I'd be crawling underneath the trees, because the branches were low, picking them up by hand. I hated it and I'd whine that I didn't want to do it.

Then, with the piggery, we'd get up at 3 a.m. I used to just love it when we turned the lights on and we'd wake up the pigs to get them up for the day. I'd help him with everything — there were four workers and they all did everything together. Cleaned up the shit and then took it all up to be sprayed over the fields for the grass to grow — like a sprinkler, but for shit. Fed the pigs, which I loved because I loved the smell of the grain. Transfer the pigs around to different sections, depending on what stage they were at — piglets being weaned, sows that are in heat and going through to be mated. Moving them to their different pens was funny — we'd be all lined up, each person in a different corner with sheets of wood to steer them in the right direction. And they'd be like, 'Okay, you got your corner? You ready?'

'We're ready.'

It was mean. I used to love that life, and yeah, those fallas taught me a lot about the different pigs and stuff like that. Pāpā was a different man because he was around those other guys, so when they were there I wouldn't be getting any hidings. That was another change, because in the old days he wouldn't care who was there.

Pigs are really intelligent, more intelligent than dogs. Even today, I would love to get me a pig and raise it like a dog. I had my favourites that I would always go and find. I especially liked one I called Pug Nose, because her nose was kind of hooked upwards, and she used to let me touch her face and her nose. I saw her go through three litters of piglets.

One time, a sow was having her first litter and she couldn't push her piglets out. She was way overdue and the piglets had grown too big for her. 'Here, you can help,' the men said to me, and I put on a long glove that went right up to my shoulders, then put my arm right up inside her, feeling for the piglets. I pulled out two piglets, one after the other. I held them for a second before passing them over; it was a cool thing to have delivered them. They were big for newborn piglets, but still so tiny, their eyes blind, so weak. I felt like the man, the big falla, and so proud. Altogether we got four piglets out, but one of the guys pulled too hard on one and its head got pulled off. The sow was in so much pain. Poor girl. She was squealing in pain. Finally, I had to go away and they later told me that they'd had to shoot her. But they told me in a way that made me feel this was the best thing for her because otherwise she would have died of pain. I was sometimes cruel to animals when I was a little kid, but other times, like this, I felt nothing but compassion and empathy.

I mainly worked in the nursery with the piglets, feeding them and cleaning them out. Everywhere inside the piggery it was all concrete, heated with hot lights, but in the piglet area there was a little kennel-like thing with a pile of sacks on the floor. I'd jump in there with them, and they'd all waddle in after me and climb on me, and we'd have fun cuddling and playing. They were so warm and cute, and I loved the little sounds they made, little grunts and squeaks. Eventually, we'd all crash out, and at the end of his shift Pāpā and the other guys would be looking everywhere for me and they'd find me asleep in the pigpen.

When it was time to wean them, we cut their tails off — real simple and it healed quick. Those weaners were the loudest little pigs.

The scariest thing was when we had to mate the sows with the boars. The boars would be waiting but sometimes the sows didn't like it, and Pāpā would make me get in the pen and make sure they were doing it properly. There was this one boar that needed help to get up on the sow. He was a giant. Standing up on all fours and me standing up straight, he was bigger than me. It was my job to hold the sow ready so she couldn't run away while he got up on her back.

I was surprised to see that my dad was really knowledgeable. He's a man of many skills. Jack of all trades but a master of nothing. Because I was the one who had to be with him all the time, I saw him do things my brothers didn't know he could do. I saw him go around all the farmhouses, butcher the animals, do all the gardening, work on the horses, asphalting, painting, building, doing the piggery stuff. Working diggers, excavators, steamrollers. Always working with his hands. I helped him build a retaining wall for our house; I got a hiding if I didn't do it properly. I had to sit there for hours when he did night-shift painting. I think he just liked to have somebody there with him.

Having me with him, I think now, was his way of saying he loved me. And I do appreciate it. Regardless of how he did it, I learnt so much stuff. I wish I'd been more attentive. But the truth was I hated it most of the time. Even though I spent so much time with him, there was no feeling of closeness. It always felt dangerous.

He was the manly man, teaching me what to do in the only way he knew. 'This is how you do it. You do as you're told. Do it now. Get in there.' Everything was forced and very tense. 'Shut up and do it.' He often still lost it and gave me hidings. If he went too far, my mum would jump in, 'Stop it, Ross. Stop it. You're a man of God, you don't do that no more.' And then he would calm down, and that was a new thing. Other times it would be too hard for him to calm down, if he went into that rage state, or if Mum wasn't around.

I was stuck with him.

So right from the age of seven I've worked. Even after getting up at 3 a.m. I'd sometimes go to school, although mostly those early mornings were in the weekend or holidays. That work ethic was always instilled in me, even if it was by way of a hiding: you have to work. And now I'm a workaholic. I love it, and I know I've got to keep working so I can pay for my lifestyle and also look after people.

I loved that outdoor farm life. Our house of course was filled with people staying with us. It was like Tamapahore in some ways, in that we could go exploring, always roving over the farm and on the motorbikes. My neighbours had a PeeWee 50 that I used to ride on with them, but one time when they were out I took it for a ride without asking and they were like, 'Never come back here again.' I was definitely a naughty kid.

My best mate at the time was an Indigenous Australian and we looked like brothers. We used to do backflips off our fence because we had really soft grass — we could do backflips for days. That was so much fun. You've got no worries in your head when you're doing backflips.

And then when I was eight we moved from that farm to another farm just a few kilometres up the road, in Bangalow. It was the same kind of thing — a piggery that my dad worked in, and thousands of chickens, and horses to ride. And it was there, in that house, that my life really fell apart.

CHAPTER FIVE

My life was stolen from me

The storm may come and the rain will fall
Fire and pain go hand in hand

— 'Find You'

I was only eight but i wasn't a normal little kid, innocent, lost in a child's world. My whole life I'd known too much about adult things. I knew what alcohol was, and drugs. I knew violence and too much anger and hate.

I also knew what sex was. I had been sexually awakened since the age of two or three.

Remember what I said: the two sides of our lives. That child life of always travelling in a gang, of loving being right in the heart of my extended family. The beauty and the violence; everything, but nothing.

Monkey see, monkey do.

Older cousins touching me. Some of them, a few years older, just boys, though, touching me like others had touched them probably. And right from when I was a little, little kid, I liked it.

That's a hard thing to say, 'I liked that feeling.' But I did, and I wanted more of it.

I had no understanding of what that feeling was. I had no understanding that my view of sex was being tainted — or of what that feeling could be if you were to choose it yourself at a mature age, when you were making the decision for yourself. That decision was taken away from me. I'm still learning about this. Even very recently I heard a man

94

speaking about abuse and he went, 'My life was stolen from me,' and it hit me, 'My life was actually stolen from me!' By the first person who touched me, it was taken.

When I was a little kid, my older cousins were touching me. Then me and my other cousins would do it, and we would do it to each other and play around with each other. It was physically nice but secretive and dirty at the same time. It was a secret thing. Touching them in places that you shouldn't touch them, and doing things that we shouldn't do, doing adult stuff as little kids. Not full-on sex because we didn't know how to do that, but everything else, oral, everything. And I craved for that feeling. It was exciting, it filled up my mind, and it made the other feelings, like rejection and fear, go away.

But it was also the thing that made me hate myself most, the way that I was. I couldn't control my feelings or my head or my emotions. I knew I was dirty and disgusting and wrong.

I would get aroused by anything. Anything. The slightest touch, no matter who from. The slightest suggestion, the slightest sight — inside my head, everything was about sex. It was how I saw and understood the world. I now know there are words for it — hyper-sexualised, promiscuous — and that it's really common in kids who have been sexually abused, but I had no idea about anything like that then, or even for years. All I knew was my own experience and that sex was a big part of the scramble inside my head, my self-hatred and disgust, my obsession. *Why am I like this? Why do I think like this? Why am I getting turned on from the stupidest, ugliest things?* That was the way it happened, and that was my first learning.

All through my childhood, from my earliest memory, I was just so sexually charged. Nothing was ever innocent. Nothing has ever been innocent since that first day.

By the time I was six, seven, eight, it took over my whole being and I believed I was fully responsible for everything I did and thought — that everything was my fault. My fault. The fault was in me. Even back at the age of three, that time I took a knife from the kitchen and tried to stab myself, I had the sense of something rotten living inside me. I was Little Evil. Now as an adult, I'm like, *Shit, I just had no control over most of the stuff I did.*

We never got talked to as kids. We didn't get talked to about sex, our bodies, where not to, where to, how to do things. We never got taught anything, because we never got talked to. We just got hidings and groundings, 'Don't do that.'

'But why?'

'Just don't, idiot.'

But now parents definitely talk to their kids. I love watching friends talk to their kids about their bodies and things like that, 'Nobody's to ever do anything to you that feels uncomfortable … don't ever be ashamed of your body … You love your body …' Hearing that sort of stuff makes me so happy.

I remember once I was with my cousin and we were touching each other, and I was like, 'Hey,' and he goes, 'It's all right, we're cousins.' He said that to me, because that was normal. It's so ugly that that was our normal.

I always say we came from the best place, having all our whānau there, and it was, but what also happened in those places was abuse and poverty. I'm the first person in my family to speak out about that. I know heaps of my family members have been either raped, molested or similar. I know heaps of rapists, and that's such a sad thing. But the questions to ask are: 'Why are they like that? What was done to them? What created them?' Because no one is born like that.

Something happened to them. This is the thing. As much as they disgust me, there's a bit of me that has empathy for them: *What happened to you, for you to be this person, for you to abuse somebody and take something from somebody like that?* I don't want to just punish these people, I want to stop it.

* * *

At our new house we had an older cousin staying with us. He was sixteen but to me he was a man. Looking back now, I'm like, *Far out, that's a kid.* But to me, spindly little eight-year-old that I was, he was a man. He was taller than my oldest brother, his voice was that of a man, and he was staunch and strong like a man.

I love nature documentaries, and the thing I love watching most, my ultimate obsession, is lions. And when a lion stalks its prey it knows, like any predator knows, which are the weak animals to target. They study their prey. They smell the weakness. They choose carefully. And I am certain that when this cousin saw me, he knew exactly who and what I was. He knew I was stuffed up. He must've seen in me that I had some issues, that I was rejected, that I wanted to be loved, or even that I was a little bit feminine. He must've been watching me that whole time for him to do that to me.

I am not a predator, but I have the same intuitive alertness. When I walk into a room of kids, I know exactly who's been sexually abused. I can sense it. I recognise it. I know because I've played every different role there is, I've used every defense mechanism possible. After something's happened to me, I've acted overly happy, I've been obnoxious, I've been the quiet one, I've just acted really normal, I've been the tough one. I was a compulsive liar, an actor my whole childhood. Kids like me, we put on these masks, to try to stop people seeing.

* * *

It's after school. I'm sitting on the couch watching cartoons on TV. He's sitting with me. There's no one else home. He starts to touch me, and that's weird. I look at him and he goes, 'Have you ever had sex before?'

I don't know what to think. I'm eight. I say, 'No.'

He goes, 'Oh, it's nice, eh.' He keeps touching me and then he goes, 'Do you want to have sex?'

I don't know what he's asking, and I say, 'I don't know.' And he keeps on going, this guy who I've known my entire life, who's so close with my oldest brother, who I love. He lies me down — makes me lie on my stomach on that couch and starts pulling at my pants so that they come right down. And that's when it happens and it's so painful and I don't know what to do. I'm saying, 'It hurts.'

I'm not crying, I'm just frozen.

And he's saying, 'No, it's all right.'

'It's sore!'

'No, it's nice, eh?'

Oh my God. To me, he's a slithery snake just prodding me and pushing into me and touching me everywhere. And I've never seen this before. I never even knew this happened. I know about sex and a lot of different things. I know how to do it, but I never knew this. It's the shock of my life.

He isn't aggressive to me. He just keeps talking, and that's what's most disgusting and confusing to me: 'It's good, eh? You like this feeling? It's nice, eh?'

After it's over, I'm in a lot of pain.

This is the first time.

* * *

It happened most days for the next nine months. He would get home from work early, so he was there every day after school, waiting for me. It was nearly always just me and him. If someone else was there, he would just act like normal and nothing would happen, except one time when my nan was in the lounge watching TV and we were in the bedroom. It wasn't the same every day. The anal thing, I would always say, 'I don't want to do that.' So he'd do something else, or get me to do something else, but sometimes he would do it anyway, even though I always said, 'I don't want to do that.' It always hurt.

He would do things to me and he'd say things like, 'You like that feeling. You like how that feels.'

And I would say, 'Oh yeah.' Because I did like the feeling, even though I didn't like what was happening. He was playing on the feelings that I liked. The things he said, he was trying to make it my fault for liking that feeling. Like he was doing it all for me; that it was my fault; that I was almost asking for it. *Yes, I do like this.* It fully stuffed me right up.

It wasn't even so much the act, the physical thing, that did the damage to me. For me, you can get over anything physical. It was what he would say to me that really stuffed me up: 'You like it, don't you? You like how that feels.'

And because I felt that it was my fault, something to do with how wrong *I* was, I would never tell anybody.

* * *

I'm walking home from school, my bare feet kicking at dust and stones, my backpack on my back. I know who's waiting for me. And I stop suddenly, frozen still. I don't want to go home. It all feels really big in my head and I'm scared. What if he does that thing to me today? I don't want that pain.

Maybe someone else will be there today. This is something I both want and don't want. It's so confusing. Have you watched slave movies? How even when they have an opportunity to run, they don't run? How when they have an opportunity to shoot their master, they can't do it? They're conditioned. And I am conditioned to this. In my young, innocent mind it is almost like a relationship. Or a collaboration that I'm part of. That's what he tells me, anyway.

I get home and go inside and he's there, standing there naked, looking at me. And I know what I have to do, what he expects me to do, and so I go to him, and it almost feels normal to me.

'Don't tell anybody,' he says to me. 'Because if you tell someone we can't do it again. And you want to do it, you like this, eh?' This is what he says to me, all the time. And so it is my fault.

Inside myself, I'm like, Far out, it makes me so … I feel so … oh shit, I don't even know how I feel. *I don't have words for it. But he makes me say, 'Yeah, yeah, I like this feeling.'* Oh shit.

I come home from school and I can't find him straight away. I go into my bedroom and he's sleeping in my bed, naked. I know what he expects, and so I go and lie by him. I know he's not really asleep. And he's like, 'What are you doing? I'm asleep.' Like I'm the naughty one, wanting it.

I'm like, 'Oh', and jump away, and he goes, 'No, come back, come back.'

He likes to play these little games with me like that.

'Don't tell anyone or we can't do it again and then I'll have to go away and that'll be your fault.'

'No, no, no, I won't tell on you.'

'If you do, I'm gonna get in trouble and that's gonna be your fault.'

I don't want him to go away. I do want him to go away. I don't want him to get in trouble. But sometimes I say, 'I'm gonna tell on you,' and that makes him get real dramatic.

I want to tell on him heaps. But I'm scared of what will happen. I'm scared I'll get a hiding.

It feels wrong but the things he is doing to me, that sometimes feels nice.

* * *

I didn't realise he was stuffing me up. I didn't realise I was a little puppet in his game.

It made me much worse inside. Because anytime I got a hiding, I would look in the mirror and I'd be crying to myself, and I'd think, *I hate you. Why can't you be normal? Why are you like this?* I hated myself. I thought I was an abomination.

I just can't believe how much I thought everything was my fault. I really did. I thought it was my fault; I thought I fully understood and comprehended everything.

Sometimes, when I was being punished for being naughty, I got left home with him while my family went out somewhere. They didn't know. One holidays, we had passes to SeaWorld and Movie World and were going every day, but I was naughty so I had to stay home with my nan. He was there, too.

And then it was over. We moved back to New Zealand and it was over, just like that. I saw him again quite soon after at a funeral and he never said anything. Never looked at me, never gave the slightest indication of what had happened between us. I stared at him during the funeral, thinking: *I wonder if you're thinking the same thing as me right now. How can you act normal like nothing happened?* When he did see me, when we were in the same group, he said, "Sup, bro?" — like nothing ever happened. 'Yeah, all good.'

Years later, when Mum and Pāpā confronted him, he denied everything. 'No, I didn't … What did Stan say? … Why is he talking like that?' He never admitted it. Ultimate denial. Ruin somebody's life, go to your grave pleading your innocence.

I was stuffed up. I was living inside a secret. From then on, I was like a little creature hiding in corners, living in nasty cracks and crevices, operating out of secrecy my whole life. I lived with so many lies and I had so many different personalities that I used to put on for different people, different crowds I found myself in. I was a compulsive liar. I was sly, I was dirty. I thought dirty.

I had this weird switch inside me, like a trigger, and I didn't know what it was.

* * *

Our cat has had kittens — so cute and fragile, grey and ginger, all meowing and trying to feed. There's one white kitten, the smallest of the litter, and the prettiest. She's got some muck from her birth sac still on her face and I'm like, 'Oh, poor little thing. Poor little kitten,' and I pick her up to wipe her clean, but something is happening inside myself. I squeeze her tighter than she likes.

It would take almost nothing.

It's like I have two voices playing in my head at the same time. Don't do that! Oh, but it feels good!

My body feels it, feels what it would be like to hurt something else. I don't understand why I would even want to. I love cats. We've always had heaps of cats, heaps of different ticklebums — that's what we call them all. I love to kiss them and rub their faces.

But now, this feeling.

I hold that tiny kitten, that pretty little kitten, and I know I could kill it, and that something is driving me to do that.

It is so helpless.

I put it down with its mum and it opens its tiny mouth to mew and I back away. My heart is pounding and my head is hot. I feel like I'm Little Evil.

* * *

That's how I was. I was at the very edge. I couldn't even acknowledge to myself how much I'd been hurt, but when I think about how I felt when I was squeezing that poor kitten, I can see it was some of that coming out. For years I thought that wanting to hurt that kitten proved how evil I was; it was hard to understand, because I love animals and have so much compassion for them — so why did I feel like that? But that's how I was. When my switch was flipped, I wasn't just coming to do damage; I was coming for your whole life. I was coming for your jugular. I was coming to end it. I had feelings inside myself — the hate, the rage — that I didn't even fully know were there. I can still feel that sometimes, if there's an injustice or somebody hurts my family, I go straight there to that feeling. But now I know to how to calm myself.

I think, 'Jesus, help me, Lord.'

The switch will always be there, but when I was a little kid I didn't understand what was happening to me or inside me. Now that I'm older, I understand more. I can catch myself and see what's happening. It's how you manage yourself and it's knowing how to turn it off. It can get flipped on but it can get flipped off. It's the same kind of thing as learning how to deal with a panic attack or anxiety. You can 'un-anxiety' yourself. I personally reckon anything that comes in can go out, you can get rid of, you can unlearn. It just takes time.

And you can learn the things you didn't learn when you were little. What happens when you're a kid doesn't have to define your whole life.

* * *

Now, as an adult, I see photos of myself from that time, and it shocks me to put those images together with my memories of then and the feelings I've carried with me right through my life. What I see is a little kid. My face has a child's softness, my eyes are bright but I imagine I see something in them that is complicated — maybe sad, maybe wary. I've got buck teeth and big ears. My hair is curly and my body is small and skinny. So little. So young. I didn't know how young I was.

I always thought I knew and understood the things that were done to me and demanded of me. I believed I carried responsibility. I always felt guilty and ashamed.

I think of a young child I know now, and how intuitive she is about her mother's feelings. When her mother feels sad, this child knows and she says, 'Are you all right, Mummy?' She understands that her mother is sad, but of course she actually has no understanding of what's wrong. How could she? She doesn't know anything about bills, or having to go to work, or anything that's a part of what adults worry about. And as I think about that, it helps me to understand what happened to me. How could I, as an eight- and then nine-year-old child, have understood about manipulation, about rape, about what is *stolen* from a person when they are raped repeatedly and their need for love and acceptance is so badly abused?

Suddenly, I understand that an eight- or nine-year-old child has no responsibility for being raped. Having that realisation is trippy.

I think it over. I let it sit in my mind for a while. And a feeling rises up in me that I've never felt before. I feel sorry for that little kid, little me, and the situation he was in, and all his confusion. For the first time ever, I want to give that little Stan a hug. *Oh, poor boy. To go through that.*

Now, as an adult I am like: How could I possibly have known? Kids are so easily manipulated to feel, to think the way a powerful person intends for them to feel and think. Kids want to please and get praise. They want to be loved. I feel like my eyes have opened to understanding more about how my feelings were manipulated.

I remember everything. I remember every feeling. I remember every good feeling, every bad feeling. And now I know: sexual feelings can actually lie to your heart and your soul. Sex is so powerful. That feeling is so powerful that it can manipulate your actual real feelings and who you really are, and that's what it was doing to me when I was a kid.

Your head and your heart are like, *What the hell? That's not good. I'm sure this is not good.* But your body is going, *Hey, this is good. This is what you want.* Your actual feelings are manipulated to the point where your self-identity is affected.

It's like the little serpent in your ear, 'I want more. Just do it. Just get it. Get your fix.'

It's funny how a physical feeling can control your mind, can manipulate you, can take over everything. That's why I think the damage done by rape is a spiritual thing. It's a soul thing. It affects your whole being.

Every time I was touched or raped, something was taken from me. It wasn't just the physical — I can recover from physical damage. But something was *taken* from me. It was like someone had sucked up something out of me. Part of my spirit would break every single time. That's what was taken. That was more than a physical thing. I learned this from my own experience, before I believed in God or anything.

Sex is tapu. You don't want to mess around with it, doing it with any person, giving it to many people. That is not right and it will stuff your head up. I've learned that from experience, and I've also learned that sex can be the most powerful, pure thing. The times that I've made love, it's like there's a transfer between two people that I think is one of the most sacred things we have. I reckon, anyway. I believe God definitely gave us that as a gift, like the utmost thing, and it should be used like that; but if it is used in other ways or taken from you in a different way, then it becomes the ultimate manipulation and lie.

For someone like me, coming from where I do and having had these experiences, it's not easy to just step into a life of easy, positive relationships, and that's something else that was taken from me. Some of my later sexual experiences have been confusing and conflicting because of the things that happened to me in my childhood.

I think sex has always been a complicated issue in my life. I say to my mates, 'Man, I wish I was a virgin.' I wish I could think pure and feel pure and not have had that experience of wanting and needing sex like an addict.

I try to understand the relationship between my early sexual awakening, the violence at home, and the rape. And there must be a relationship, because it had to start somewhere. I was a certain way, maybe giving off this thing, wanting that feeling, wanting to be loved — maybe certain people, predators, can detect stuff, can sense what you know, if they've gone through similar things or something's happened to them when they were young. Maybe they can pick up the same trauma, just like I can recognise it in kids.

And as someone who's been through all the stuff I've been through, you're a little bit attracted to it, even though you hate it. This is like women that keep going back with the men who keep smashing them. It's a stuck mindset. They don't have self-worth. It's something they've always known, so there's something about it that attracts them.

It's familiar. You know it. And yet you think nobody loves you, and you hate yourself. You're disgusted with yourself. But you don't know what else to do.

They are hard feelings to get rid of. *There's something wrong with me. I'm disgusting.* I was so scared that those feelings would haunt me all my life. That they meant loss — that I would never have the thing I've always really wanted, to have a wife and kids and that whole thing. I'm like, man, I don't want to just be stuffed up and not give them the purest version of me.

I don't want that ugliness to come into my life with my family. As I grew up, I was scared about that.

I don't know which parts of me are what I was born with, and which parts were created through the things that have happened to me. As an adult now, I understand that little kids respond to what's thrown at them in the world. They grow into the shape that the world shows them. But it's still *me*. What happened to me, happened to *me*, and I'm the one who has to live with it. I'm the one that has to live with this Frankenstein vision of myself.

And that's how I felt — like I was Frankenstein's monster. I was made up of all these things that had been done to me and that were part of me; nothing made sense and nothing belonged to me. But it was me.

I often felt rejected as a kid. I've already written about how much I wanted from my mum, how I wanted hugs and kisses, but she was too wrapped up in the things happening to her to give me that kind of love. 'Get away. Go away. So annoying.' I felt unloved, and maybe that made me more vulnerable to someone who seemed to be showing me attention and affection.

Kids have a massive need for love, and the way they're loved in childhood fully moulds and shapes the way they are able to love, and the kind of person they're going to be.

As a kid you just learn from what's around you. You only have a child's understanding, no matter how worldly wise you think you are. But we don't have to be stuck in the old ways of understanding. Anyone can change. I've learnt a lot as I've grown. I know love now. I know what love is and what it isn't. And I make sure to tell the people that I love, that I love them. I try to make sure that everything is open. I don't want that closed-off way of being. Some of my bros are so staunch, they would never show affection except in the staunchest ways. But I've broken them down. I'm like, 'I love you, bro.'

My best mate, he once said to me, 'It used to be annoying when you always used to say, "Love you, bro." I wasn't brought up like that.'

'Neither was I, bro.'

'Yeah, but now I love it.' And then he said, 'I love you too, my brother.'

* * *

I wish I could give that little Stan a hug.

That feeling I have now, my recent feeling of being sorry for little Stan, is not a feeling I usually carry around with me. I've never felt like a victim, in that way of having a victim mentality. Yes, I've been a victim, but what's the point of living in that? I see people who live in that and their lives are so shit. They're getting nowhere, they're staying in the same place. Sometimes they become the abuser themselves — constantly blaming other people and not taking responsibility for their own self and their own feelings. You cannot change what has happened. You cannot change the things that are out of your hands. You can only change your own self. It's the only thing you actually have control over.

There are heaps of things I might change, if I could change the past. But I *can't* change it. And all those things that happened, I've learned from them and I've grown from them so at the same time, maybe I wouldn't change them because I am who I am.

When I tell my story, I don't tell it to say that I'm a victim. I tell it because it's my story — it's mine alone to tell. That's my testimony of where I have come from and to show I am who I am, and where I'm at today. I have to own my story.

Of course, when I'm tired or down, I sometimes get dramatic and all 'poor me'. I go through stages of mourning, sadness, hurting and feeling lost. I have had hard times when I struggle, when the old bad feelings get their grip on me, but I take responsibility for myself, and I hope to get better and faster at getting back to a state of acceptance.

'When I was a child, I spoke as a child, I understood as a child, I thought as a child: but when I became a man, I put away childish things.' (1 Corinthians 13:11)

I am still learning.

* * *

I need to explain something that's hard for some people to understand. First, we don't all come from homes where things are talked about openly, or even at all. We don't all come from homes where it's accepted that you can be whoever you really are and that's okay. In my home, growing up, everything was black and white, no explanations. In a world like that, you are not given choices. You don't have the information to make choices.

I come from a place where if you are gay, it's because you were raped or molested. And if you're a boy, and you were raped or molested by a man, then that means you are gay. I didn't know better than that until I was quite old, definitely adult. As I got older, I was drawn to women. I am attracted to women and that's who I want to make a future and a family with. But inside myself, I had this secret, that I must be gay because I'd been raped by a man. It was a dark secret because in my world it was evil to be gay. That's what I experienced.

It wasn't until after Idol, I was talking to a producer one day, and he mentioned his partner and said 'he'.

I was really shocked, and I asked, 'Are you gay?'

He goes, 'Yes.'

'Really?' Because he wasn't what I expected … he wasn't bad or anything like that. This was me coming from where I come from. And I asked again, 'Eh? Are you sure?'

'Yeah, I've got a boyfriend.'

And then I asked him, 'Oh, did you get raped, bro?'

'No.'

'Really?' I was astonished. 'Oh, did you get touched up?' I was trying to understand. *What do you mean, you didn't get raped and you didn't get touched, but you're gay?*

'Bro, I tried, I tried to go with girls, you know, and I just couldn't. I just love the company of a man.'

I was like, 'Wow. I didn't know.' It was like going back to school.

I was lucky that he took the time to explain his story to me, because I know in some situations gay people would not get where I was coming from. They'd just think I'm ignorant, that I was just bigoted. But I was never wilfully ignorant; I just never had the opportunity to understand. Now I understand that gay people don't have a choice about their identity. So, you can't ever assume that people who don't share your opinions or attitudes do so out of bigotry or hatred, or from having a closed mind. It could just be that they haven't ever heard that other story.

Since I became an adult, I have had a lot of amazing friends and teachers for different paths and I understand myself and the world a lot better. The most broken part of my life has become one of my biggest tools for learning.

When I was little, the joke was always that I was a little 'beeitch'. I was feminine. I just had my mum and aunties to be safe with, and I used to hang with my nan all the time, wear a tea towel on my head like I was doing the karanga like the ladies. My nan let me bake bread with her and I liked that — I'd knead the flour and water and she'd cook it in the oven. I used to like girl stuff, but I was a little boy.

And then behind the closed doors, from when I was little, being sexually awakened, being touched and prodded by older male cousins, and then doing it with cousins and mates, and not knowing what it was, but liking that feeling.

I don't even know how or why it started, if it was from being touched and stuff like that, but I kind of used to act feminine. I had a way about me that looked gay. I actually didn't even know or understand, I just always thought that if you're feminine, you're gay. If you're too nice and touchy, you're gay. That was my belief. There's no in between. I acted like a girl and I'd get teased for that or beaten up. I didn't know that there are actually lots of ways of simply being male.

As a little kid, I used to think, *Was I supposed to be born a girl? Why am I like this? Why do I have the feelings I have?* I always knew deep inside me that there was something wrong with me.

Now, I know some fallas who are hard and staunch who are gay, and others who are the softest, loveliest people, and who aren't gay. There's no black and white. But I didn't know that then. Now, I don't care. I can be whatever I want.

These days, I look at people and I see them being all ways. I've got a lot of girl mates who dress like boys, and boy mates who are soft and feminine, but it just does not matter. I love seeing people be whoever they want to be.

Pāpā was so afraid I was gay. If I acted a certain way, if I was acting girly, he would smash me. 'You're acting like a poofter.'

At school, they were like, 'Oh, little fag, little poofter.' I would take it all because in my mind, I'm like, *Nobody's ever going to give out a hiding like my dad, so go hard. I'll never cry.*

People would make comments like, 'Is your son gay?' And Pāpā would give me a hiding because he didn't want to believe that.

One time, when I was twelve, I was in the car with my mum and she asked me, 'Are you gay?' I got so angry at her for asking me that. Her asking me that meant she understood nothing about my life and what had happened to me. She didn't know about how my cousin had raped me. She knew nothing, but she was asking this question that felt like a judgment on the way I acted. I didn't know how to change. I couldn't explain what was wrong, even to myself.

It wasn't ever a question of my sexuality. It was a question of me being a kid who was completely stuffed up and didn't understand anything that had happened to him.

Now, watching my audition for *Australian Idol,* I see that there are still remnants of that time in the way I carry myself. I am a bit feminine, I have certain ways of behaving, mannerisms, that are whispers of what I'd been through. I was still evolving, as I will always be evolving. It was a little bit left over from that earlier time, stuff that I still had to grow out of. I have many physical scars; I had many invisible scars on the inside, and at that time I still had physical vestiges, behaviours that were also like scars — reminders of how I'd been when I was little.

* * *

Whether you're a girl or a boy, being penetrated, manipulated, dominated in rape is ugly. It's stuffed up and bad, no matter who it's happening to. But there are particular issues in there for boys getting raped by a man. That's what I know, so that's what I'm going to talk about. I feel sorry for young boys. When you're a young boy being handled in a certain way by a man like that, it's just shame. Shame that you got raped. It's total domination by another man, so it changes the way you see yourself as a boy or a man. It kind of makes you an outsider.

The way boys like me were brought up, to talk about rape, or anything about feelings, was weakness. If you grew up like me, you got to be tough. 'Don't be weak … Don't you cry … You're crying … Don't you cry, little pussy.' The old way of having to 'man up' was to be staunch, be silent, talk with your fists. It was made even worse because of the homophobic culture that we grew up in. People thought that being weak, being feminine, being 'unmanly' equalled being gay.

Most fallas from that mindset don't want to talk about sexual abuse. It's too much shame. We never talked about that stuff. If it ever did come up in conversation, it'd be like, 'Ah, shut up,' or, 'Don't talk about that,' and they make it into a joke.

There's a change happening now, and it's a change that teaches young boys how to be men that respect, that love, that feel, that talk, all that stuff. The old way of being a man is to pretend there's nothing going on inside. The new way is to change the definition of strong.

Me and my boys, we've got a group of men, we're called the Kings. We've got All Blacks in there, we've got business owners, we've got artists, we've got producers, and we talk about all this stuff. We sit together and we talk about the things that are real in our lives. We say, 'I love you, brother.' Man, saying that back in the day! It could never have happened. I tell all my cousins, 'I love you, my cousin.'

'Ah, chur cuz,' all staunch and awkward. Hopefully, we're the last generation.

CHAPTER SIX

Hurt so bad

I cry myself all night to sleep
Cos I was hurt so bad
And every second I wish I was dreaming
That this was for real

— 'Missing You'

THE WHOLE TIME BEING IN AUSTRALIA WHEN I WAS SO little, I missed my koko. I missed my cousins, I missed life back there at Tamapahore, but most of all I missed Koko. He came to stay with us at Christmas, the year before he died when I had just turned eight, and he was alive and well.

I have a memory of him, my mum and me all lying down together on the bunk in my bedroom at the first pig farm. It was so warm and safe, and he was using his cute cheeky humour. I was like, 'Koko, can I please have two dollars?'

'Oh, go have a shit,' in his playful, jokester voice. I'd be giggling and laughing.

'Koko, can I please have two dollars?'

'Oh, you little fat thing ... Oh, shut up, boy ... Ooh, shut up.' It's like mocking, but also being cute to the kids. We loved him.

For me and my brothers, he had been like our dad. He was with Mum to do everything. He would take me with him in his van when he needed to go down to Bayfair, the mall, and he'd always get me PK chewing gum. It was his favourite, and now it's what I chew because of him. I prefer PK over anything. He took me with him wherever he was going, except when he took my two brothers up to see the Warriors in Auckland, driving in his little old van. I was too little to go.

'I want to go with you guys!'

'You can't, boy.'

I was like, 'No!' and I chucked a tantrum.

The only time he ever growled me was when I was chasing my brother with the chains. My brother had hurt me and I'd switched into my out-of-control and wanted to smash him, so I was chasing him with the dog chain, trying to hit him with it. Koko made me stop.

Koko always seemed like an old man to me, but he was only 54 when he died. He was so loveable. He always wore his stubbies with his skinny little legs poking out and his feet in these ugly big jandals. He'd have his stubbies held up with a belt, and a button-up shirt tucked into his shorts. He would wear his cowboy hat or his bucket hat, and he would have his glasses on and his big moustache. He was brainy — he was an accountant; he was also the man for whakapapa and knew all about the land and the shareholdings. Everybody loved him, everybody. He didn't have any issues with anybody.

He hated the way things were between my mum and dad. He hated my dad. But when he came over to Australia to visit that time, he saw that Pāpā had changed. He saw it — no more drinking and drugs, no more hitting my mum. And I remember them hugging. Oh, my gosh, I remember them hugging at the airport, Pāpā and Koko. I think that's my last memory of Koko before he got sick. I had never seen them hug before, never. And he went home and he told everyone that Pāpā had changed.

It must have been late April the next year, 1999, that I was eating my lunch at school when I looked up and saw Pāpā coming in the school gate. *What's he doing here?* And

Pāpā goes, 'Stan, come over here. We got to go home.' And we jumped in the truck and he goes, 'Koko's dying. We got to go back to New Zealand.'

Next thing, we were back in Tauranga and going straight to the hospital. He was lying there in the bed, in a coma, with all these tubes coming out of him. I was crying and Mum was telling me, 'He can hear you,' so I said, 'I love you, Koko.'

He was in that coma for two weeks before my mum and Uncle Whiti had to decide to let him go.

Koko's death was actually even sadder and more poignant than I really understood at the time. For many years, our whānau had been plagued by death — in the thirty years leading up to the mid-1990s, more than one hundred of us had died of cancer. Our urupā is full; our houses are empty. There were some in our family who believed it was a mākutu, a curse on us, for having taken money when the quarry was put on our land.

But in 1994, my Nanny Maybelle McLeod, who is a nurse, got funding from the Health Research Council to employ a scientist to look for answers. She was so proactive: she knew we had a problem, and she went out and found the resources and the people who could help her solve it. She started working with a geneticist at Otago University, Professor Parry Guilford, and again, our whānau was very active in that process, using our whakapapa, the registry of Births, Deaths and Marriages, hospital records, gravestones and blood tests — and eventually Professor Guilford and his team identified a genetic mutation that was responsible for all this cancer, the mutant CDH1 gene.

It meant we could now get a blood test to see if we had the gene. And we learned that a person with the gene has almost an eighty per cent chance of developing stomach cancer, and women with the gene also have a thirty-nine per cent chance of getting breast cancer.

My koko was one of the first in the family to have the blood test, and it was discovered he had the gene. He wasn't surprised, as he had already lost so many of his family to cancer, including his own father, and one of my cousins, who died at just seventeen. He told Professor Guilford it wasn't bad news because now he could lead his family into the screening process. He then had a gastroscopy and it confirmed that he had stomach cancer. The only possible treatment was for him to have his stomach removed. He had this done, but there were complications that led to his death two weeks later. So we all felt like he had died for us, died so that we would understand more about this disease that was killing so many in our whānau. Since his death, there have been many more operations and no one else has died.

The full significance of his death came home to me more as I got older, and at no time more powerfully than when I was diagnosed myself, the fifth generation of my family to inherit both the gene and its high risk of cancer, and I had to have the exact same operation that had killed him. But that was nearly twenty years in the future.

At the time, as he lay in that coma, I went to stay with my Uncle Stan and Aunty Leonie. I'd brought my recorder with me from Australia — I'd been learning it at school and I used to play it everywhere. I was playing 'Amazing Grace', and thinking, *I want to play this at my koko's funeral. If he dies, I'll play it at his funeral.*

He died in the middle of the night. Mum and Pāpā came and picked me up so we could all be together with him at Tamapahore.

I didn't play my recorder at the funeral, too shy, but me and my cousin went out and picked flowers for Koko to put inside his coffin. But what I also remember is how his dog went missing. For my whole life, Sooty had always been with Koko, but then after Koko died Sooty disappeared. Dogs have this thing where they know that their owner's dead. And I remember somebody saying, 'Oh, I think he's gone to die.'

I wish Koko hadn't died. He would be so proud of us today and how far we've all come as a whānau.

After Koko's funeral, we went back to Australia, back to Bangalow and the second pig farm. But Mum wanted to move back home, and so the decision was made that we would move back to Tamapahore. It took several months to get everything sorted. So I was stuck with the cousin who was raping me and there was nothing I could do about it. It happened right through that year, through Christmas and New Year.

Somewhere in there, during those months, I had my first cigarette. There were some older boys at my school and I knew they used to go to smoke under a bridge. One day, I ended up walking with them, I just followed them there. They offered me a smoke and I was like, 'Yep.' I had a puff. I coughed, and that was my first experience. After that, I smoked with my older cousins, especially after we came back to New Zealand, just passing the cigarettes around to be cool. But I didn't really get started properly till I was twelve.

I couldn't wait to do those things. I couldn't wait to smoke. I couldn't wait to drink. I couldn't wait to do whatever I wanted to do. When I was nine and still in Australia, I had my first puff of dope.

So we moved back to New Zealand, and that was when the raping stopped. I loved being back at Tamapahore with all my cousins, nannies and koros. I guess it was weird going from that situation of being raped every day, as I had been in Australia, to it not happening anymore. I don't really remember. I was still a little kid and I don't think I ever really dwelt on it — I just kept moving. No one knew so it was easy to just pack it all away.

I no longer had Koko to run to. That was hard. I missed him, but at the same time I was getting older and I was getting into older kids' stuff. That little Stan had gone. The only time I went out my bedroom window now was to sneak in and out to be with my cousins, or to smoke ciggies. I didn't do that much, though, because I was too scared I would get a hiding.

During the day I went with my cousins to school at Arataki Primary at Mount Maunganui. In the winter, we'd walk to school in those freezing mornings, frost on the grass. I never used to wear shoes to school, so to keep my feet warm just for a little moment, I'd find a nice fresh cow poo and wiggle my toes into it.

I was the only one out of our cousins who wasn't in the full-immersion Māori unit. In Australia, we spent a lot of time at Māori gatherings — whether it be a rugby game, a barbecue, a birthday, a party — but there wasn't really anyone that, as a child, I could speak Māori with, even though I'd been to kōhanga. So at Arataki I went into the bilingual class, where we were actually learning Māori, and it came to me quickly, like it was always there. It's natural to speak our own native tongue. It just felt natural and familiar to me. I've always loved te reo, I've just never had time or the opportunity to focus on becoming really fluent.

School can be a hard place for a kid. A kid doesn't even have to do anything wrong, but the way they look, the way they dress, what they've got for lunch can make their whole life difficult. It's so sad and kids don't deserve that — nobody deserves to be bullied just for some little difference between them and the other kids.

I used to get bullied for acting like a girl, for my hair, for my buck teeth, my crooked nose, my big ears. Our cousins were ruthless. My nickname was Crooked Nose. ''Sup, Crooked Nose? Oh, you black shit. 'Sup, Black Arse?' Just the worst thing you could think about someone, that became their nickname. I think that's what made me tough. I could handle anything, because I grew up in an environment where you had to argue and fight, otherwise you just got extra picked on. You had to fight back. I was one of the smallest kids but I was quick with my mouth and quick with my feet.

* * *

Things continued pretty badly between Pāpā and me. I can see now that I was a mess.

124

My dad's brother, Uncle Stan, and his wife, Aunty Leonie, lived across at Matapihi, just on the other side of the harbour; they were the ones who took me in the most. They would always fight for me. They knew how often I was grounded and left home by myself, and also they knew I was getting hidings, so they often used to try and take me. They would come over and beg Mum, 'Come on, come on, sister, let him out.'

'He's not going.'

'Oh please, sister, let us take him.'

I spent many weekends with them on their farm, and I was with them every holidays. They were my hiding place. Everything about their place was old and rugged, very worn down, but we didn't look at things like that. It felt like home to me. There was a broken-down truck out the back and my uncle's ute and fire pits, and at the front was a caravan with an old man living in it — he wasn't whānau but he was always there, our whole lives, and my older cousin used to be good mates with him; he'd just go in all the time and take him smokes and have a smoke with him and see if he's all right and hang out with him. And so I used to go over there sometimes as well.

Stan and Leonie's daughter Jacqueline is the same age as me and we were best friends. To start with, I was always called Bubba Stan, then I was Little Stan, and Uncle Stan was Big Stan. (Now Jackie has had a son and she named him after me, so now we got three Stans. So it's Big Stan, Little Stan, Baby Stan. When she told me, I was buzzing out. He'll always have a little special spot in my heart because he's like the little us.)

At the back of their farm is a big farm with a paddock that we used to spend so many of our days in, racing around, doing relays, playing with their dog — they had a Rottweiler called Tui; we used to put a leash on her, and she would chase the cows and drag us all through the cow shit. You'd honestly have about five kids hanging onto this long lead, and she's running, dragging us. But eventually the farmer came and got her because she was killing the cows.

There were orchards there and we'd play in them, making huts and having wars but still being best friends. We would just roam around Matapihi.

Me and my older cousins would smoke in the orchard — that was when I was still at primary school, around ten, eleven. My mum and nannies all smoked rollies, so I knew how to roll smokes. My nanny had this rolling machine and she would ask me to do it for her — you'd put the paper in with the filter, then the tobacco and roll it up, lick it to glue it. Us kids used to go into town and pick up butts and get the tobacco out of them — roll them up and make a couple of ciggies out of them, and you'd get the different flavours. It was yuck, but we'd pass them around and after the first time or two I didn't cough anymore. I used to 'bum puff', like, not fully inhale, just to be cool. But then I just got to like doing it.

On Sundays we'd go over to Nanny Arlene and Koro Paul's for Bible studies. Nanny Arlene is Aunty Leonie's grandmother. While the Tamapahore whānau were Rātana, the Matapihi side were staunch Christians, and she would run these Sunday school classes for us, all in Māori. All the mokos would come around for it, all the grandkids and great-grandkids. She would give us Bible verses in Māori, and we would have tests and hand it back in. I didn't connect with the Christian message at all back then, but it was fun because we did it all together.

Being with Uncle Stan and Aunty Leonie felt more than safe. It was the funnest place ever. My Aunty Leonie is my favourite aunty. She's the funniest person. And my Uncle Stan is the loveliest, softest man. I suppose it was a relief to me, after being on edge at home, but I didn't really think about it then. I was a kid and I just lived in the moment, and it was fun and free. I didn't get smacked there and I would hardly ever get growled, and I think they were soft on me because they knew that I was getting hidings at home, so they let me get away with things.

Being around the older cousins, me and Jack knew they used to smoke dope as well as tobacco, and I couldn't wait to try that again. It definitely felt like the natural thing to do. The first time I remember getting really stoned I was eleven, around the back of the Hungahungatoroa Marae at Matapihi, hiding behind a toilet cubicle with my cousin Jack. At first I was like, *Oh, nothing.* Then it got me in the head and we ran home the whole way and I was light-as on my feet. When we got back, we lay down and I said, 'I'm falling through the ground, hold on!' We were looking at each other and we saw our eyes were bloodshot, and we hopped up and ate some toothpaste and went straight to bed so no one would see us. *Whoaaaa.* I was just tripping out. I don't know if I liked it, but I wanted to do it anyway.

* * *

I was always a thief. My whole family were thieves. Even my mum used to be a thief; that's one of the reasons she went to jail.

I used to do it to get things, but also for the thrill of it. I used to just love stealing. It was one of my greatest gifts. The first time I did it I was probably four and it would have been lollies from a shop. After that, it was just all the time. Even now, years after I've stolen anything, it's still a bit of a habit in my mind. *I could steal that if I wanted to.* Or I can catch a thief out, notice someone else doing it in a shop. *Oh my gosh, what a dumb thief.*

I broke into my first house when I was five or six. It was my friend's house, and I just went to their fridge and drank all their milk real quick. I thought it was so funny. After that, I just broke into houses all the time. When I was younger, food was the main thing I took. I'd break into somebody's house and go into their fridge and take their food. I did it by myself; sometimes I did it with other cousins. I'd make sure nobody was there, check all the windows and the doors, get in, run around and grab what I could. If I saw something else I liked, I'd take it. Get out as quick as I could. If there were a few of us, we were like little dogs, running in, taking the stuff, fighting over the things. Leave a mess. Oh my gosh, so stupid.

I'd be a little bit scared but excited at the same time. You're on the edge, you could get caught any minute, but it's so exhilarating. I loved that feeling.

I was so lucky I didn't get a record. I was caught only once, and that was in a supermarket in Australia when I was waiting for the bus. I was seven or eight. I nipped in to get myself an ice block and the shop guy saw me. 'Put that back! Don't you ever come back to this shop …'

Sometimes I'd break into brand-new houses not even to steal but to walk from room to room, looking at things and not even taking them, but just dreaming of how I wanted my life to be one day. I was always a big daydreamer. *I want a house like this.* I'd walk around rich streets, rich neighbourhoods. *That's the kind of car I'll have, that's the kind of neighbourhood I will live in.* I always wanted a five-bedroom house with two lounges and a pool and two bathrooms. After I won Idol, I bought a house just like that for my family to live in.

When I was at intermediate, like eleven or twelve, I stole my brother's car and went for a drive around Hamilton, but that's what we all did. Everyone in our family has stolen a car to drive. It was normal. If you got caught you got a hiding but you're like, *Yeah, I drove!*

My favourite thing was to go stay with Leonie and Stan because I had more freedom. I could get away with everything, have fun, stay out late-ish. 'Be back before the sun's gone down,' that was always our thing. 'You better be back before it's dark.'

Me and my cousins would walk all the way into Tauranga, over the railway bridge. Leonie might give us $20 to share for pocket money and, if she did, we could get a feed at Burger King and get some slime, which was the trend then. But if we didn't have money, it didn't really matter. I'd just steal what I wanted. Then we'd go to Burger King and wait for people to leave their tables and eat the rest of their food, and then grab their cups, because there was free refills. Or somebody would buy one drink and one chips and we'd all eat it.

But for everything else I was like, *I don't need money.*

We'd all go our separate ways, picking up butts from the streets of the town, going into shops and stealing what we wanted. Jack didn't like stealing, but some of us others were good. One time, when I had just turned twelve, I stole a couple of grand's worth of clothes from the one shop. I couldn't believe it. *How do you not know that I'm stealing?* I'd steal clothes for me, and my girl cousins, too. So we were just getting everything. Getting stuff for all of us. Then we'd head back home with our new merchandise and make rollies and smoke them in the orchards that were all around Aunty Leonie's place, looking at everything we had.

The same day I stole those thousands of dollars' worth of clothes, I caused another catastrophe. It was a really hot, dry day, and me and my cousins had got back from town and were hanging out in the kiwifruit orchards behind Leonie's. It was nice and shady, and we were just lounging around, looking at the stuff we'd got, passing around some smokes. I was playing with the lighter, lighting little fires out of piles of dry grass and leaves. It was fun to watch how the flame crept through the grass and then flared up really quick and sudden. After a bit, we got bored and decided to go down to the water. I stamped out my fires, and off we went. Someone had some dope, so we get stoned down there, and I don't know how long it was before we headed back. But as we came back, near the orchards, we saw three fire trucks. I was so off my face I just thought, kind of giggly, *Oh, that's trippy.*

But we soon heard that three orchards had burned. Someone had got trapped in a shed and was almost killed by the flames. Later, walking in the orchards, I saw the trunks of the vines were blackened.

On the way back from that, my little cousin said she was going to tell on me, and I had to bribe her with some pens I'd stolen. Anyway, somehow my aunty and uncle found out about the fire and what I'd been doing, and then my little cousin told them about the stealing. Lucky for me she only told them about the pens, not about all the clothes.

It was the first time I'd seen my uncle get angry and disappointed at me. He told me they had to take me home. He'd never said that before. And I was saying, 'I'm so sorry, I'm so sorry.' They didn't even know I'd stolen those clothes. 'Please don't tell on me,' I begged Leonie. 'Pāpā's going to give me a hiding.'

But she had to. She just felt like it was too big of a thing. We got home, and I remember my dad saying, 'Get into your room now.' There was no doubt what was going to happen. He knocked me over. I fell to the ground and he was punching me, yelling, 'So you want to steal? Eh? You want to steal?'

My mum was furious too, but was more upset about the fire. She was going, 'Babe, hun, hun, yes he stole, but he burnt three orchards down and almost killed somebody.' And Dad's saying, 'Yeah, yeah. But he *stole*.' Boom, boom, boom in my face, blood all over the place.

To his knowledge, I'd only stolen two pens, but now that he was a Christian he hated thieves. He didn't even care about the fires. But that's the thing about my dad: when he homes into something, that's it.

Every birthday I'd get presents, but then they'd be taken away from me, every single time. I'd do something naughty, like talk back to Mum, and that was it. Toys, clothes … gone. 'I bought that, that's mine, I own this and I own you.' Pāpā would take everything and either break it or hide it away; the only way I'd ever see it again was if I managed to find the hiding place. One time, he'd taken all my birthday clothes and I found them by accident. I was looking to see if there was any money in the cracks of the couch, and I felt underneath the cushions … looking, touching. *What can I take, what can I get?* My fingers found a little hole in the lining over the frame, and I felt inside. *What's this?* And there were my birthday clothes. I found them because I am my father's son — he's always hiding, spying, looking, and so was I.

As time went on, he became even more intent on catching me out, on teaching me a lesson, and I became even more defiant. I was wearing my cool new clothes that I'd just got for my birthday. I love the feeling of new clothes, of looking good. But I put a step wrong — what did I do? I can't remember. Answered back, grumbled about something. He tells me to get out of the house, but when I go to leave, he's like, 'Where do you think you're going? Get those clothes off, those are my clothes. I bought them. Get them off.'

'Here, take them. Stuff yous.'

Boom. Boom.

* * *

After we got back to Tauranga, I had two years at Arataki Primary, and then one year at Mount Maunganui Intermediate before we moved again. That took me from nine years old to just on twelve.

I was already pretty out of control, getting naughtier as I grew into being a teenager, but with all these feelings inside me, of hating myself, which nobody knew about or would have understood.

We moved to Hamilton, and there I did my second year of intermediate. Mum and Pāpā tried to get me to see a counsellor that year but I refused. I wasn't telling anybody anything. Then came two years at Hamilton Boys' High School, where at last I got to be in the Māori unit, which I loved. My reo got a lot more developed over that time. But even there, Pāpā exerted his control. Now that he was a Christian, he'd turned hard-line religious.

'You're not doing kapa haka,' he told me one day. 'I don't want you to learn about those Māori gods. There's only one God.'

I tried to tell him kapa haka was nothing to do with that, but it was no use. He was fixated. He went to the school and told them I wasn't to do it, and that was that. Oh man, I was so angry at him. But I hated him anyway, so it was just one more thing.

At the end of 2004, the end of my first year at Hamilton Boys', there was a massive change in our family fortune.

For two years, Mum had been working on behalf of our tribal corporation, which included 147 individual shareholders, to sell the 27-hectare block of land between Mangatawa and Pāpāmoa Beach. At a local gathering, she had bumped into a guy named Steve Short, the son of a local pastor, and he said, 'Do you remember me? You used to bully me and beat me up at school.' It turned out he was a property developer, and he and Mum got talking. Anyway, after two years of negotiation, where Mum convinced all the other shareholders to sell, it ended up with him signing the deal to buy our land for a 100-year lease. It was a good deal and we were one of the bigger shareholders, so it changed our lives.

Mum and Pāpā bought a brand-new house in Hamilton, which felt really flash. It was cool. *This is our house.* They also bought a unit to rent out, and we always had a nice car after that. Both my parents, but especially my mum, are really good with money — still really good savers and really careful. Not like me — I couldn't save ten cents.

Personally, though, I think it was the wrong thing to do, selling that land. It was a sale, instigated by us, not taken by force, but it still makes me angry and sad when I go back there and see all that construction — all the development that has become a well-off new suburb. Our tūpuna fought and died for this land, and look what we've done. We're not going to see our land back in our lifetime.

A few months after that, something terrible happened. When we moved to Hamilton, I didn't know that Mum had actually sold our house at Tamapahore to one of our relations. I was still going back to Tauranga in the school holidays, but I'd stay with Uncle Stan and Aunty Leonie at Matapihi so I didn't realise someone else was in our house. But then there was a family meeting in the food court at Bayfair Mall, and Mum told us not only that she'd sold the house, but that our relative had gone on a massive bender after getting his big payout for his section of the Pāpāmoa land, his money was gone, and now the bank was claiming back what had been our house.

That's what happens when you give money to a poor mindset. We all erupted there in the foodcourt — shocked, raised voices, lots of tears and anger.

Mum didn't care about not living at Tamapahore anymore. She'd always been desperate to get off the hill. 'I can't stand that place. I couldn't wait to get off. I'm a city girl. I want to be done with that.'

I was angry with her. 'You don't even care about us. You lost our house. You lost the whenua our tūpuna fought and died for. You lost our homestead. You literally just gave up our connection to our home. What about your mokos that are still to be born?'

I'm still so sad about this. Land has turned into business. I understand that people are desperate and need money, but it is short-sighted and does not benefit us in the long term. Poor people with a poverty mindset just want a quick buck. They forget the land is literally priceless. It's not something to be sold. And yet our house *was* sold — by the bank, to a family who didn't even come from the hill.

One day I will buy it back. I'll put it in trust, so that no matter how desperate somebody gets, it can never be sold. So my kids can always go back there, to their home.

Looking over Pāpāmoa now, that sea of roofs and tidy grey streets, I remember what it used to be like. Land stretching to the sea. I hate how it is now, and after that meeting at Bayfair I felt a change inside me. I still loved going back to Tauranga and seeing whānau, but for my true sense of home, I began to turn to my Tūhoe side, to Rūātoki.

In the years after that, Mangatawa became almost eerie — so many people had moved away, like we had, or died. The hill's seen a lot of sorrow and sadness. To me, it felt lifeless.

But in the last few years, something wonderful has happened. In partnership with Housing New Zealand, our tribal corporation has developed Mangatawa Pāpākāinga, a new housing project at the foot of the Mangatawa hill, just a bit below where our old house is. New houses have been built for our kaumātua, our older people, and new four-bedroom houses for other whānau. And there are rules: no alcohol, drugs or violence.

People have come back home, and it's brought kids back to the hill. When I go there now to visit my Nanny Maybelle, I see groups of kids wandering around for the first time in years. The life is being brought back to the hill. Mangatawa is coming back to its glory.

* * *

As I reached my second year at Hamilton Boys, things were not looking good for me personally. My mum couldn't handle me; she used to threaten me, saying she would send me to a boys' home. She was always kicking me out. 'All right, that's it. I can't handle you. Get out.' And I'd have to go and stay with Aunty Leonie or someone else. Next thing, Mum'd be like, 'Come back home, Stanny. I want you to come back home. I'll come and get you …'

I got suspended from every single school I ever went to, from primary school right up to high school. The first time was when I had just started school in Australia and I stole this girl's pet snake. It was in a glass jar, which I buried in the sandpit. When you were suspended, the school usually wanted you to spend a few days at home away from everyone, but my mum never allowed that. 'Nah, he's not coming home.' So at one school I had to sit on a chair during interval and lunch and not move at all. Another school, I stayed in a little room all day, through all my classes, and I just had to do work, only allowed out to go out to the toilet. Another school, I had to stay down the back of the class and not interact with any of the kids. I was disruptive, I argued with the teachers. I was deceitful, sly and naughty.

I was actually even naughtier than anyone knew.

I still stole stuff all the time. As I got older, it was mostly so I could have nice clothes. I always had ugly clothes, cheap market stuff, and I didn't want to look poor. I'd steal whatever was in the trend. At one point, when we were living in Hamilton, I often used to go and steal all the mean rugby shorts, long rugby socks, and the thermals to wear underneath your T-shirt. That was the look. Even undies. I'd steal anything and everything every day.

My parents had both been thieves but when they became Christians they turned against that way of life. They certainly would not have tolerated me stealing. I had to hide everything I stole. I couldn't let them see me wearing any of the clothes I stole, so I hid them in places they would never ever look or go to, often not even at home. Pāpā was always poking around, looking for stuff, so I had to be really good. I kept them at friends' houses; or I put them in a bag and hid it in a tree, or in a bush down the road, where I was clear to get in and out. I'd get changed wherever I was going to, then later on take it all off again, chuck it back in the bag, and go back home as if nothing had happened.

I hid everything. I was good at hiding everything. My life was full of secrets. I hid the stuff I stole and I hid everything that was going on inside me. It was exhausting but it was all I knew.

I took money out of a wallet I found at a skating rink, when I was there with a church group. I went and bought me some McDonald's. *Yeah, I feel so rich.* I stole money from the church — they had an offering plate upstairs, like an honesty box, where people put money if they bought soft drinks. My mum worked up there at the time, so I used to see where they put all the money. No one realised it was me who took it.

I took my mates in and showed them the ropes. One time at Hamilton Boys', I took my mate stealing, teaching him how to do it. Then he went and did it without me and next minute he was brought to school in a cop car. I laughed! I was like, 'You're an idiot. I don't think you can do it by yourself yet.'

I was probably seventeen the last time I stole. I wasn't breaking into houses anymore by that stage, but I still loved to steal clothes from the mall. I'd go in with what I had on and come out with a whole different outfit. Different shoes. It was easy.

Anyway, back in Hamilton, when I was fifteen, Mum had had the final straw. I can't remember if I did anything in particular, or if it was just a whole lot of the usual things, like answering back, but I got kicked out and had to go and live with my Uncle Andrew and Aunty Denise, who welcomed me into their home. I loved it there. I was like another son to them, and they will always be like parents to me. Their son, my cousin Kaha, was the same age as me and we did everything together. We were like brothers. We liked the same things, we liked the same girls. But he was always the more handsome one, stronger and faster than me. I will always remember living with my aunty and uncle as one of the greatest times of my childhood. But eventually, my mum wanted me back home. That didn't last long. It was maybe only a few weeks before Mum once again was fed up with my behaviour and, this time, she did what she'd always threatened me with and sent me to boarding school, to New Plymouth Boys' High School. This was just after they'd sold the Pāpāmoa land, so they had some money. I was there two terms before I got suspended.

Boarding school was good and bad. I loved the freedom from my parents. I stayed with an aunty on the weekends but I could sneak out, go to parties. That was the best part of it.

But I was still getting plenty of hidings at school. I've got a mouth on me and I don't back down to people, so I was getting into fights. One of the rules among the students was you can't look anybody older than you in the eye. You had to call everybody by their last name. I didn't follow the rules and I was opening up my mouth and not respecting the older students, so I got jumped in the middle of the night. That's where the older boys ordered my friends to attack me when I was asleep. Turned my bed over, beat me up. Not in a friendly way. That was a normal thing. Everybody experienced that. You got the beats.

You get tough skin after years of being bullied. And none of those beatings were as bad as what my dad gave me, so I didn't really care and I wasn't scared of them.

I was only little but I was tough. One night, one of the prefects chucked me in a bush and I jumped up and grabbed him. 'You think you're tough? Try me. Do it. And my brothers will smash all of yous. They'll come here and waste you.'

After that they were always trying to get me, and my boys would be looking out for me: 'Bro, just run. They told us to beat you up. Just go.'

It was very hierarchical. Biggest, toughest, oldest.

But after two terms, I was suspended for fighting and my parents brought me back to Hamilton. I was so happy to be back in Hamilton. I loved my mates there, and I loved my life there. At that time, I was full-on smoking dope, smoking ciggies, stealing. I was in the fourth form at Hamilton Boys' but I often didn't bother to go.

Aunty Leonie had moved next to the school, so I'd get stoned every interval with one of my cousins, and then climb in Leonie's window and make myself scrambled eggs on toast. Stoned all day. The teachers didn't say anything, but sometimes my mates would be like, 'Oh, what are you up to?' I don't know why I always did it. But I just liked the whole thing — leaving school, getting stoned.

Other times I'd go with my mates to someone's place and get stoned. My parents were always angry with me. I remember one night, I got chucked out of the house when I was just in my undies and I had to run like that to my mate's. Stayed there a few days. I was always getting kicked out and crashing at mates' or cousins' houses.

I did some stupid things during those years, but one of the stupidest things was what happened when we jumped a taxi. Oh my gosh, everything went wrong.

Taxi jumping is when you pick up a taxi, get your ride, and when they slow down you get out and run.

The first time I did it I was fifteen. Me and my mate were going to this party. I was staying at Aunty Leonie's; I stuffed something in my bed so it looked like I was still there and I snuck out. We got the taxi, and then, just like we'd planned, we jumped out and ran. But the falla chased us, so we dived into this hedge and we had to stay there for like half an hour while he looked for us. We were so scared. We finally got to the party but almost straight away there was a big brawl between different gang members, the Bloods and the Crips. The police came with their dogs and they started going hard. It was scary, so we left and we walked all the way back home — literally about twenty kilometres. It was *far*. And it was freezing. We stopped at a fast food place in town just so we could go underneath the hand dryers and try to get warm. When I finally got home, I walked in and there was Aunty Leonie waiting for me. She was just sitting there at her computer playing solitaire, looking furious. 'Where the fuck have you been?' Oh my gosh. She just sat there and stared me down.

I did naughty, naughty things. I just was a naughty kid. I wanted to push the boundaries. I couldn't wait to do naughty things. I couldn't wait to smoke, to drink. I wanted to do stuff that I knew I shouldn't do. I wanted to do that for no other reason but to feel what it felt like to do it. For the experience. For the thrill of it.

It would be really easy to tell my story like everything was the fault of the treatment I got and the things that happened to me. And I definitely feel like that had an effect on me, I'm not saying it didn't. But I've always just been mischief. I've always been a tutū. I've always been a little lone ranger, like I've always just been on my own buzz, walking around doing my own thing, finding my own things. That's not a result of hidings, or being raped, or being abused, or being rejected. It's something *in* me.

The abuse might have magnified certain aspects of my behaviour, or added something to certain situations. But you'd think that if I was getting beaten up all the time, that I would think, *No, I won't do that naughty thing because I'm going to get a hiding.* But instead I was like, *I just want to do it.*

I know how my nature is. Sometimes now I still feel like that little kid. Someone will say, 'Don't do that, Stan', and I'm immediately thinking, *Don't tell me what to do.* And I do it.

That said, I never reacted to all that violence by being so rebellious that I just said, 'Give me your worst' — never to my dad, or my brother, or even my mum. I wasn't that stupid. I said it one time to God, though, and I really regretted it because he *did* give me his worst, and I'll tell you about that later. But to my dad, never. I was too scared. More scared of my dad than of God!

* * *

Through all those years, singing was always still a thing for me. I always sung on the marae, at funerals especially. I'd sing with all the other little kids as a group, or sometimes they'd get me to sing by myself. My parents would make

142

me sing at their church things. Everyone always said I was a mean singer. But I never had any musical lessons of any kind, and the first time I sang in public, away from the marae, was at Fairfield Intermediate in Hamilton.

I went to audition for the choir but the music teacher liked my voice, and she put me in as the lead singer for the rock band instead. Mrs McKenzie. She was just awesome. From then on she championed me at the school.

The first songs I ever sung in front of an audience was in that rock band; I did Delta Goodrem's 'Born to Try', Good Charlotte's 'Lifestyles of the Rich and Famous', and Renée Geyer's 'It Only Happens'. I was nervous, but afterwards the other kids would come up to me in the playground and say, 'Stan, can you just sing, please?' I become popular after I started singing. It was good, but it was also: shame. It was a feeling deep inside myself that stopped me taking any pleasure in my own success. How could I, when I thought I was disgusting? When I believed I was an abomination?

When I got to high school, I saw there were singing classes and I realised I could get out of my normal classes if I went to them. And that's where I learned to do the warm-ups I still use today. They were the only singing lessons I'd have till I got to Idol.

I can't remember the music teacher's name, but he was the man. Such a good falla. He told me I was amazing. It was like with Mrs McKenzie at intermediate — they both fully championed me. I'd never been championed like that, believed in and pushed forward. I both liked it and was shamed by it.

I didn't want anyone at Hamilton Boys' to know I sang. Not only was the feeling of shame almost overwhelming, but I thought I would get mocked. *They're going to think I'm soft if I sing.* Intermediate had been a co-ed school, but Hamilton Boys' was obviously a different story, and I didn't want to look like I was soft there. *I'm not going to take that risk.*

But near the end of the year, the music teacher said to me, 'I want you to sing at assembly.' Somehow, he got me to sing 'Circle of Life' for the last assembly of the year. It went okay, although I'm sure if I heard myself now I would cringe. But after, as we walked out, everybody was like, 'I didn't know you could sing!' Then my two best mates wanted to start singing, too, and they were rugby players. It just pulled down so many barriers with the boys, and this is something I have learned always happens with music. Everything kind of changed. I'd been at the bottom of the food chain at school and then suddenly was at the top.

But I didn't take music as a subject. I tried it. I thought you just went in there and sang but instead found out it was all theory; it wasn't for me. I was a practical person.

* * *

For most of my years at school, I was switched off. If you'd asked most of my teachers what they thought of me, they'd probably have said: 'He's disruptive, he's ignorant, he's naughty. He's going nowhere.' Being in the classroom was never good for me. And yet I've always been competitive. Under all my shame and the self-hatred, there was still something in me, secretly, that never wanted to just be mediocre or just exist. I always wanted to be amazing. That was the side of me that came out in my crazy daydreams, in my little-boy self singing on the top of the hill.

Mostly, though, school just did not cater to me and my needs. I didn't know what my needs were, but what I needed wasn't there. Ultimately, school failed me, and I failed school.

Through primary, intermediate and then even into high school, the area I had most success in was sports. In fact, after I won Idol, the deputy principal of Byron Bay High School, Ian Davies, commented that I was very social and good at sport, and not such a 'bad boy' at all.

I did athletics and swimming my whole life. Loved running, loved swimming. My mum, when she was fifteen, she qualified for the Commonwealth Games, for 50-metre breaststroke, but she didn't want to do all the work. So, without knowing, I had that in my blood. I was good at breaststroke, too, and in Australia, I made it through to the state competition — the levels are school sports, then inter-school, then regional, then state. I made it through to state competitions in athletics as well — cross-country, 800 metres and the relays.

But I never actually went to the state competitions. 'No, you're not going there,' Mum would say. No money. A waste of time. 'You're not going to need that.' Mostly it was the money. Going to those competitions cost a lot, just getting there but you also had to buy gear.

Of course, I moaned and cried to Mum, but there wasn't the money then, or maybe I'd been naughty, so I wasn't allowed anyway. So when teachers or coaches would ask why I couldn't come, I'd just say, 'I'm not allowed.'

All that side of sport was impossible for me. Even at primary school, I was aware that the other kids were having lessons and special training or belonging to sports clubs. I never had lessons for anything — except from my father — and when it came to school sports, I didn't even have Speedos, like we were supposed to. I had to wear my undies. I remember the kids saying to me, 'Those are undies.' And I would say, 'Well, my mum told me they were Speedos.' I stole my cap and my goggles.

But I was naturally good at it. It was always: go hard. Show up on the day and go hard.

In the playground at school, I practised my gymnastics, doing backflips off the monkey bars. I got banned from the playground for that. Banned from the jungle gym. Man. I was just like a little monkey. I needed to jump around all the time.

So I've always been a sporty person. Always played touch, volleyball, rugby, league, a bit of tennis with my mates. Hurdles, triple jump, discus. Me and my boys, ever since we were little, we lived in the outdoors, and I always loved that. Even today, I love to have sports days with my bros. We play all those games and finish up having a beer at the end.

I like winning. I love competing. I love the camaraderie of team sports. So, anything competitive, I love to do.

In general, whether I'm playing sports or playing music, I like to surround myself with people who are way better than me. Then I become better. I can't excel if I'm not surrounded by people who are better than me. And I'm always trying to get better at what I do.

Some people say they feel insecure when they're working with people who are better than them. Not me. It makes me feel like I have to work more. Run faster. Sing better. Like I said, I want to be amazing.

* * *

Those teenage years, I was stuffed up. I still didn't know what I was, who I was, what I was supposed to do, where I was supposed to be. When I got hidings or got in trouble, I'd go in my room, and cry and look at myself in the mirror. *You're so ugly. I hate you.* Then I'd just go back into my normal world, go to school, act like nothing ever happened. Go and hang out, go and smoke, go and wag. I used to wag school a lot.

I had an identity crisis in every way, and for so long. I don't wish that on any kid.

I figured I'd settle for a life of just having babies at fifteen, stay home, smoke dope, and that's it. Everybody else I was hanging around with did that. All the older teenagers did that. So that's all I could see in front of me and all I could see around me. That's all I wanted to do. It could have easily happened.

But then, halfway through my fifth-form year, that's when Mum told me we were moving back to Australia. I was fifteen. I didn't want to move but they gave me no choice. Turns out I wasn't destined to be a teenage dad after all.

CHAPTER SEVEN

How sweet the sound

Amazing grace, how sweet the sound
That saved a wretch like me
I once was lost, but now am found
Was blind but now I see

— 'Amazing Grace'

I HAD WAGGED MOST OF MY DAYS BACK IN NEW Zealand, so I failed every class automatically, because of poor attendance. So when I arrived back in Australia, at Byron Bay High School, they looked at my records and put me in the special education class, called the SPED class. Everyone knew it was the dummies' class.

One day, not long after we'd moved back, I was in my science class when I saw I'd missed a whole lot of phone calls from my dad. I left the class and called him. 'Pāpā, I'm in class—' He just came out with it, no preparation. 'Nana got killed.'

His mum, my nan. Ever since Koko died, all those years before, she was the one who had been my everything, a still centre in my life. I couldn't bear it. It was like my guts sunk into my bum. I broke down, started hitting the walls, crashing against the lockers. People were rushing out of the classrooms, asking if I was all right? I can't remember what I said.

It turned out she had died in a car crash — she was doing a U-turn and a truck went into her car.

Oh, I missed her. Even now, every single day I think about my nan. If I hear a certain song I'll sometimes think, *Far, she would love this. She would love this song.*

A few months later, I wrote a song for her and I recorded myself singing it, playing my guitar, and I put it up on YouTube. It's called 'Missing You'. *In the morning, in the evening, and tomorrow in the afternoon, it doesn't matter when, I'll be missing you.* There I am, mullet hairdo, my troubles and grief there on my face, classic teenager in his bedroom. It's the first thing I ever put up online.

I still mean every word of that song.

I often think about Nan and how simply she lived in her little bach. She was so content in having nothing. All she wanted was her nets and her fishing rods, her kūmara patch, her rīwai, her gardens. Put her nets out, roll her smokes, have a little money for the pokies. That was it. She was happy.

The Bible says that it's easier for a rich man to go through the eye of a needle than to go to heaven.

When I think of my nan, I wonder if we've made a mistake about what's important. Three years after she died, and just a few months after I won Idol, I had the opportunity to go to Haiti. They had recently had their massive earthquake. It was a catastrophe for that tiny little country. They already had ultimate poverty and corruption, and the earthquake brought even more devastation. I was taken there by a Christian charity to offer support and fellowship through music. On the way into Port-au-Prince, I saw people eating mud. I saw people drinking from mud puddles. I met a woman who had AIDS, and I said I would pray for her. And she said, no, she would pray for me. I couldn't believe what I was hearing. 'Why?' I asked.

'Because you have everything. We have nothing, but all we have is God to hold on to. Your everything distracts you from God.'

That was profound for me, and I thought of my nan, who was content with so little.

I always wanted nice things, I ain't going to lie. Nice things were what I dreamed of as a kid, when we didn't have the things other people had. I still want nice things. I want to be comfortable. I want to be successful in my business, be successful in my art, one day be successful as a father, as a husband, as a family man. I want to make money so I can reclaim some of our land back.

But mostly, I want to be content.

Definitely, if you'd asked that mullety kid in the YouTube video what he wanted, he would have said a nice house, nice car, nice clothes. And yet, even then, it wasn't just that stuff. I always wanted love, security — the warmth of whānau. The acceptance I'd had from Nan and Koko. Peace. Forgiveness.

* * *

I knew I wasn't dumb. I was in the SPED class because of attendance and behaviour. But most of the teachers treated us all like we were stupid. Our maths teacher was different. Mr Watt. He was one of the most inspiring teachers I ever had. He was very strong and firm but he had a good heart, and he actually cared. I'm not saying that the other teachers didn't care, but when you're a kid like me, you know who *really* cares.

He would call me out. He got angry at me when I acted dumb and disruptive, like I didn't know how to do what was being asked of me. He'd say, 'Stop acting like that.' He somehow saw my big act. 'Stop acting,' he would say.

Most teachers taught in a way that I couldn't understand. It was like they were speaking gibberish. So I would turn off. I had a short attention span anyway. I wasn't learning about the world I actually lived in, nor learning skills I actually needed. We were learning history that wasn't our history, in both Australia and New Zealand. We were given options of trades: mechanic, building, bricklaying. None of that was inspiring me. *Is this what life is?*

But Mr Watt taught in a methodical way that I really got, and I actually loved it. He made Pythagoras' theorem so logical and simple that I found it easy to understand. I'd always liked maths, but now it was my favourite subject and I ended up getting the top score in my whole class, scoring at the same level as the two extension maths classes.

But one day in class he caught me on my phone, and when he went to take it off me I hit him. When he caught me, I knew I was in the wrong, but something in me decided to just go with it. I got suspended.

At the end of that year, I turned sixteen and wanted to leave school. My parents did not want me to leave. The only thing that would get me back to school was to do maths again, and I said if I didn't get Mr Watt the next year, I was out. They won, and I turned up at the beginning of the next year of school. And it was lucky I did because I got my first opportunity to sing on a big stage.

The music teacher at Byron High, Darko Milic, was the bomb and helped me a lot with my singing, and encouraged me to enter a talent quest. The prize was to sing on the APRA Stage at the Byron Bay Bluesfest. I won the talent quest, along with a girl from the school, and we put a band together with my cousins and brothers singing backing vocals. Our guitarist was actually the legend Willy Hona, who had played with Herbs. Mum and Pāpā had met him at the Mullumbimby RSL and got talking. He was Māori, they were Māori, that's how things go.

The Byron Bay Bluesfest is a massive event, one of the biggest music festivals in Australia, with lots of international stars and that year, 2007, it included Ziggy Marley, Ben Harper, Missy Higgins and Bonnie Raitt. To be honest, I didn't even realise how massive it was until I got there. I got a shock when we arrived and it truly sunk in that we'd be singing in front of hundreds of people.

We played seven songs, including 'It Only Happens'. It was my first experience of people just sitting there listening as I performed. Just wanting to listen to music. Trippy.

But when I walked into my maths class, Mr Watt was not there. Instead, I got this lady and I was like, *I'm out*. I left school that day.

* * *

It was just before then that Pāpā hit me for the very last time. He was gearing up to give me a proper hiding as usual, when I felt the courage and pushed him away from me. I had never ever reacted to him like that before in my whole life. I always figured he might kill me if I did, so the best thing was to just take it and wait for it to be over. But this time, I knew my oldest brother was in the house, as well as my other brother and my sister-in-law, so that gave me the courage to stand up to him. Sure enough, he went completely psycho and he grabbed me and was about to start smashing me. I didn't really know if my brother would help me, but I started yelling and suddenly Mike was there. He ripped my dad off me, and said, 'Not today. Don't you touch him.'

Then they had a massive argument. I was crying and my sister-in-law took me into my bedroom and just held me. Then Mike came in. He told me, 'I love you, and I will always protect you.' I never heard those words from him. I never even knew if he loved me.

Mike was so much older than me and, while he tried his best to protect us, he had his own troubles with our dad; they would nearly always end up in fights. Mike used to give me the biggest hidings, too. So I never used to think he liked me or loved me.

He took his own anger and pain out on me. That's a weird thing, but I understand that. I did the same to our youngest brother. But now Mike was saying: 'He's not going to hit you again.'

Really? It was hard to accept. My life up to that point had been dominated by my fear of my father. My fear and hatred was not going to just vanish. I didn't trust him. I was still on alert. It was a long time before I really believed that that was the last time.

I would still get scared when we argued and he would get loud and angry. I'd think, *Here we go. He's going to hit me.* It must've been the same for Mum for years. He'd use that tone and what followed had always been: boof, boof. I couldn't change the way I thought or acted just because he'd said he wouldn't hit me anymore.

Soon after that, there was a big argument one morning at home. I was answering my mum back; Pāpā was there and it turned into an argument. He never actually touched me, but he tried to — he probably would have if his arms were longer. I got out of the house but I missed the bus, so I went down the road to hitch to school.

I was standing there with my thumb out and my dad showed up in the truck. He goes, 'Get in the truck.' I was just like, 'Nah. I don't want to get in the truck.' He goes, 'Get in the fucking truck before I fucking kill you.' The way he says it, it's like he *is* going to kill me.

'I don't want to get in. You're going to hurt me.'

He yells, 'Get in the fucking truck now before I fucking kill you, you fucking little cunt!'

That's the old Ross, that voice. When he gets to that voice, that's when he's ultimately angry. It's like he's been bodysnatched. His eyes had changed colour from hazel to bright yellow. It was so scary, it put more fear in me than getting hit. I was scared to get in the truck, but I was more scared of what he'd do if I didn't. I jumped in the back, and he chucked a few things at me, but that was all and he just kept driving.

Sometimes after hidings, I'd just go to school like nothing had happened. Other times, I'd go and hang out, go and wag. I used to wag school a lot. This time I hadn't actually had a hiding but I was all churned up. So once he'd dropped me at school I decided I wasn't going to go that day. Instead, I went to the beach with some mates to go body surfing. And just as I was catching a wave I looked up, and Pāpā was in the same wave looking at me. I nearly shat myself. I thought, *He's going to kill me.*

But he just said, 'Oh, I had a feeling you were gonna come down here.' After he'd dropped me off, he'd gone back home and calmed down and started to feel so bad. He goes, 'God, I'm sorry, son. I'm really sorry, you know? You just keep answering Mum back, and I couldn't handle it.' Usually when he said things like that it would make him angry all over again, but he didn't get angry at me again this time.

He was trying. He had a whole lifetime of abuse and hurt, so it was going to take him longer to recover and undo, to reclaim his life. I wasn't ready to forgive him, though. How can you forgive someone else if you can't forgive yourself?

But as time went by, I realised that Mike was right. I don't know how he knew, but Pāpā never did hit me again.

* * *

My parents were so angry when I left school. They told me I had to start paying board immediately.

I got a job at a supermarket. Mallams 5 Star in Mullumbimby, a tiny little town a few kilometres away from where we were living at Ocean Shores. My job was stacking shelves and doing all the orders. I was glad to be working and making money that I could actually spend. I never regretted leaving school.

When I moved back to Byron as a teenager, it was the first time I'd experienced proper in-your-face racism. A guy at school was always taunting me, trying to make me do the haka and joking about Kiwis. Bloody sheep-shaggers. One day I had enough, and I picked him up and slammed him on the ground and booted him.

But now, at the supermarket, I encountered the same kind of thing. It was more about being Kiwi than it was about being Māori. They just kept on saying, 'Oh, you sheep-shagger … bloody Kiwis … hey bro, fush and chups.'

And then one day, the two managers were discussing something that was wrong with some of the checkout equipment, and I could immediately see how to fix it, so I tried to tell them. And one of the managers turned to me and said, 'Stan, what would you know? Just piss off and go and rape some sheep.'

I lost it. Little sixteen-year-old shelf-stacker, yelling at my boss. 'Who the hell do you think you are? Don't you ever speak to me like that. You're lucky you're not a man, I would waste you.'

'Stan, Stan,' the other manager was trying to calm me down.

I was like, 'No, shut up. All of yous try and bully me, you're racist to me. You think that you're better than me.' Ugly yelling. It's amazing they didn't fire me. They were actually saying, 'Oh, sorry, Stan.'

I stayed there nine months. One of the other managers, Janelle, used to complain about me because I'd always be humming and singing in the aisles. 'Stop singing in the aisle. Shut up, Stan. Do your work. Productivity, Stan.' She was hard on me, but she had this soft spot as well.

Until she came along, I never heard that word in my life. Productivity. She said it every day. 'Come on, Stan. Productivity. Stop talking, Stan.' Here we were in this little old supermarket — it was about a hundred years old, literally — and she'd be talking away about productivity and excellence. She always wanted excellence in the way I stacked things, in the way I got the orders together. And it did appeal to me, me with my pedantic cleaning habit and my desire to be amazing.

By the time I left, I had a little crew of friends and I knew all the customers. I went back for a visit after I'd won Idol and I said to Janelle, 'Hey, look, it worked out.' And she was like, 'Oh, man. I'm so proud of you.'

* * *

Despite the chaos of our family home, it might surprise you to know that my mum has always been a clean freak. Our house was the cleanest, tidiest house, spotless and immaculate. That's how she brought us up, and I'm like that now, too. In my life now, I always want people to come over, but then I also don't want them to come over because they're just messy, and I hate it. I'm not a filthy slug, like some of my cousins, and some of my best mates. They're just the most lazy useless things. My mum drilled it into me to be tidy and clean, and she was strict, man. The strictest parent you ever came across.

Literally, after school, my mum would be waiting for me and if I didn't come home *directly*, she'd say, 'Where the hell do you think you've been? I told you to come home. You got your chores to do.' I had to do them straight away.

The morning wasn't so bad, unless I had to do the washing and hang it out. But when I got home, I always had to get the washing off the line and fold it. Then it was dishes, cleaning up, vacuuming. Everything was done properly. The kitchen was spotless, the benches were wiped down, floors vacuumed, toilet cleaned, shower cleaned.

Sometimes if I had to stay home by myself I would clean the whole house from top to bottom, make it spotless, and I'd wait for them to walk in, and they'd be like, 'Wow, that's amazing.' I'd be back in the good books.

We were brought up to use Jif and disinfectant for everything. We used to shower or bath in disinfectant if we had sores, like school sores or scabs, or grazes. When it came to cleaning the house, Jif was for everything. Everything. For the windows, for the walls, for the benches, for the floors, for everything. Jif and disinfectant were my only cleaning products. I would vacuum everything: every corner, every crevice that I could get into. I would do all the couches and the cushions properly. That is, they've got to be straight. If I'm in your house and I see a book that's just a little wee bit not straight, I want to straighten its edges. I would make the beds exactly, put the sheets on properly. I would clean all the gunk from the drains of the showers. I would do the washing, I would vacuum everything, mop everything. The slightest mark on a wall, I'd clean it. That would be me doing a full-on clean.

When I start, I'm like, *Oh, I'll just do a little clean-up*. But then I get into it and I have to do everything to the extreme. And I'm glad I'm like that.

I just love looking at a clean room. Nothing better than a clean room, clean house.

As soon as I left school at sixteen, I had to start paying rent straight away, and if I didn't have enough money to pay rent, then I would have to do the house from top to bottom.

I remember once I left my bed unmade and Mum rang me while I was at work at the supermarket and she was shouting down the phone: 'Where are you?' I was like, 'I'm at work.'

'You better get home now and make your bed. If you don't come now I'm going to chuck your clothes out.'

And when I got home I found all my clothes there on the driveway. So yeah, that was quite hilarious.

* * *

During the time I was working at the supermarket, my life had started to change.

Everyone else in my family had found God. I was the only one who hadn't but I was still being dragged along to all the church things, and to the youth group that was part of my parents' church. I didn't have any real interest but it was the only thing I was allowed to do.

It was so boring. Dumb people; dumb songs — that was my mindset at the time. I was like, *I'd rather go drink and smoke.* When I look back now, I know that I actually did love those people and I did have some good times, but I needed something that was my own, that I could feel was my own choice.

One day my parents took me with them up to Tweed Heads, about an hour north of where we lived, to catch up with some of their friends, Uncle Pete and Aunty Lynette. They belonged to a different church and they were having an outreach day. We were invited along to their sausage sizzle.

The Tweed Heads church was called Ganggalah, and it was like no other church I'd come across. Its core mission was to raise the next generation of young indigenous leaders. It's a very multicultural church — 'serving God and celebrating cultures' is its motto. It's about bringing all the different races together. Its leading pastors are a couple, Willy and Sandra Dumas, and they are both Indigenous Australians. So at that sausage sizzle, there were all sorts of people, and lots of young people. There were Indigenous Australians, heaps of Māori, Fijians, Sāmoans and Torres Strait Islanders, along with the white Australians.

These fallas looked cool. They were all playing footie on the field and going surfing, I'd never seen that before in a church.

'Come to our church,' they said to me. 'It'll be awesome as.' My parents weren't sure because it was a long way away but Uncle Pete said, 'Stan can come and stay with us on the weekend.'

So I started hitching up to Tweed Heads every week. I'd take my bag to the supermarket on Friday so that after work I could just go straight up there from Mullumbimby. I would end up staying for the whole weekend.

I loved it so much. I felt at home, and I felt like I was being myself for the first time. It was all these young people who loved Jesus, who weren't weirdos. They weren't what I thought church was like. The music they were playing, the band — it was gangsta. *I love this.*

I quickly became best mates with Pete and Lynette's son, Nahshon, who was the same age as me, a real chill creative musician with no real bad issues in his life, and with this guy Tim, who's awkward and funny and hilarious, like me all angst and ready to go. We were the three musketeers. Even though we all now have whole new lives, time, location or life choices don't change how we are with each other. I love my brothers.

At Ganggalah, there were heaps of naughty kids like me, but they were coming to church and the pastors treated them like normal people. They were never, 'Bless you, brother. Don't be naughty. God sees you.' Here, it was more, 'You little idiot, what are you doing?' You know, it was real. It was real.

The youth pastor, Sam, he changed my life. He was the opposite to me. Sam was this Aussie white boy from a really lovely family, one of four brothers who all surfed and fixed up cars together. They were the lads, the boys. Sam, who would have been in his early twenties then, made me feel like he saw something good in me and he just gave me time. He was the first person who showed me the example I've always wanted, needed, the first person to ever 'do life' with me, which means to talk real. I didn't even know what that meant. But listening to him speak, he made me think about stuff differently. It was very captivating.

One day as I left work, coming out into the little main street of Mullumbimby, Burringbar Street, there they all were outside my work, Nahshon, Tim, Sam and one of the other boys from Youth Group, Reece.

I was puzzled. 'What the hell are yous doing here?'

'We've just come down to see you.'

'What? You drove all the way down? For what?'

'Just to come and chill. Do you want to go and get a feed?'

'Eh? So you drove all the way down just to come and hang with me?'

I'd never had that before. I'd never had anybody go out of their way like that to show me: you matter; this is for real; we're not doing this because we have to, we're doing this because we want to. We're actually believing the best for you and out of you. *This is weird.* But I loved it.

I still wasn't very interested in God, but I found these people incredible and I loved these new friendships. And now I know, it's the people who lead people to Jesus. That's the key. As Christians, we're supposed to be the bridge to Jesus. We ain't Jesus, we ain't the judge, we ain't the ruler. We're just supposed to reflect his love, his grace, and only be a bridge, and help people across the bridge. But the relationship that people have with Jesus is their own.

These people turned out to be my bridge because they were like me, but they were free. They were fun. They lived life to the fullest. And they loved Jesus.

Sam asked me, 'What are your goals?'

'Eh?'

So he taught me about goals. No one had ever talked to me about that stuff before. He taught me to write my goals down so that I'm clear in my mind. If you have them written down in front of you, then you have something to be accountable to; you can't make excuses or get lazy. I live by that now. I teach that to people.

I can't remember exactly what I wrote on my first goals list, but what I would have been thinking back then was: I want to get my licence, I want to get a car, I want to get a good job, I want to save money for a road trip to Sydney with the boys. Buy a house, act in a movie. And once I'd set my goal, I did it. I saved up and I went for my first road trip with all the boys from youth group, to a big church conference in Sydney. That was truly one of the best trips of my life. We had so much fun and it was just normal fun, like not smoking and drinking. Stopped in all these different spots, stayed in a hostel in Sydney, and went to a conference at Hillsong, which is a huge Sydney church. Learnt so much, met so many people.

They didn't know too much about me, of course. I still had a lot of my stuff locked away inside me, and I still believed I could never recover. I thought I was always going to be stuffed up in my head. I still believed I would never tell nobody, ever. I would take it to my grave, be in pain but just hide it all. I thought that was it.

But I loved these new people and I was starting to trust them. *Faar, this is so cool.* I didn't know it yet, but change was becoming possible.

* * *

At my parents' church back in Byron Bay, there was a young woman I'll call Carrie. To me, she seemed like the kind of person who would have a perfect life. She had quite a high-profile job, a beautiful spirit, was stunning to look at, softly spoken and kind. Her parents were millionaires. But one day she gave her testimony in church and she told us that from the age of five to eighteen she had been raped by her uncle, her dad's brother. When she finally told her father, her father denied her experience. He didn't believe her. He chose to believe his brother.

Whaaaat? Oh my gosh, I would never have known she had that inside her. *You?*

Sitting there in the church, I cried. I cried because I understood what she'd been through, and I cried because for the first time, the penny dropped for me. Because up till that moment I had never heard another story like mine. Carrie used the word 'rape'. I had never said that word to myself. Rape. That's how in denial I was. I thought about what had happened all the time, I remembered everything, I suffered the pain, but I hadn't had the words to know what it was. I just lived in the sticky, dark mess of shame. But now here was Carrie — beautiful, awesome Carrie, who was kind of the opposite to how I felt about myself — who had had the same thing happen to her.

At the end of her testimony, she asked if anybody had been through similar things and I did put my hand up to go and get a prayer. I almost let it slip out of my mouth that night. I couldn't. The words didn't know how to come. But that night was my first step. Carrie's testimony, her sharing of her story, was the first thing that encouraged me to allow myself to be free.

Her story showed me something else, too. She was sitting there, not broken. She was free. She was forgiving. She had a faith that was unshakeable. That was my first inkling that God was real.

It was a few months after I'd started going to Ganggalah that I got a ride home to Nahshon's house with Reece. We got to Nahshon's but we just sat in his car talking. I loved talking to these people because they always talked about real things. Interesting things. The first time ever talking about my feelings about anything was with them, and it was weird to start doing that, but at the same time it was just so cool.

But now he was telling me about his experiences. And just in the middle of it he goes, 'Yeah, I was raped, blah blah blah.' Like, he just said it. He'd been raped, he'd been a sex addict. And I was like, *What?*

Oh my gosh. It was the most incredible feeling. *I'm not the only one going through it.* Carrie went through that. Reece went through that ... but they look so happy and free. I felt a terrible fear inside me, ultimate fear, but also excitement, and I realised: *I'm going to say it.*

I heard myself say it, telling this new friend who had been so open with me. 'I got raped, too.' I said it out loud, but quietly, and the words just kind of fell into the open air. And the feeling inside me straight away — it was like I'd just spewed up some bad blimmin' cancer or something. I was liberated. Liberated from my secret and my lies. My journey since then has still been a long one, but that was my first step, like breaking out of jail. Reece was just really calm and empathetic. He really understood because he'd been through that, too.

There is a lot in the Bible about the power of testimony. This is what I know from my own experience: when free people are able to speak, it actually sets other people free. Because Carrie and Reece were able to be open about stuff like that, they allowed me to be free. I don't think I could have done that in any other kind of space.

My bros now, we speak to each other from our hearts. But where I come from, we never talked in those ways: honest, open, real. We just shrugged stuff off or laughed about it, but never actually looked at what we might be really feeling. We had to be tough all the time. This was a new experience for me, and straight away I loved it. I was free as soon as I stopped lying, as soon as I spoke that truth.

Now I believe it's always better to talk honestly with people, to tell them what's inside you, but it has to be the right people. You've got to be fully careful. You've got to know that you're in safe hands.

* * *

I have to tell my parents. I want to. But I'm so afraid.

Me and Mum were sitting in the lounge. My heart was beating so fast it was almost knocking all the breath out of me, but I knew I had to say it. And I said, 'I need to tell you something. Mum, this is going to shock you.'

She had no idea what was coming, so she was just like, 'Yeah, yeah.'

I asked if she remembered how, when I was twelve, she'd asked me if I was gay. I reminded her how angry I'd been, and I explained that at that time I hadn't known who or what I was. 'I was so stuffed up. I'd been raped. This person raped me. And he was doing that for nine months.' And as I said that, despite how scared I was, I felt that same incredible feeling of liberty.

She didn't know how to take it at first. It was hard for her to compute what I was saying. 'What? What? What do you mean?'

The more she thought about it, the more real it got, the more angry she got. She called out to my dad, and she told him, and then Pāpā just lost it. He was crying and swearing

168

at me. In our family, you always blame the person who's the victim. He was saying, 'Why didn't you ever tell me? Why didn't you ever tell me?'

We're all crying. 'Because I thought you were going to do *this*. I thought you'd beat me up.'

'I wouldn't do that. I want to kill *him*. Why didn't you ever tell me? You little cunt, you little cunt.' All the frustration and hurt coming out as anger. And we were just all crying. He didn't blame me for the rape; he was angry I hadn't told him. He was angry because he was hurt.

I was scared more than anything. I was scared to tell them. I was scared of their reaction. I was scared that they would not believe me. I was scared that my dad was going to beat me. I was scared of being rejected. I was scared of looking like a monster or like a little faggot to them. Most of all I was scared of rejection, I was scared of the hiding.

But none of those things happened.

In amongst his anger, Pāpā was crying. Hugging me. He blamed himself. 'That happened under my roof. That happened to my son.'

I remember they said, 'Our relationship's going to change from now on. Because we didn't know that.'

For the first time, they understood me and why I might have been like I was. And they did change. But it took a long time, too, because they didn't even know how to change. Because we were never talkers, although I am a talker now. I just wanted to be accepted for who I am and for them to not judge me. And to just love me. I know they do everything out of love. We're just tough love people. It's real tough love.

They decided to go and confront the guy. I didn't want them to. I just wanted to be done with it. *I don't want to see him, I don't want him dead.* I just wanted to leave it.

But I knew that they were going to do it anyway. And when I found they had, I felt the old shame feeling. *Oh, what did you do that for? Now he knows I told you.* Shame.

They yelled at him but I was actually surprised they didn't kill him. To be honest, though, if it was my kid, I would be worse. I just wouldn't be able to think straight. It nearly killed my dad, though — he had heart palpitations at work and had to come home and we were worried he was going to have a heart attack.

And now that my parents knew, it took the whole thing out of that dark, shadowy corner it had been in for all those years. It was in the real world now, for me but also for the rapist and I understood that because he knew that my parents knew, it put him in a jail — not a real jail, but a jail of fear. *He's been called out. He's been exposed. Maybe he'll be less likely to do it again.*

My parents wanted him in a real jail. They pushed me into taking a court case against him. I didn't want to, but I agreed. And the next minute I was with a police prosecutor giving my statement. It made me scared. I got so scared. They asked me so many questions and they wrote down all my answers, and then I had to read it back to them. Every detail was in that statement — the temperature, the position, where the hand was; what color was the couch, was I sweating, where was the leg, how heavy, what was on TV? Everything. What color hair did you have? How long was it? It was all written down and then I had to read it all back out loud. That was very weird to do.

I cried when I read it back, and I realised, *There's no way I'm letting my parents read this.* I couldn't do it. I simply couldn't handle it. And it was very clear to me. *There's no way I'm going to do this.*

I just abruptly stopped. 'Chuck that away. I'm not going to court.'

I know this is why a lot of rapists get off. I knew, and I felt so guilty. But the shame around bringing the family in. The shame of having to say all this in front of my parents and them having such a clear and vivid picture of their son, that they would never be able to un-see, and un-know. I was a minor still; they would definitely be in the courtroom. I couldn't do it.

He can go to his grave denying it happened. But when I told my brothers, and after they'd got over their shock, they each told me they'd also been molested — by this guy's brothers. So now, I'm not just angry. I actually have empathy and I want to understand. Something happened. Man, what happened to him? Because he knew exactly what he was doing, when to do it, how to do it, the words to say. How do you know this? 'You like this, eh? Don't tell on me or we'll get in trouble …' All the games he played with me. Was that done to him?

So I just think back now, and I'm sure: he studied me. Because you don't do what he did just on the spur of the moment. He would have known I didn't have anything. He would have seen my rejection, where my weak spots were. The fear I had of my dad — that I would be too afraid to tell. He probably sussed that all out.

Now that I'm older I realise he was only young himself. Surely that must've happened to him, or he must've been shown how to do it. Maybe he'd done it to other people before me.

That's really scary. He was taking advantage of an eight-year-old kid who he knew got beaten up and rejected all the time. He was just taking advantage of the weakest person in the room. And maybe he'd been in that exact same situation himself.

* * *

After the experience of telling Reece, and then my parents, I felt so empowered and excited that I couldn't stop talking about it. The biggest secret of my whole life was now, 'Yes! This is my badge, everybody! I was raped! I was raped! I'm good now.'

It was weird to tell my cousins. I told two of my cousins I'd grown up with, one my age, one two years older.

The older one started laughing. 'Shut up, man. No you didn't.'

I said to her, 'Cousin, why would I say that? Why would I, as a falla, say that I was raped by another man? What does that do for me? Where does that get me?'

And then I reminded her of something I'd seen happen to her, when the same guy who raped me was touching her up. We had never talked about it before. And she just went quiet.

'Yes,' she said. 'I remember.'

We were all quiet then.

She had that first reaction because of shame. She would rather push it from her mind. My people, they come from everything that is shame. Don't stand up, bro. Don't shine.

Don't be awesome. Don't try. No, no. Everything's shame. She didn't want to believe it. It was too hard to accept.

When I told my brothers about my rape, I was sixteen, but they are a few years older and were just becoming parents. If I had never said anything, they probably would never have said anything about their own experience. Would that have altered the course of their life? Would they have brought up their kids differently? Because I was able to tell my secret, I feel like it opened the door for all our lives to change for the better.

CHAPTER EIGHT

Leap of faith

Search my heart
And know me God
As I lay me down
I can rise and stand

— 'I Surrender'

PASTOR WILLY, THE SENIOR PASTOR AT GANGGALAH, IS the man. He's so funny and a great leader of the church, fully committed to mending the lives of broken people. He and his wife Sandra not only founded the church, but they set up the Ganggalah Training Centre, which is a Bible college, and Pastor Willy encouraged me to do the six-month course there. It was full-time, so I left my job at the supermarket and moved up to Tweed Heads.

There were twelve of us doing the course and we all lived in two apartments, one for the girls and one for the boys. We were Fijian, Maldive, Greek, Tongan, Indigenous Australian, Torres Strait Islander, Polish, Sāmoan, Māori. We were such an eclectic group. Tim and Nahshon were doing the course too, and we lived together and did everything together, and that was perfect for me.

I worked part-time to pay my board and fees — got a job at Nando's just around the corner. Tim worked at Baskin-Robbins. So I would get the chicken to take home and he would get the ice cream.

It was three months of theory and three months of practical. For the theory, obviously we were in the classroom and I'd always hated studying, but this was actually really cool, because everything always came back to real life.

Different teachers would come in for different bits — such as 'the father heart of God' or different parts of the Bible.

But the practical I really loved. We went out all around New South Wales, Queensland, to different missions. Missions are basically the Indigenous communities. I loved going into those communities, because they reminded me of Māori people in so many ways, It was just second nature to me. Often in the Pākehā world, I've found myself very awkward, almost like I just don't know where to put my hands, I don't know how to look. I'm a fish out of water. But with the Indigenous people, I felt completely at home and comfortable. Laughing, joking. Loving all being together.

We'd go into the schools and talk to all the young people. We shared our stories and did skits and sang and danced and did our cultural stuff. My role was to sing and to share my testimony up to that point. I hadn't yet had my full-on experience of God, but I felt like my life was changed through the relationships I'd formed at the church, and the way Jesus manifested in the people there. I felt like I'd met God.

Also, we'd go out and do outreach on the streets. 'Can we talk to you or do you know Jesus?' And some people were, 'I'm good, sweet as.' Some would reject us and be rude. But others would want to talk, and we'd share our stories and sometimes we'd lead people to Jesus and they'd end up coming to church with us.

All this stuff that I'd so hated doing with my parents — the outreach, the sausage sizzles, the creative outreach — I loved doing with my new church. It was my space and I loved it because I didn't have my parents hovering around me or making sure that I was going. This was completely my choice and they supported it.

But then I fell in love with one of the girls who was also doing the Bible college. Her name was Sefina, a Sāmoan girl, and we bonded over music. We fell for each other through singing together, laughing together. We were like best mates. But my parents didn't like her. They thought she was going to stuff up the path I was on. My dad had seen us getting a little bit too close, and he knew what was going to happen. He gave me a hard word: 'I don't want you hanging with that girl.'

He didn't want us sleeping together, didn't want us having sex. He just wanted us to do things the right way. Because my parents had had the lives they'd had, now they were very strict about everything. Pāpā had become a traditionalist. Old school. So he was hard on us.

Me and Sefina slept together on the last week of Bible college. We got caught out and word travels fast. That was definitely against the rules, and everyone was angry with me. The church and my parents insisted we break up, but I refused. I put Sefina before the church, before God, before my family.

I was expelled from Bible college and kicked out of home. Sefina and me, we were Bonnie and Clyde.

I was angry and disgusted with everyone. I was seventeen by that stage and in love. I didn't realise how young I was in years but also in my head. All I could see was that we were being judged and that the people at the church were not showing love to us. I didn't think they were very good Christians. I didn't know that people were concerned, I had no understanding of that.

You're just judging me. Stuff you all. Stuff the church. Stuff God. I turned my back on everything. My brother took me in and I slept on his couch. I got a job with him in a chicken factory.

Dad was ringing me up. 'You better not go with the girl.'

'You don't have nothing over me now. I don't live with you. I don't owe you nothing. I got my own job.'

He goes, in his evil voice, 'I own you.'

'No, you don't.' My brother got on the phone. He goes, 'Shut up, eh? You don't own him. He's with me now.'

I carried on seeing Sefina. And because she was Sāmoan, and came from a full-on strict religious family, things weren't easy on that side either. But I was allowed to go to her house, and I was prepared to live that Sāmoan life and abandon my life for hers. I've always been like that in relationships. I just go all in, go hard.

Both of us knew nothing about contraception, and I found out later she'd been pregnant twice and had miscarried. All I knew was that she'd been sick sometimes, and once when I was with her she was in a lot of pain, but she just told me she had a heavy period.

So for a while my life was cut off from both my family and the church, until one day my youth pastor Sam rang me. 'Hey bro. What are you doing?'

'Why are you ringing me?'

'I'm seeing how you are.'

I didn't understand that. I thought when you were done with people, you were done with people, but that was actually just me. I was angry at everybody; he was part of everybody.

I don't want to talk to you. I was done with people, but I was shocked to find they weren't done with me.

Being done with people was an approach to life that I often used. If things got hard — if I had an argument with someone or if I suffered a loss — I did what I'd learned to do, and that was to channel it all through anger. I cut people off, I cut myself off. I did this after my cousin died of our inherited cancer when he was seventeen and I was sixteen. I was with him when he died, and I sang to him, and helped lay his body out after he passed, get his body straight before rigor mortis set in. And then because I couldn't face my feelings of grief, I was just angry with everyone, told my friends to piss off, didn't want to talk to anyone. Anything emotional: get angry, cut people off, get behind my wall. But in my mind, it was everyone turning against me. And usually people were pretty happy to leave me alone.

But not Sam. He pushed on. He asked me if I wanted to come to youth camp.

'No'.

'Come on, bro. Come with me.'

'I've got no ride.'

'I'll pick you up.'

'I've got no money.'

'All good. I'll sort it out.'

Anything for free. I gave in. 'Whatever, sweet as. I've got nothing else to do.' So I went with him to the youth camp. It turned out to be one of the biggest decisions of my life.

* * *

Lennox Head, where the youth camp was held, is so awesome — it's this big white beach just south of Byron Bay, with a freshwater tea-tree lake and tennis courts and all sorts. There were different youth groups there from all over the North Coast, probably 250 people, and I already knew everybody because we'd done this heaps of times. I'd been full on with the Ganggalah Church for about a year and a half by the time I got kicked out of Bible college.

I brought my nasty attitude along. On the first night, we all gathered in the auditorium to listen to the preacher as darkness came down outside the windows. I sat down the back of the hall with my arms crossed feeling salty. *Yeah, whatever. You should be glad I'm here.* I knew how it all went.

The band was up there and I knew all the songs by now. And at the end of his sermon the preacher was just like I knew he'd be: 'If there's anybody here who wants to have a relationship with Jesus … You could have done this many times, this could be your first time … Just give it a try, and see what it is for you.'

Despite my attitude, I just suddenly thought, *Why not?* It was something in me, something that, despite everything, was sick of the old me. But when I was walking down the aisle past everyone, up towards the preacher at the front, I was thinking, *Okay, God. This is your last chance. If you don't get me now, if you don't show me that you're real now, I'm done. I'm walking out. I'm never coming back.* Arrogant as.

When I got to the front, I sat there with my arms folded tight against me, like they were my armour. And the preacher led us in prayer. 'I want you to close your eyes.' I'm still thinking, *Yeah, yeah, I know how this goes …*

Then he said, 'Imagine that it's you and Jesus.'

I closed my eyes.

'I want you to imagine that it's you, Jesus, and there's an altar. I want you to imagine yourself taking everything out of your life, and putting it on this altar before Jesus.'

And I imagined the whole thing. So I started getting things out of me, from things that everybody knows, to dark secrets that nobody's ever known, from the good to the ugly. Hurt, pain, happiness, loss, fear. Most of all, my shame. My whole life. I found it all. I was exposing it all to myself, maybe for the first time ever. The walls I usually hid behind, hid myself from myself, hid myself from the world, they had gone. It started to hurt. I was getting tears in my eyes and then I was crying. Crying my life out.

Then the preacher goes, 'There's one thing that you're not putting on that altar. You're too scared to put it on. I want you to put it on the altar.'

And I knew, for me, it was Sefina. *I'm not giving her up for nobody.* But then suddenly I thought, *Okay.* So I put her on this altar too, and I looked at her, and I fell to the ground. It felt like I literally ripped out my rib.

Then the preacher goes, 'Now I want *you* to jump up on the altar.'

For me, it was the last bit. He was right. I had done this before — gone up the front to be prayed over, to commit to God. Even though I'd had many incredible moments, everything I'd done while I was with the church, all my hallelujah, praise God, it had always been ninety-nine per cent. There was always something I held back. That was why, when shit hit the fan, I left church, blamed God, blamed the people who represented God, when it had nothing to do with God. It was all to do with me. I had always left myself a bolthole.

But now, I jumped up. I put myself on that altar. I finally surrendered. I blacked out and I went into a dream, a vision.

I was standing at the front of a crowd and before me was this black stage with these white lights, and there was a band. I blinked, and then I was on the stage, and I was singing. And as I was singing I saw people coming through the crowd, a sea of people, my whānau, seeping through the crowd like a draught, their heads bowed. And I heard this voice so clear, like if you were talking to me, and it said, 'I've called you to sing my people back home to me. I've called you to woo my people back home to me, so they can be healed.'

I had never heard the word woo before, ever in my whole life, but I understood what it meant.

I blinked again, and now I was at my marae, at Tamapahore, on the steps of the wharenui, still singing, but now I understood the people in front of me *specifically* — I saw the fatherless son, the single mother, the abuser, the rapist, the murderer, the drug dealer, the alcoholic. They were all bowing. I was like, 'Eh? Is that before me?'

'No,' the voice said. 'They're bowing to me. You're going to sing them back home to me.'

I blinked one more time and an image flashed before me of all my whānau just surrendering. There were tears but they were tears of like, *I'm free*, tears of joy, tears of happiness.

And then I opened up my eyes. *Holy shit, did this happen?*

I was still at the camp, still had all the people around me, but I was so gobsmacked I couldn't speak to nobody. They all went off to have supper, I just went and sat by myself, singing to myself, and saying thank you to God for that experience, which I was struggling to understand, but which felt more real than anything that had ever happened to me before.

The very next day my faith got tested.

The biggest fear my whole life has been hearing about more deaths in my family. There were always so many deaths. Death was often the thing that had made me turn away from God, blaming God, getting angry.

I woke up that next morning feeling like I was dancing to a whole new tune. *What's up? Hallelujah! I'm back!* Me and some mates went swimming, diving through the waves, but then we heard some voices. Screaming. And we realised there were two girls further out, stuck in the big waves and they were in trouble. We swam out. I got one on my back and held onto the other one, swimming with one arm. Pāpā's tough swimming lessons, all that time swimming at school — it all came into play that day. I brought those girls in until I reached where my mate was, and then he took one, and together we brought them to shore.

Hallelujah. Another blessing.

But when I got back to my phone, I saw I'd missed a whole lot of calls from my mum. I called her back. Nanny Lanni had died, sister of my nan, one of the very last of the twenty-three siblings who'd grown up in Rūātoki.

My worst fear. I hung up the phone. I was bawling my eyes out, yelling at God: 'Fuck you, God. I finally come back to you and you do this to me. I'm done with you …' Blaming God again.

But then I heard a voice. I know I might sound like a crazy person. I *heard* Him say, as clear as if he was standing

My great-great-grandmother Ngapera Taahu, the last Tūhoe kuia to receive the ancient tradition of female facial tattooing, moko kauae. (Supplied by author)

My great-great-great-grandfather Taipari McLeod (front row, centre). Taipari was a Ngāi Te Rangi chief, the paramount chief at the time, who fought against the British at Gate Pā in Tauranga, and went on to be a member of the Tauranga Māori Council. When he died in 1916, his tangi was so massive it went on for weeks. (Supplied by author)

Māmā and Pāpā back in the day. Early 1990s, Melbourne. There were always lots of parties going on, and the photos captured the laughs and the good times — but never what happened after. (Walker family archive)

Me. My mum used to call me her 'little bulldozer'. (Walker family archive.)

From left: my grandfather Rangimarie McLeod, his sister Raukatauri, my cousin Pīpī, my great-grandmother Nana Ngawaiwera, Pīpī's little brother Pumau, and my uncle Vince. Rangimarie McLeod, my mother's father, was my koko, my favourite person, my safe place. I could run to his house any time of the day or night. (Walker family archive)

Me and all my cousins at kōhanga reo up at Tamapahore Marae. Kōhanga helped to save our language — but all I knew was how much fun it was. All my cousins were like my brothers, sisters and best mates. (Walker family archive)

Me and my cousin Jade at kōhanga reo up Tamapahore Marae. (Walker family archive)

Me (left) and my next older brother Russ at Bi-Lo supermarket in Ocean Shores, Australia, shopping for Easter eggs. (Walker family archive)

Me at four years old with my little cousin Maddison. I was lucky that I grew into my ears! This was at my uncle and auntie's wedding in Trangie, Australia, 1995. (Walker family archive)

Another 'new beginning'. This time, back to Australia, to Ocean Shores, near Byron Bay in New South Wales. I didn't want to go. And, of course, everything just carried on the same as it had back in New Zealand. From left: Mike, my cousin Pete, my brother Russ and me. This was about 1996, not too long after moving into this big five-bedroom house. (Walker family archive)

My two older brothers Russ and Mike, my mum and me, Byron Bay, 1996. I'm five or six, and as usual I can't stop acting. (Walker family archive)

Ocean Shores Public School, 1996. I'm in the middle row, second from left. I was suspended from every school I ever went to, and this was no exception. (Walker family archive)

Me and one of our family's Kiwi mates in Ocean Shores, 1998, when I was seven.
(Walker family archive)

In Byron Bay with my baby brother Noah, 1998. Noah represented the new life my parents had found in the church. I had just turned eight not long before this photo — I recognise the clothes that had been given to me for my birthday. Not too long after, my dad took them back off me. (Walker family archive)

My mum's mum Nana Raewyn and me when I was almost eleven. I was nine when we reconnected with Nana Raewyn. I see so much of myself in her. We're rebellious. If someone says don't do something, we're going to do it. (Walker family archive)

My oldest brother Mike, back in the day. He was my protector against our dad, but he'd experienced so much violence himself that he sometimes took it out on me. Monkey see, monkey do — we were all victims of that. (Walker family archive)

We had a lot of hard times, but photos are always there to remind us of the good times. I always love having fun with my whānau. (Supplied by author)

Our 'outreach' team from my parents' church C3 in Hamilton. I'm sitting in the middle. I hated being in this group because at that time I hated doing anything with my family. The only thing good about being in this group was spending time with my two cousins Tira and Rarauhe, who are like my sisters. (Walker family archive)

Me at fifteen, in Byron Bay, soon after we moved back. I hated moving back to Australia. Not long after this, my nana girl was killed in a car crash. Two of the worst years of my teenage life. (Walker family archive)

Sixteen years old, at the Ballina Idol singing competition, near Byron Bay. (Walker family archive)

Me and my little sis, Mary-Grace. So proud of her — she became the first of our whānau to finish school. I was sixteen, I had dropped out of school and had started working at Mallam's 5-Star Supermarket in Mullumbimby. (Walker family archive)

November 2009. From high-school dropout to 'the guy who won *Australian Idol*'… Here I am at the very beginning of my career, just around the time my first album *Introducing Stan Walker* hit the charts. (Supplied by Sony Music New Zealand)

Filming *Mt Zion*, in 2011. It was my movie debut, and I loved it, maybe even more than singing. From the director to the crew, almost all were Māori and there were a lot of native speakers so we could talk to each other in te reo Māori. (Supplied by author)

Whānau after my Aunty Mary's tangi at Tamapahore Marae, 2012. (Supplied by author)

The day me, my oldest brother Mike and Pāpā went to speak at Man Up in Auckland, 2016. For me, it was all about the kaupapa, and the chance to say to 1000 men from all backgrounds: 'Look at us. Change is possible.' (Supplied by author)

First time round: me and my love Lou Tyson, back in 2016. Here we are at the top of Mount Maunganui, with my family's traditional land, Pāpāmoa and Tamapahore, behind us. (Supplied by author)

My parents' twenty-year wedding anniversary, Gold Coast, 2016. (Supplied by author)

From left: my sisters-in-law Tammy-Lee and Missy, my mum, my sister Mary-Grace, Lou, and my beautiful nieces, at Māmā and Pāpā's twenty-year wedding anniversary. (Supplied by author)

Māmā and her sons. (Supplied by author)

next to me, 'You didn't experience me last night to give up now.' I know this sounds so impossible. I never believed in this stuff. Yet it was more real than anything else.

I just went quiet. I went from hysterics, swearing, crying, to quiet. And because my mates have seen me go through this before when I've lost people, they were looking at me like I might bite, but saying, 'Are you all right?'

'Yeah,' I said. 'I'm all good.'

I assumed me and Pāpā would fly back to New Zealand for the funeral. But Mum said, 'Stay there, son. You stay there. I think this is going to be good for you.' And I said, 'Okay, Mum.' I couldn't believe those words came out of my mouth so simply. I felt an absolute peace.

I said to God, 'Okay, God, I don't know what's happening, but I want to trust you. I know I felt something, so I'm going to trust this feeling. I'm here. Thank you.'

That night was the last night of camp, and there was another service. Everyone was there, hundreds of people there in this big auditorium. The pastor was speaking and I was in the congregation, in my own buzz of feeling thankful and that feeling, the best feeling there is, of being close to God. But then, out of the blue, the pastor said: 'I want to stop the service for a second. I want Stan to come up here and lead the song.'

Eh? I wasn't even part of the worship team; I had no actual role in the band. I'd been thinking I'd sunk those ships. But I walked up there, already feeling tears, already snotty nosed, you know, all shy, a bit giggly. The song was called, 'I Could Sing of Your Love Forever'.

I started singing, which quickly turned into crying. I had my eyes closed, weeping on the mic, just basically talking the lyrics. It was overwhelming me, the knowledge that I never really knew what love was, something I'd only had screwed-up, false versions of. But the love I felt from God was the love that I'd been craving for. I had always wanted to be accepted, and to be free, and that was how I felt, and that was why I couldn't stop crying.

At the end of that song, I opened up my eyes, and everybody in the whole auditorium, and the band, were on their knees weeping. And I was standing on that black stage, with those white lights, and it was as I'd seen in my vision.

Oh my God. You're real. You're actually real. And I promised him, and I promised myself, that no matter how hard it got, I was never turning back.

Impossible. Possible. Who really knows the truth of those words? Things that are impossible turn out to be fully possible. Look at our whānau today. Look at my life. These things are beyond the usual way of knowing. For me, my relationship with God made the impossible possible. It's not about rules or regulations or reading stuff in a book. It's about me having my relationship with Jesus, who is love and forgiveness. People are people and they stuff up. I stuff up all the time, but my relationship with Jesus is always there.

I had grown up around church stuff most of my life, in it but not really of it. The only time I talked to God was to yell and swear at Him, and to tell Him, *Kill my dad.* But I had never believed.

Now, my personal experience of God's grace was the realest thing I'd known in my whole life. It was my *experience.* I believed. I trusted.

You might think that everything was going to be easy for me from here on. I might even have thought the same then, that it was going to be easy, that I would carry that feeling of lightness forward into my whole life. But it's not like that and as you will see my old feelings of hating myself, of struggling with my old habits, continued to eat at me down through the years. I don't have the answer to that, why loving God is not enough to make me love myself all the time. I think it's not so much about loving God as knowing that God loves me, and knowing that that's an infinite agape, pure love, that he died for me. That's what I now knew. It's impossible for us as humans who are so faulty to understand or to give love that pure, especially to ourselves, when we can be so self-destructive. It is not a straightforward path.

But that night, I was filled with the knowledge that God is real, and I was certain about what I needed to do. When that night was over, I went home and I broke up with Sefina. Not because of my parents but because I knew she wasn't the one. I knew in my heart it wasn't right. My whole heart had changed and she wasn't part of my revelation, and that's pretty much what I told her. It was so bad, the way I did it. After fighting against everybody to go together, I brutally dumped her.

I feel bad about that. You know, I was a kid, and I was just running with the truth. I was running with my heart for the first time. It was a giant leap of faith.

* * *

I moved back home. I got a part-time job in a men's clothing shop.

It was just around that time that my Uncle Dean, who was involved with the Gold Coast music scene, heard me singing. He took me along to a jam night at The Avenue in Surfers Paradise. I got up there and sang 'Ain't No Mountain High Enough' with my cousin, his daughter Jadey-girl. And everybody was like: whoa. My uncle believed in me. He was a big inspiration and a big push for me. He started taking me around to meet people, getting me gigs, like residencies at cafés, restaurants, clubs and even a shopping mall — we'd turn up with our little speakers. Sometimes it was just me with my guitar, and sometimes I was with my cousins. Always covers; I had a repertoire of about fifteen songs.

I sang at church all the time, too. I always had, because my mum and aunty ran the outreach groups at their church, so I always had to perform for those. I used to hate it, though, because at that stage I hated doing anything with my family. Singing in front of them had all been tied up with hidings and shame and getting forced to do things. But at Ganggalah, where I was in the creative arts team, I loved it, although I'd never been the lead singer in the church band.

Now that I was gigging, I started to really love singing and performing. It was fun. I wondered if I could earn my living from it.

'Nah,' Pāpā said. 'You're not singing.' He'd always worked with his hands. 'Get a real job. That ain't going to pay the bills. That crap ain't going to take you anywhere.'

And then I found out that Sefina was pregnant. She did a test while I was with her and it was positive. And that was it for me. I was committed. If there was going to be a baby, I would be there, even if Sefina and I weren't actually together as a couple. But my mum didn't believe Sefina was pregnant. She decided Sefina was only pretending so she could get me back. She didn't believe me that I'd actually seen the positive pregnancy test. We argued and I got kicked out again. Back to sleeping on my brother's sofa.

It wasn't long after that that I began the Idol audition process. As I made it through the different rounds, they began developing their story about me — that I was about to be a young dad. That was the whole core of the story.

When I made it from the top one hundred, down to the top twenty-four, I got my first tattoo — the word 'Ataahua', tattooed on my neck. Ātaahua — Beautiful — was to be the name of our baby, and I was happy and excited to be becoming a dad, no matter the circumstances. I had gone back to Coolangatta, where my parents were living, on a visit before the next phase of Idol began, and on an impulse went into a tattoo studio. I showed the guy what I wanted, he drew it on my neck and I was like, 'Sweet,' and he got started. It was such a spur-of-the-moment thing; I hadn't really looked into it and didn't know you're supposed to drink water and have something sweet to eat first, so pretty soon after he started I got dizzy. 'Is this normal?'

'Nah, not really,' the guy said.

'I feel like I'm going to faint!' He had to stop while I had some water. But soon after that, I was tatted up.

I kept trying to get in touch with Sefina but she wouldn't answer my texts and calls. Something wasn't right. I hadn't seen her for ages, although we had been in touch by phone.

But now I couldn't get a hold of her at all. That evening, I went to church and everyone was gossiping. 'Oh, have you heard?'

'Hmm, yeah, well I heard she wasn't even pregnant.'

I said, 'I beg your pardon? Who're you talking about?'

'Oh, Sefina. Was she even pregnant?'

My mother had opened up her mouth, telling the ladies at church, 'Ugh, I don't trust her. She's not even pregnant. She's just a liar.' She hadn't thought about the effect on me of what she was spreading around. You see, that baby was real to me. There was a baby shower being planned by some of the girls at church. I had the baby's name tattooed on my neck. But here was everyone doubting.

Then my mate Tim told me. He didn't want to. He thought Sefina should tell me, but no one knew where she was. So he told me: 'Sefina lost the baby. She had a miscarriage.'

I wanted to rip the tattoo off my neck. I'd been wearing it so proud. Now I felt embarrassed. Ashamed. Caught in this situation where my mother was telling everyone Sefina was a liar and there had never been any baby, and my own hurt and sadness. I had lost a child, yet no one asked if I was okay and Sefina herself had vanished. It was years before I was able to talk to her about what had happened. Meanwhile, most people at church were so caught up in gossip, in wanting to be right, they forgot their empathy. My mum hurt me the most. In her way, she thought she was protecting me, but it hurt me so much when she kept saying, 'I knew it. I knew she was wrong.'

Even the guest pastor who was staying over with us acted like nothing happened. I think they thought that because I was the guy it didn't affect me.

But Tim, he really felt for me. I just remember him being there for me and saying, 'Are you all right, bro? You'll be all right.' It meant a lot to me that he was thoughtful in that way. Empathy is more important than winning a debate.

It was a lot for an eighteen-year-old to take on board. And then I realised, oh my gosh — all the stuff the Idol team had put together about me being a young dad was just about to go to air. I rang them in a panic. 'You need to take everything down!' That was my whole story, and they had to change it.

It was not long after that day that I had a dream — one of those dreams that was clear as day. Everything was white, and then there were three little girls, all slightly different ages, which was weird; I hadn't even been thinking about the fact that Sefina actually had three miscarriages. I couldn't see their faces properly but they were brown and they had hair like mine and Sefina's, and a face shape like Sefina's. It was so vivid, and when I woke up it stayed with me. I felt at peace.

Now, my tattoo is so much a part of me, and what I feel now is that it's all part of my story, part of what I was supposed to go through.

A friend told me something really cool recently, 'Don't allow your knowledge to take away your heart.' And I relate that to my tattoo: I got it out of my heart. I got it out of love for that child. That's the only thing that counts.

* * *

Australian Idol was a real circus right from the start. Executive Director Greg Beness travelled all over the country, to cities, to tiny little out-of-the-way places, auditioning people through

April and May 2009. And on Saturday, 9 May, he came to Brisbane, the nearest auditioning location to where I was living in Coolangatta. I turned up at Brisbane Stadium with my friend Jillian as my support — she'd been my friend since we were neighbours, back when we were at the first pig farm. She was the only person I'd told I was going to do it. We were absolutely shocked at how many people were there — more than 10,000.

I saw a few people I knew there, and they were like, 'Are you auditioning?'

'Nah, nah, just with a mate.' I didn't want anyone to know I was doing it. We had to wait hours and I fell asleep on the seats. I was saying to Jillian, 'Let's just go. It's taking too long. Look at all these people.' The whole thing seemed pointless. She made me stay. Finally, when there was hardly anyone left, it was my turn.

Auditioning for Idol is quite a long process. But the first step — and the one where most people instantly fail — is when you go into a little room with three people from the TV network, Channel 10. The way it works is you sing until they say 'stop', and after that you're given a card that reads either yes or no. Instant death, or the chance of life.

'Circle of Life'. Just how I'd planned it back when I was twelve years old. I opened my mouth and out it came, and I sang till they told me to stop. I lived. I got the 'yes' card, and then on I went, into a bigger room where the big hitters were waiting — the producers, the heads of department, the vocal coaches and the big boss, Greg Beness.

When I walked in, a senior member of the production crew looked at me and virtually rolled his eyes. He would have seen a shy, badly dressed kid with a rat's tail who couldn't stop his nervous giggling. He said, 'You know what? You Polynesians think you can just walk in here and sing, but you're all lazy.' He was so brutal. It could have killed me right there.

I was nervous, of course, but when he said that, I was taken aback. I became *un*-nervous. My whole life had prepared me to fight, and I thought, *Cheek! You don't know me! Don't you ever compare me to anybody else!* Only I knew that underneath all my giggling, I was probably the most competitive person he'd seen all day.

Maybe there had been bad examples of Polynesian people on that show who had been lazy, who had gone late to every rehearsal and stuff like that. Maybe he was speaking out of actual experience. I don't know. But he was pigeonholing us as a people. I can't stand generalisations and I hate racism. I don't know why that guy said it, but I'm glad he did. I had been shy and soft before, but his comments were perfectly timed for me, to push me, remind me. Boom. *I'm here for a purpose.* I had that feeling: *I'll show you.*

He tested me hard, running through the different theme nights of the show.

'What are you going to do when it comes to rock week?'

'Metallica, "Nothing Else Matters".'

'Sing it.'

I sang it.

What are you going to do for country week?

'Johnny Cash, "Ring of Fire".'

'Sing it.'

I sang it. I was fully prepared.

'Okay. What are you auditioning with?'

I said, 'I'm singing "Circle of Life".'

I sang it and at the end of that, they told me I was through to the next round.

Life at that time didn't look that hopeful. I'd been kicked out of home for the hundredth time. I was sleeping on my brother's couch. I worked part-time in a men's clothing store. My ex-girlfriend was pregnant. I was only eighteen. But I'd got through the first hurdle of Idol, and I had that inside me to keep me going. There was a few weeks' wait, and then I was called back for the televised interviews in front of the three people who were going to be the actual judges — the stunning African American singer Marcia Hines, TV presenter and producer Ian Dickson and radio host Kyle Sandilands (although Kyle later got replaced by Sony executive Jay Dee Springbett).

Oh my gosh. I was sweating with nerves and heat, dressed in a T-shirt and a waistcoat with front pockets that I kept jamming my hands into so that my elbows stuck out at the side. I had a checked scarf wound around my neck, and I sat there crushed up against the other nervous contestants also waiting their turn, trying to pray and focus while I waited to be called. 'Eighteen-year-old shop assistant Stan Walker, whose singing is mostly done in church …'

'Why are you all giggly?' the show host Andrew Günsberg asked me, as he roved around the waiting room with his microphone. 'Is it because you're nervous?'

I was so hot, and I was mopping my forehead, giggling, laughing, nervous. 'Yeah,' I told him jokingly, 'I'm just thinking about what's going to happen when I walk into the room. I'm going to forget what I'm going to sing and then just sing a random song.'

'Breathe and relax,' Andrew advised me. I tried.

Eventually, it was my turn. 'Stan, this is it, mate,' Andrew said, ready to usher me in. I didn't know it, of course, but those were the exact words he'd use a few months later when I won.

'Am I going in?'

'You're going in.'

'Like, actually?'

And there were the judges, the three of them sitting there, looking deadly serious, shrewdly sizing me up. 'Oh, I'm so nervous,' I told them. I couldn't stop giggling and then I tried to calm myself. 'Pull it together,' Dickson said, and I breathed and calmed. They were just watching me, smiling a bit. God knows what they expected. Maybe not much. I got on with it. I sang 'Circle of Life' and thought I nailed it, but then Marcia asked me: 'Do you have anything more modern?' I wasn't expecting that. I hadn't planned a second option.

But then I thought about John Legend's 'Ordinary People'. They found a guitar for me, and I sang that as well — and that became the song that was on the televised audition, even though it hadn't been part of the plan.

The thing is, they thought I was dumb, and to be honest, I was acting a bit that way. Maybe I only knew how to act as if I wasn't taking myself seriously. But that was my coping mechanism. Giggle. Laugh. But my brain was on, and I was taking myself very seriously. I think when I sang they realised that, because as soon as I sang, my demeanour changed and

I became very focused. One minute I was giggling, the next second I was focused — then as soon as I finished singing, I giggled again. They were very intent, very serious, all the way through that second song, and at the end Kyle said: 'Mate, you are a must-have on this show.' Then he said, 'I really did think you were going to be a crazy.'

'This whole room was just captivated by your voice,' Marcia said in her lovely, quiet way. 'You could have heard a penny drop. And I'd like to say, welcome to *Australian Idol*. Welcome.'

I needed to check what I was hearing. 'Like, *in* it?'

'Big yes,' Ian Dickson said.

And I knew: this was going to change my life

Somehow I got myself back out to where everyone was waiting. 'I got in!' And they started screaming and hugging — and that's really when the journey began properly.

Next up was the top one hundred in Sydney, where they weeded us down to the top twenty-four. They had us all standing in rows and would randomly call us to step forward and sing something. For this part of it, I sang 'Jesus Loves Me', a cappella — I just thought of it on the spot. It didn't feel childish. That old song just felt true. Jesus loves me. I absolutely knew I was in his hands and that, whatever happened, it was all for a purpose that went beyond my own personal ambitions — it was about setting an example for my whānau, for my people. I was getting my chance.

Then they were like, 'Sorry, second row, you didn't make it. But you, you're through to the next round.' And I was like, 'Yo!'

The whole Idol format is about creating stories about the contestants, who are really like characters in the show. He's the shy one. The giggly one. The unfocused one who doesn't take it seriously. That was the story they were all creating around me.

It was around that time we met Delta Goodrem. That was incredible to me. The first song I'd ever sung with a band had been her song, 'Born to Try', when I was still at intermediate school. She'd obviously been told by the producers that they thought I wasn't focused because she pointed at me and said one word: 'Focus.' I was like, *The hell?*

At the end of that process, of getting from one hundred to just twenty-four, I sang 'Let's Stay Together'. My performance came at the end of the evening, after a really long day with lots of waiting around, and was the moment they decided whether I'd made it or not. Once again, Ian Dickson acknowledged the concerns about my focus, and my need to prove I had it. He asked me about it at the end of that night — you could tell he was puzzled about the difference between the giggling, apparently unfocused me, and the absolute focus they saw when I sang.

'What happens when you sing?' he asked me.

My answer then was the same as it would be now: 'When I sing, it's the expression of who I am, without having to mould myself to anybody else's idea of me. It's my way of showing where I've come from, to who I am now.'

They couldn't see my ambition. I kept it all hidden away inside me, but it was there. I'd had a lifetime of acting. Nobody knew anything about me — not the real me, not about what was really going on inside me. I was still a really closed-up person. I used a fake smile and a fake laugh to protect myself. I was the master of the masks. If I had been my real, everyday self, I'd have been too nervous to perform. Acting got me through life, and that's what had got me onto that stage.

Dickson was still testing me. He asked me if I wanted to go through or go home. 'I wanna go through,' I said. I was in. I made it out to the waiting room out the back, where my cousin Tira from Rūātoki was, there to support me. 'I got in!' And Tira and I were hugging and crying and we both had the same immediate thought. Our grandmothers are sisters, and they had both passed on, but we knew how proud they would've been — that I'd come this far and that we were both here in Sydney, adults now, starting to live our own lives. And that was all there between us in that amazing moment.

From then on, it got really intense. The live shows were starting in a couple of weeks, so we were divided into four groups of six, each group performing over four nights. I was in the first group and sang Alicia Keys' 'If I Ain't Got You'. And that's when the nerves struck: I was shaking and my throat was wobbling and I was sure I'd completely ruined it. Something about the pressure suddenly got to me — the cameras, the live audience, the performing. *There's no way in hell I'm going any further.* But somehow I was chosen to carry on into the top twelve. *Whoa.* I was completely shocked.

My life had already changed by this stage. As the top twenty-four, we'd been staying in a Sydney hotel, getting driven around in a bus, meeting famous people like Delta Goodrem and Michael Bublé, doing photo shoots, living and breathing music and performance every day. And the food. We could eat whatever we wanted, and so I did.

By the time the twelve finalists moved into the Idol mansion, a massive, five-level house at Mosman Beach, I was living my best life. I was being paid $600 a week, which seemed an incredible amount. I was like a kid in freaking Disneyland.

All the way through, I got amazing feedback from the judges. At one point, on the night the top twenty-four were chosen, Kyle Sandilands told me I was the only one of the contestants who he'd told his family and friends about. And yet it didn't really touch me. I was so aware of my shortcomings, the way that nerves were affecting my voice. I didn't want to get thrown off.

My manager, David Champion, who became my manager at the end of the Idol process and is still my manager today, later told me he got a message really early on from the show's producer: 'We have the finest voice in the country — one that will blow your socks off and he could win. But we have a note of caution … he will be unmanageable. He is feisty, has strong views, does not appear to be driven by money or fame, and to top it off probably has OCD or ADHD.' So that's what they were thinking, what they were seeing in the way I carried myself at that time. And that's what I was seeing reflected in their concerns about focus.

But all I could do was commit to the next performance, and the one after that, and I was almost always dissatisfied with myself, no matter how kind the judges were. But I loved the whole thing and how much it was pushing me.

On Idol, as in the industry itself, the big fight was always to stay true to who I was. After the top twelve were selected, we got to go home for a bit before the next phase began, and the cameras came home with me, to meet the family, find out where I'm from. They came to my work, came to church, filmed me out singing at the beach. We did three days of filming, and at the end of that they pulled me aside. 'Ah, Stan, we can't use any of the footage of you talking. We cannot understand any of your English. We're going to have to put you through speech therapy.'

I was just like, *Hell no*. So I taught myself. I was from Byron Bay, and I knew how to talk like an Aussie. I'd always put on different accents to go with my different masks, so it was easy for me. But other things they said showed me that they actually thought I was dumb. They'd put me in a box. After watching the interview clips, they'd say things like, 'Man, you're so philosophical,' and, 'The way you talk is so wise,' like it was a big surprise.

In those days, I had a problem with people taking me for granted or underestimating me. It made me mad, like, *I'll show you*. It still happens. Ironically, I get underestimated because I came from Idol, or because I'm a pop artist, but now I love it. I love that look on their face when I perform, or talk, and it's so much more than what they've expected. But back then, to be honest, I guess I presented to the world as if I didn't take myself seriously. It was a lifelong habit.

On the night of the final three, I chose to sing 'Amazing Grace'. For me, personally, it's a very important song. *I once was lost but now I'm found*. I was thinking of everything that had happened in the time between watching Guy Sebastian, the first winner, and now. I couldn't really believe I was there. It felt like a miracle, a very unlikely thing. It had become clear to me that the Idol journey was not about winning, not in and of itself. I wanted to win Idol because I knew I could do it. It could be done. It was about an incredible feeling that was strengthening in me: *I can do it.*

* * *

When I first met the *Australian Idol* vocal director Erana Clark I was like, *Yes* — I knew who she was. She was a legend in New Zealand. She began her career in Auckland when she was just twelve and had sung on all the early TV talent shows, and even toured with The Supremes and Dionne Warwick before eventually moving to Australia. By the time I met her, she'd been vocal director on Idol for every one of the seven seasons, and she had become ruthless. She would say, 'There are thousands of kids who have this dream; some of them are totally deluded. Some are pretty good, and a small percentage have star quality.' She'd just come right out and tell someone if they couldn't sing.

Not only all that, but she was Māori, and here I was, a brown boy in a white man's world. But she didn't seem to give me anything for that. We all knew she was tough, but I felt like she was especially tough on me. She said I had a short attention span. She criticised me for being a sugar freak. She would sometimes say, 'Shut up!' Or, 'Sit down!' But she was training not only my voice, but also *me*.

I'd never had a music lesson and I couldn't read music, but I always knew exactly what I wanted in my arrangements.

I never wanted to do things just like the originals. I would hear a song and just somehow hear it in my own way. I always wanted to be different, take risks. That's one of the reasons I chose songs by female singers. I did 'Umbrella' by Rihanna, 'If I Ain't Got You' by Alicia Keys, and 'Sweet Dreams', 'Single Ladies' and 'Halo' all by Beyoncé. I'd have battles with the music director but I stuck to my guns and I always got props from the judges for the way I did stuff.

Sometimes there'd be a bit of an attitude, 'Who do you think you are?' I was just this kid who couldn't even read music. But my point of view was: it was going to be me up there singing, me up there being judged, and it had to be sharp, excellent, tight. It had to reflect me. More than that, I had to feel it. I'd be thinking: *You might know music when it's written on your piece of paper, but music is not reading. It's feeling and if I don't feel it, I don't want to sing it.*

At the final, Ian Dickson said, 'I love your voice, I love your heart, but the risks you've taken every week have made it one of the most thrilling rides ever.'

When it came to music, I didn't have any self-doubt. There have been many things that have happened to me in my life that have left me finding it hard to trust even the people nearest to me — to really trust that they won't abuse my kindness or my love. My heart. I have trust issues. However, I never have any trust issues with music.

I didn't connect with Erana properly for a while. Then after a few weeks, she pulled me aside and she goes, 'Why do you think I'm so tough on you? You have to work harder than everybody else because of who you are, because you're Māori, because you're brown and you're from New Zealand.

You have to work harder than everybody else, so I'm going to be hard on you. I expect more from you. You have to work harder than all these people.'

I hadn't understood that about this industry I was getting myself into. She was the one who told me.

I knew then and there that this is something none of those other contestants would ever have to experience. There were actually two other contestants like me earlier on — there was a Māori girl before the top twenty-four, and a Sāmoan, and we all rallied together. That's a natural thing. You just find your own people.

But one girl was too big, the other girl was too sassy; they'd seen similar traits in previous contestants who were Polynesian. Being outspoken is trouble, being confident is trouble, knowing your worth is trouble. It's a lesson I learned fast.

Later in the competition, when it was getting near the end, Erana said to me, 'You're going to win this.' So she pushed me even harder. But it was encouraging because I understood why she was doing it.

It wasn't until the grand final night of *Australian Idol*, just before I had to walk on stage, that I had a moment where I thought, *Am I actually going to win?* And then I prayed, *Oh God, let me win!* It seems weird to say it, but it's true; that was the first time I had prayed hard for that. I was on the show because I loved singing and I knew it was my calling. I wanted to use my gift in the world to help people. Most importantly, I wanted to be a light for my whānau. If my people ain't winning, I'm not winning.

I didn't know anything about fame. I didn't know anything about what it would mean to have a career. Our family didn't talk about stuff like that. I thought I knew what I was getting myself into. I didn't know.

My prayer throughout the whole Idol process had simply been: *God, wherever you're going to take me, then take me.* It wasn't until that last night, by myself in the changing room, when the realisation struck me that I could be going all the way, that I asked: *Is this the plan, God?* It was so trippy. *Oh God, let me win!*

* * *

After it was all over that night, my whānau came back to celebrate with me, and I was bawling my eyes out. We were all crying and laughing and hugging, and that's what it was all about for me — about us all being here together. 'Look at us,' I said to them. 'Look at our family that has come together.' That, for me, was the power of God, that he could use a little broken person to bring all the people who are broken together, and be mended. It was one of the most incredible times.

People often ask, 'Why are you a Christian? Why do you believe in God?' And I say, 'Have you seen my family?'

From the minute I got into Idol, and at no time more than on the night I won, my voice — my gift — was at work, healing relationships within my family.

Mum supported me by coming along to every night except one of the competition. But the miracle was that Pāpā also came a few times, and on the last night there he was in a place of honour next to Mum. He hadn't wanted me to sing. He thought I would fail. He just didn't understand any other way of living a life but his way, working with his hands, until he saw me in that context. Since then, he's been my biggest supporter. Far out. He is really proud of me. My whānau came from all around Australia and New Zealand, coming together to celebrate, with joy. When I win, we all win.

And that's one example of how my singing broke down barriers. Old barriers. It brought everybody in our whānau to better relationships, reconciliation, healing.

'I've called you to sing my people back home.' When I think about that voice I heard so clearly that night at youth camp, what I understand God means by 'back home' is back home to ultimate freedom. And what is freedom but peace and grace. What is 'home' but serenity, joy and love. That's God's home.

And I have seen that. I saw that on the night I won Idol. My voice is a healing tool. I'm helping to bring our family closer.

My success has given us more opportunity to dream bigger for ourselves. My whānau can see that the world is so much bigger than our little world that we've lived in. We can do anything and be anything we want.

Also, when I sing, I remind my whānau of the old people. I carry the voice, the spirit, the blood of my ancestors, and that also binds us together. When my family hear me, they'll say, 'Oh my gosh, it's like listening to ...' and they'll name some old falla who had a beautiful voice back in the day.

'Well,' I say, 'he wasn't as good as me. Let's be honest.'

'Oh, you sound just like him.'

'Yes,' I say, 'he was amazing. He was beautiful, but he's not me.'

CHAPTER NINE

Take me as I am

This is who I am, if you look within
You will see this is from the inside out
Take me as I am, this is all of me
You will see this is from the inside out

— 'Inside Out'

AUSTRALIAN IDOL, BASKET OF DREAMS. THE WHOLE experience was the highest of highs. But don't let anyone tell you reality TV is easy. It ain't. It's a marathon and a sprint all wrapped up into one.

Over those months, my life changed completely. Gone — wiped out completely — was the kid working in the menswear shop. I was off on my new path. Idol threw me in the deep end of the music industry, very like when my dad chucked me in the deep end of the swimming pool when I was four. Sink or swim both times. Lucky I was tough because it ain't no place for the faint-hearted.

I learned everything on the job: everything from stagecraft to media work and everything else involved in leaping from nobody to star, from singer to artist.

And the horrible truth is, winning something like Idol puts you straight at the top, it definitely does, but the fall can be just as fast, and it goes all the way to the bottom. Can you imagine that? One minute, people saying you're a star; the next, you're nobody again. I was determined that wouldn't happen to me.

I quickly realized that I needed to be the director of my own future because it didn't matter if I had the greatest voice in the world, in the end it would be down to how much I was prepared to work for my career. I could never stop.

So after I won, I went straight to work.

Idol was like the first kiss in a relationship. Figuring out how the industry works was like when the relationship has gone a bit further and you realise, *Oh man, you're grumpy in the mornings.* You stop dressing up for each other, you stop being on your best behaviour, then you start getting into arguments. Then you have to figure out, *How can I make this relationship work?*

* * *

Introducing Stan Walker. The cover of my first album, featuring a close-up of my face, beamed up on the giant Idol screens as I sang 'Black Box' in public for the first time ever. Little me, with the word 'Ataahua' curling around my neck like a reminder of a life that could have been very different.

Of course, *Introducing Stan Walker* didn't actually exist yet, apart from the single 'Black Box' that I'd already recorded. So the morning after the Idol final, I was straight into the recording studio and in two days it was done — eleven tracks, nine of them covers I'd sung during the competition, and two originals: 'Black Box' and 'Think of Me', which was produced by none other than my old hero Guy Sebastian. That was amazing to me. He was my hero, hard out, and now here we were in the studio together and getting on so easy, human to human. Obviously, I contained all my excitement, but inside I was like a little kid — *Oh my gosh!* The song he produced is one of the songs off that album that I still really like.

The album was such a rush I only heard it the day before it hit the stores. The video for 'Black Box' — filmed to look like I was at a pool party among the beautiful people — was made in one day after less than two hours' sleep after a full day of interviews. Literally, everything was non-stop. If I wanted to go to the toilet, I had to run there and back. During that first busy time I was always asking God for strength.

Sony had the digital download of 'Black Box' released the same night I won Idol, 22 November 2009, and it went to number two on the Australian charts, number one in New Zealand. The album was released two weeks later on 7 December and it went to number three in Australia, number two in New Zealand. It eventually went triple platinum.

It's the power of the music industry to get things done. To make stars. I was swept along in that and it was incredible. It doesn't matter that those things — the album, the single, the video — all make me cringe now. At the time, it was just exhilarating, and I was beaming. To go from being nobody, singing at church, to all this — to know that people were listening to me, listening to my music — it's a buzz that's never gone away. That first year after Idol, every moment was new for me. Every day I woke into a reality that was better than my dreams had been. I felt like I was this little superstar.

As always, the question was: what next? Through all the post-Idol stuff — the tour of Australia, doing in-store events, getting interviewed all the time, doing live shows — I knew I couldn't rest with all that had been given to me. I was a singer but if I wanted a career in this industry, I had to become an artist. I had to carve out my own identity. This is the blessing and the curse of shows like Idol. They make dreams come true, but they also stamp an identity on the winner that's very hard to change. I needed to carry on learning about stagecraft, how to dress, how to speak, how to perform with confidence. I needed to focus on writing my own material, and I needed to insist on my own identity.

I had always written songs. Mostly they were worship songs for church. One of those, 'I Surrender', I wrote just before I did Idol — but I still sing it and I included it on my 2018 EP *Stan*, in gratitude for having survived my cancer operation. With 'Missing You', the song for Nan, I had only gone so far as to put it up on YouTube.

But this was a whole lot more serious now. I was pumped to start writing more and to collaborate with other writers. I knew I had a lot to learn. Almost straight away I was thinking about my second album.

* * *

When it comes to music, I'm like a bag of Allsorts. I'm like a box of Favourites chocolates. Music is music. I've been moved by country music, I love Metallica, reggae music, Beyoncé. I love opera. Black gospel music. Māori songs and island music. I love it all. It's all part of me. They are all pieces of the puzzle that makes up *me*.

I don't know why you have to be this or that when you can be everything and anything and create your own space. I'm forever changing, forever growing. Why can't I put it all in?

But, of course, I know the answer to that — it's about marketing, about packaging, about control. And you know me, I always hated being told what to do. I've had a controlled life nearly my whole life, so now I'm like, *I am not going back in that box.*

Don't tell me what to do. It's an attitude that was always going to get me in trouble with the industry. It's the thing the Idol producers saw in me right at the very beginning, when they told my manager-to-be David Champion: 'We've found the best voice in Australia, but he might be unmanageable.' That first kiss was always going to lead to trouble.

Me and Champo have had plenty of break-ups and make-ups through the years. But a relationship like mine and Champo's is a career act, a lifelong one, and our fights have only made us stronger and given us more understanding of who the other is. It's through those tough times and adversity that we've really grown. He's been the realest, strongest relationship I've had in my life, outside family and friends. Talking about first kiss, our relationship is like a marriage: it's not always easy but it's worth fighting for. I feel like we're a team and I know he's *always* got my back.

To whom much is given, much is required. This is what Erana Clark told me, in one of our vocal sessions during Idol. I didn't understand what she meant then. But over the years I've learnt she was right.

The music industry is incredible. It offers platform, money, opportunities, but it demands so much in return. It demands the whole of you, and many people don't make it out. It's an industry that's full of addiction, suicide, breakdown. The highest highs, the lowest lows. People lose themselves. They forget who they really are underneath the industry version of themselves.

The moment my first album cover flashed up on the screen during the Idol final, the industry had its grip on me, shaping me, creating my public image. It gave me plenty, but it demanded a lot in return. Right from the beginning, I knew I had to fight to be me: my own version of Stan Walker.

At the age of nineteen, I stepped into a whole new world. My gift allowed me to get into this world, but I'm not *from* that world. I had to assimilate and that was hard because so much about me wasn't what they thought of as 'right' — I spoke wrong, my hair was wrong, my body was wrong, my attitude was wrong. Often I would have arguments that left me lonely and also afraid that I could lose everything and be nobody again. My dad had said he owned me; now this industry owned me.

A boardroom. A table. And around that table, a crowd of executives, people who didn't look like me, didn't have the same hair texture as me and didn't understand what was fashionable in my community. Me, with my naturally curly Māori hair and my background that couldn't have been more different to the expectations and priorities swirling around this room. I was ready to make the most of this opportunity but very sensitive and defensive about my difference. Feeling like an alien. Like I was being judged. The man appointed at that time as my new marketing manager told me I needed to cut my hair.

I read it as him saying he didn't like my look. I felt he was saying, 'You're not good enough.' I started to feel they all thought I was all wrong — too brown, too Māori. That the more I was myself, the less I appealed to the industry.

I was very young. I didn't want to lose my chance. Now I see that I had to find a way to compromise, to manage the situation, to give and take, but at the time I struggled. It was my youth and inexperience against their experience. I would argue, respond angrily, and that would lead to threats.

Grow your hair. Oh no, cut your hair. Style your hair like this. No, like this. If you don't do as we say, you'll lose this opportunity. Undo your top button or we stop filming.

It was really a battle over my image but I experienced it as a battle over my soul, my identity, and too often they won. I felt it was an industry with old mindsets. I think there was some truth in that at times but, to be fair, it's changed a lot now.

My second album, *From the Inside Out*, was very different to my first. I was happy with it. It was all originals; I had co-written some of the songs, in particular the title track. The first single released was 'Unbroken', written by Ryan Tedder who wrote 'Halo' for Beyoncé and 'Bleeding Love' for Leona Lewis — one of the best songwriters in the world, and I was honoured to record his song. But the video that accompanied that song, I still can't watch it, because of the way they insisted I look. That hairstyle. It's not me. It never was.

The title track was written with Audius Mtawarira, and I wanted it to reflect who I was and what I was going through. It's very literal: 'Maybe I'm not the one you thought I'd be … There's nothing you can ever do to break me … Take me as I am, this is all of me.'

Despite all the pressure coming from the industry, in a really important way I was never confused about my purpose. Yes, I wanted a career. I wanted to sing. But most of all, I wanted to use my gift in the world. To whom much is given, much is required. At the most important level, I was very clear: I had a gift and I wanted to use it to break down barriers. I wanted to help people. God had shown me I could help my whānau; I believed I could help other broken people, too.

And two days after I made the video for 'Unbroken', I got on a plane with my brother Mike and our friend, the singer Taya, who's now one of the lead singers of Hillsong United, and we headed to Haiti.

* * *

I have a hunger to learn, to understand the world. And for me, knowing and understanding are not about my head — they are about my heart.

I already knew Haiti was one of the poorest countries on the planet. I already sponsored two kids from there. But then when the earthquake struck in January 2010, one of my kids, a boy, died with his mother. It was a big realisation for me, and such a sad one: this is real. So when the Christian charity Compassion asked if I'd go there to help, I couldn't wait.

I wanted to go over there because I wanted my heart to break, I wanted to feel it. I wanted to feel it so I could understand.

And yes, my heart did break. You watch World Vision ads and you think it's so sad, but when you're there and you smell it — sewage, rubbish, death. It is the smell of despair.

We were taken to a big hākari, a big feed, there for all the aid workers and big people coming over to do stuff —

a luxurious spread in an area protected by armed guards. Armed guards protecting us from who? Outside this area were people drinking from muddy puddles. Me and Mike went around a corner and started crying. How can we eat? We can't eat.

We learned not just about Haiti in that situation, but about ourselves, and about the rich world we come from. This us-and-them world. We went out to a tent city to sing to kids who had been enslaved by people who had bought them with false promises to their parents. The children sang back to us and danced back to us. Human to human, with the power of music and love. Music breaks down barriers.

These kids were crowding around us, so happy we were there, and we were hugging them and picking them up when we were told, 'Don't touch them. You'll get sick.' I couldn't believe it. It was the most dehumanising thing I'd heard. If I get sores, if I get the runs, who cares? We're Māori. We do not care about that stuff. We saw a lot of similarities between ourselves and these people.

When we got back to Australia, I did media work, talking about what we'd seen, about how amid all this ultimate poverty, kids were being raped and beaten. I told this to morning TV, and got a call from a record executive saying, 'What the hell, Stan? You can't say rape on morning TV.' These kids are dying and all you care about is the word 'rape' in the morning?

In Māori culture, you call a spade a spade. Otherwise you can't deal properly with the issue. Did he think I should have said 'sexually violated'? What does that even mean? For me, using the right word acknowledges what has happened and doesn't downplay it. The right word can set us free — that was definitely the case for me, when I realised that 'rape' was what had been done to me.

I had to tell those stories as I saw them. I'd seen camps full of kids who had been enslaved. I had learned, and I needed to tell people, because otherwise how would they ever know?

I'm determined to be educated, so I can make change for our people. Then I can empower, change the hearts of people. I need it to be that when I speak of the issues I care about — about rape, or suicide, or poverty or climate change — it's more than an empty opinion.

*   *   *

Through my whole life, things that are totally contradictory have lived right up alongside each other. It was no different working in the music industry. You can often be having everything going good, but you still feel a sense of emptiness and loss.

I had so much success in the first few years. Two albums within the first year, my first headlining tour in New Zealand in early 2011, a trip to Los Angeles for writing and filming my single 'Loud'. I became close friends with one of the other past winners of Idol, Jessica Mauboy. She's like a sister to me. I think it's natural for those of us with that experience to so easily connect. I sang with her on our hit single 'Galaxy' and we were to double headline a tour together in early 2012. I particularly admired Jessica because as well as being an awesome singer, she has starred in a movie, *The Sapphires*. Acting was very much something I also aspired to do.

The goals that I'd set back with my youth pastor Sam at Ganggalah: buy a house, be in a movie — impossible, right? At the time they seemed impossible. But in 2011, at age twenty-one, I bought my first house, on the Gold Coast, for my family to live in — a five-bedroom house with two bathrooms and a pool, just like I'd fantasised when I was breaking into other people's houses.

Then the next part of my dream came true, too. Film director Tearepa Kahi invited me to do a screen-test for his movie *Mt Zion*, alongside Temuera Morrison, Troy Kingi and others. I got the part, so I had that to look forward to in 2012. On the surface, things couldn't have been better.

But underneath, despite how happy I was at the way my life was going, I wasn't coping with the pressure. From quite early on, I began having insomnia and that plagued me for years, so that I was regularly having only two or four hours' sleep a night. Then one day, some time in 2011, I was in my apartment by myself and I felt so ill I thought I was dying. I was having a heart attack, I was being attacked by demons — I didn't know what it was. I panicked. I yelled like I was trying to fight something off, 'No!' I rushed out of my apartment, downstairs to where there was a busy shopping mall and I stood there, comforted by having people around me, even if they were strangers. Breathless. My heart pounding. Gradually, I got myself back together.

That was my first panic attack. I used to think anxiety wasn't a thing. Now I know better. And it was different to the experiences I'd had as a child. Then, I had things done to me that I couldn't control. Now I was an adult, I had so much responsibility, to myself, to the goals I'd set myself, to my family, to my industry, to the public. There was no one else to lean on. The pressure was mine. I didn't talk to anybody at all. Just kept it inside; kept the masks on outside for happy and successful Stan Walker.

The pressure from the industry and my fear of being dropped was a constant. Every argument I had left me feeling desperate and a bit scared, and yet I couldn't just roll over.

Every criticism, every time I wrote a song and it wasn't good enough, my soul was tested. *Maybe just keep working on the song. Hmmm, maybe just keep writing.* What does that mean? I could read the criticism and I hated that they couldn't be direct. So, is this shit? Or isn't it? I'm a black-and-white person, that's how I was brought up, and I found those grey areas confusing. I could handle it better if they were straight with me. It's the little scratches that are eventually going to get into your heart, and it will stop beating.

My music and my art is my ultimate expression of who I am, but now I was laid wide open for people to say, 'That's not good enough.' They thought they were doing the right thing but they didn't understand they were mucking with my soul. I couldn't handle it. Sometimes I lost it, reacted badly, exploded, and that levelled up the stress as well.

Since becoming a Christian when I was seventeen, I had not smoked anything, or drank any alcohol. But some time in that first year, I had a puff on a mate's cigarette — *Ooh, that's nice* — and before you know it I was borrowing smokes, and then I was buying my own. I found it helped me calm down, and soon I was smoking like a train, only never in public. I'm not proud of it. It's been my biggest addiction, the hardest thing to stop, and it kicked back in even after one puff. My advice to young people: don't have that puff.

* * *

I always felt like I was doing this all on my own, but the people around me did notice sometimes. My mum said to me near the start of 2011, she must have noticed I was not sleeping or I was stressed: 'Boy, you're not a super-Christian. You can't do this on your own. No one can do it on their own.'

But I thought I could handle it all. I thought I could be there for everybody, handle all the challenges.

Towards the end of 2011 things were coming to a head. I had done a third album that was released in November that year. I had worked eight months straight without a day off. I was feeling more and more strongly that I was on a treadmill — same circuit of releases, interviews, promotional gigs, charity gigs as a favour to somebody.

When was I going to get off this treadmill and start running? They were always saying, 'Yeah, you're going to go to America and we'll pitch you over there.' But they didn't; I was watching other people go over there. I never felt they didn't believe in me, but I felt more and more that they saw me a certain way — this crooner, this boy next door — and I wanted to be more than that. But they were getting good money from me being a crooner.

It was an ongoing battle. And then, following a massive argument with my manager, they took my name off the 'Galaxy' tour. I was still doing the tour, but instead of a double headline, it was Jessica Mauboy supported by Stan Walker. I didn't even really mind being a support for Jess because she is the queen, but I felt the insult; I felt degraded and angry.

* * *

Early afternoon. Broad daylight. I'm in a taxi, scrunched up in the left-hand corner of the backseat. I can see the back of the driver's head. He can't see me and he's not thinking about me anyway, just like I'm not thinking about him. I've just had a fight with my manager. And that's it. My career's over. I'm done. Nobody cares. I'm not crying, but tears are streaming down my face. There's no hope. All that's in me is numb disbelief. How could this happen? Me, the great example. Tired and dead.

I don't want this no more. I open the car door and go to jump out.

I've been in this place so many times before. Since the age of three, there have been many times I've tried to take my own life. I have failed, been interrupted, or gone right up to the line but not quite over it. But this is the first time I've been this low since winning Idol. Who would ever have thought, seeing me that night with the world before me, that I would once again get to this point of hopelessness? In this moment, I forget my purpose. I have nothing, am nothing.

But then the door slams shut and everything goes black. I am in darkness but a light is coming closer and I see Jesus, hanging on the cross, all bloodied up, and a voice says, 'I already died for you, so you don't have to do that.' And that is it. I come back to consciousness. Open my eyes. The taxi driver is still driving.

The cars are still streaming past. And I know, He's still got me. I don't have to do this on my own. Thank you, Jesus. I'm so sorry.

* * *

I went home to my mum and dad and lay on the couch and hugged Mum and said, 'I'm tired. I need help.' Of course, I didn't tell them how bad it got sometimes. No one at all knew about that, but just for that short time it was so good to be there with that feeling of home.

I carried on. But the exhaustion and stress of 2011, plus going from virtually nothing to working 24/7, resulted in me losing my voice. I was scared but I was also too impatient to nurse it properly, and even though it was mean to be with Jess, I struggled through the 'Galaxy' tour, sounding like shit. But the show must go on. That's my whole ethos. In 2010, that amazing first year, I was sick more often than I was well — glandular fever, bronchitis, tonsillitis, root canals, wisdom teeth out. I kept going through it all. The show must always go on.

* * *

It's funny, when we did Idol, and it got down to just two of us left, me and Hayley Warner, I remember what Michael Bublé said about both of us. He said Hayley's big strength was that she fully knew who she was. Imagine that! On me, he said my throat was kissed by God, meaning my voice was beautiful. I wonder if he could tell, though, that I didn't really know who I was.

I've been an actor my whole life. I had to be. I had to put on so many fronts. It started from when I was a little kid pretending I hadn't been beaten, not wanting people to know what my home was like. 'I forgot my lunch on the bench at home ... Anyway, I'm not hungry ... I fell down the stairs ...' I changed school so often, and every time I told new lies about myself, about the kind of house I lived in, the famous people I'd met. 'I was in the first fifteen at my last school ... Oh yeah, I used to go with that girl.' Just trying all the time to be cool. It was constant and it was everything and anything, for no reason at all. Lie after lie, all the time. I was fully conscious of what I was doing. I would make a decision. I'll be *this* person. I would have a whole new accent, different things I would say about myself. I lived in those lies. I put on so many masks, papering over the cracks from the last mask, that I didn't even know what was real underneath. When new friends met up with old friends, I'd get caught out. Caught out in my lies.

I hated myself, so it was easiest to lie. Quite a relief, in fact.

When I was doing Idol, living in the mansion, one of the things us competitors had to do was a daily video diary, so we could connect with our fans. I was pretty silly on mine and when I watch them now, they are funny. When I first actually met Guy Sebastian on the night of the Idol final, that's what he said to me: 'We've been watching your video diaries. Bro, you're the funniest thing.' But I can also see my masks — I'm sliding from one front to another, sliding, sliding seamlessly from one accent to the next, trying out this act then another character, constantly sliding. A full range of expressions within every sentence. 'You think I'm nice, I'm cheerful, but I'm not. I'm angry.' Hysterical laughter. I hid behind something then popped out. 'Can you see me? Now you can!' More laughter, then instantly serious. 'Far out, can't believe Scotty's gone, man. Far out, I was so depressed. He was fully crying like a little girl on stage. Gosh, who does that? Liza Minelli, minelli, frenelli, I love you, you love me.' From serious to joking to serious, from talking to singing to talking, without any pause. I just can't stop.

On the video diaries, it was fun. Crack-up. Frenetic. In real life, it could be exhausting, but it was a habit from my whole life. I was often described as a compulsive liar, which I was. But I would like to say it was acting training.

After the disastrous tour with Jess Mauboy, my voice slowly came back to me, but different from before. It came back with a whole new power, but I lost my high and I had to learn how to sing falsetto. I had to practise, test out how it worked now, like a kid in a candy store, honestly: try this, try that. It was lucky I was having a break from gigging during that time because my focus was on my role in Tearepa Kahi's *Mt Zion*. It was the door into a whole new world.

I played the role of Turei, part of a family of potato farm workers. Turei is a talented musician who dreams of being the support act for Bob Marley's 1979 New Zealand tour. But Turei's dad, played by Temuera Morrison, is against the idea, so Turei finds himself set against the values he grew up with.

Being in *Mt Zion* was such a Māori experience, from beginning to end. I came back to New Zealand for a couple of months, living for the first time ever in Auckland, hanging out with all these actors and crew the whole time, creating a new family. From the director to the crew, almost all were Māori and there were a lot of native speakers so we could talk to each other in te reo. Tearepa directed us in Māori a lot of the time and, whether you knew it or not, you just had to go with it, so we were all picking up and learning more.

Tem Morrison — we've got a lifelong bond now. Poppa Tem, easily the most hilarious person in the world.

It was scary working with such talented people when I knew nothing, but I had constant coaching and I quickly found I loved acting. Sometimes I feel like I love it more than singing. Just like it was for me when I was a stuffed-up little kid, the joy for me is I get to be somebody else. I don't have to be Stan Walker. I can take a break from myself.

We released a soundtrack album featuring songs from the fictional band Small Axe. And, together with the Australian songwriting team DNA, I wrote the song that was the single release from the album, 'Take It Easy'. 'Open road, broken down, Bright lights, dark town, Stand up then you fall again, You will find a way in the end.' It went to number five in the charts, and double platinum in the end. Sharp and ready. That was our motto in the movie, and that's how we were.

Since then I've done five more movies. Next was *Born to Dance*, which I worked on in 2014. It's a hip-hop movie directed by Tammy Davis, and I played Benjy: naughty boy, good heart, caught up in the wrong stuff. When I accepted the role, I somehow missed the fact that I was going to have to dance. I turned up to rehearsal and there was Parris Goebel, the awesome dancer/choreographer who took the dance crew The Royal Family to three world championships. I was not prepared. I came straight from doing interviews and I was wearing boots and jeans, and Parris was diving right in. 'I want to see where you're at with your dancing. I'm going to teach you this routine.' I had to dance in front of the whole Royal Family. Embarrassing. I said, 'Are you going to make it easy?' and she said, 'No. You just need to catch up.' I feel I did good in the end, even though I ain't no dancer!

I used to dance during my performances, do choreographed moves in my shows and in my videos — and actually, the young actor Tia Maipi, who I met on *Born to Dance*, he and his cousin Whare and the O'Neill twins I met on that movie came on tours with me and danced all over the world in my shows. But around 2018 I stopped doing that. I love to dance but I am not a dancer, and I realised that having choreography was masking my connection with the audience. My band was hidden behind the dancers.

I used to dance and sing for two hours, and that requires talent, don't get me wrong. But I started to realise I wanted to be a proper solo artist, a performer who could capture the crowd without having to do moves. I still dance, move a lot on stage, but it's not the highlight. My performance is me connecting with my voice, me commanding my band, us together as a unit.

The difference is that for dancers like Parris Goebel and The Royal Family, and a lot of the other young dancers I met on *Born to Dance*, the dancing *is* the connection to the audience.

In 2015, I was so excited to get a part in Taika Waititi's *Hunt for the Wilderpeople*, in which I played one of the hunters the main characters encounters in the bush. I was on set for a few weeks, back and forward between different locations in the Waitākere Ranges and the Central Plateau around Tongariro. Watching and learning from the heavy hitters. Taika is a genius — there's no other word for it. Watching him direct was one of the most inspiring things ever. He's so efficient. He's in charge, the big boss, he don't mince his words. He's got no time for small talk; just very matter of fact and super hilarious. If there's a problem, he doesn't have time for people saying they can't do that. He'll go, 'Just wait,' and he'll think a whole new scenario in his head. 'Okay, this is what we're going to do.'

I watched him deal with a problem that way one time, where we got to where we were going to shoot and it was snowed out. That was not the plan. One of the assistant directors goes, 'We've got to move, we're running out of time.' Taika said, 'Hang on', and he sat there and thought for a minute. Then he turned that problem into one of the best scenes of the movie — got everyone in, all the body doubles, and he put the camera on a pole and he just moved it around, an in-camera one-shot montage. We were all hiding and popping out for our scenes as the camera moved around. It was my favourite shot in the whole film and he did it off the cuff.

I'd been in awe of Taika since me and Russ watched *Boy* back in 2010 and we felt like he was spying on our lives, from the beauty to the sadness. These narratives are everywhere in terms of te ao Māori, the Māori world. I could see even then that Taika is so intentional about every little thing he does. I love that. Everything has a reason. And for me, that takes me back to being Māori, too, to our language and our

227

protocols, where everything has a reason, everything is done with intent. Everything has a purpose, deep and spiritual. And it's all just a millimetre away from being hilarious.

In 2016, I acted in *The Stolen* and that was a very different experience. I flew in from Los Angeles, where I'd been writing and recording, to Canterbury, where it was really cold. The movie was directed by Niall Johnson, an English director, with English actors like Alice Eve and Jack Davenport, so a very different cultural experience for me. I played a native Māori warrior, and it was fun playing that big falla, but I got into conflict with the head make-up artist. 'This is going to be your moko,' he told me, and showed me these moko stencils he'd got from Paris. He wanted to draw them on me in black ink.

'What's that? This is not a moko,' I told him. 'If I wear that, I'm going to get in trouble.'

And he goes, 'Well, it's in my instructions.'

'Who told you those instructions? Was he white? I'm not using that crap.'

Instead, I copied the moko of my great-great-great-grandfather Taiaho Hōri Ngātai, and had the other make-up artist draw it on me every day, in dark green. So there were a few hiccups, but I did my best, even if it was a far cry from the warm environments of my first three movies. Mostly I hung out with the guys who looked after the horses.

In 2017, I worked on my first Australian feature film, a comedy drama called *Chasing Comets*. I was Reece, over the top but a good guy, contracted to play in the AFL. That was the gag, because at the same time my little brother Noah actually was contracted to play AFL.

I want to do more acting in the future. I would love the challenge of doing a character that's far from myself. We'll see what the future brings.

* * *

In 2013, I came back to New Zealand as a judge on the TV show *The X Factor*. It nearly didn't happen, thanks to an episode my manager calls 'tweetgate'. It so happened that just as my team was locking in my role in *The X Factor* New Zealand, I got together for an evening in front of the TV with my friend Jessica Mauboy, to watch week six of *The X Factor* Australia. Some of our friends were competing in the show, and their band Fourtunate had made its way week by week. Me and Jess were huge supporters of those boys, but this particular week they got eliminated. We were gutted, and without even thinking I tweeted about it. '#xfactorau that is a load of crap … THIS IS RIGGED maaaan … Fourtunate r the best 4 realz.' Jess said much the same, also using the word 'rigged'. We didn't really mean rigged in the literal sense; we were expressing that we were disappointed and wished it had turned out differently. To us, it was the equivalent of screaming at the TV, except of course it wasn't, and before I knew it I was in big trouble. I hadn't taken the time to figure on the power of Twitter, and next thing it was headline news in the mainstream media and, almost immediately, my upcoming job with *The X Factor* was in jeopardy. I learnt a big lesson: that 'private' comments made in jest carry legal weight when a mentor claims publicly his own show is 'rigged'. There's no such thing as private on social media. I knew it, of course, but in the heat of the moment I'd forgotten. There was quite a furore over that, but in the end I think we all understood each other better and I kept my job.

The months back in New Zealand doing *The X Factor* were a time of reconnection for me. I'd been back for movie work on *Mt Zion*, but this was an extended period and I was able to take a proper look at what was happening in the music industry. The country, my culture, the way they did things in my industry — it all had a very different feel to Australia. I liked what I saw and what I heard.

As it happened, just before I came back, I'd written a song I really liked, called 'Bulletproof', co-written with Vince Harder and Lindsay Rimes. It was very much a pop song but I'd mixed up a few different influences in there, and it had that reggae skank. 'It's been a while, I'm back again, I'm stronger now, I'm not afraid ...' It just felt good to me and more a reflection of my true self than other songs I'd written up to that point. The underlying message was powerful — *I'm at the turning point in my career, and the turning point in myself, and if people are not going to roll with me, I'm out.*

I took it to Sony Australia and they didn't react like I'd hoped. Reggae isn't a big mainstream genre in Australia like it is back home in New Zealand. One of the executives told me, 'Reggae is for Polynesian people. We don't think it will work.' I was surprised and disappointed, as I knew that the reggae market isn't as simple as that.

'Man, I really think this is going to be something,' I told them. I could see real potential in the mainstream market for this genre, and nobody else was doing it. 'This is my own lane,' I said.

But the same thing that excited me — that no one else was doing reggae at that time — was a worrying factor for them and they rejected my song. So when I came to New Zealand for *The X Factor*, I took 'Bulletproof' to Sony New Zealand, who loved it, released it and it went straight into the top-ten singles charts, where it stayed for seven weeks, peaking at number two. I was stoked. And then around six months later came that song by the Canadian band Magic!, 'Rude', which was way more reggae than my song, and it went to number two on the Australian charts.

I found that really frustrating. I wanted to lead, not follow. For a while, I'd been feeling I wasn't on the same page as the team in Australia at the time. We wanted different things. I was acutely aware that this is my life and I have to do what I want and need to do. I increasingly felt, rightly or wrongly, that I wasn't valued as a creative, and as I got older and surer of myself and my direction, I sometimes felt we were heading in different directions.

My mate Shae Sterling, who does all my videos, came up with the concept for the 'Bulletproof' video; we shot it in Vanuatu using only people of colour, and that really set the tone for my future — representing the Pacific and people of colour in my videos properly; that is, prominently and strongly. That felt right, like coming home, and it's a central aspect to all my work now. It clarified for me the need to take charge of everything, take control, and lead my team in every way. We did that instinctively to begin with, then it became a conscious strategy.

I still have my Sony Australia team, and I love them. So much has come together for me over the last few years. The team's changed over time and now we have a lot of diversity and forward-thinking creative executives. They get me, and I get them. They're my Aussie whānau: Petrina, Mo, Olly and Shelley.

And now I have my Sony New Zealand team as well. Kim Boshier who heads Sony up, Taryn, Lizzie, Gareth, Laura and the whole team — from the moment I met them they wanted me there.

Bringing my focus to New Zealand never seemed like going smaller. On the contrary, it has opened things up for me. I felt like I was stepping into something way bigger.

That time of doing 'Bulletproof' and then refocusing on New Zealand, that was a landmark for me in that long struggle I'd had for creative control — the struggle to look and sound like I wanted to; to look and sound like myself.

* * *

Towards the end of 2013, I released my fourth album, *Inventing Myself*. It was the first album I'd worked on with New Zealand A&R — A&R stands for 'artist and repertoire', and is the industry term for the division of a record label that takes care of the artistic and musical development of an artist. When I moved to the New Zealand arm of the company, Jaden Parkes took on the role of my A&R manager, and I've worked with him ever since — a really awesome, creative guy. This new album included 'Take It Easy', the song from *Mt Zion*, which had come out

almost a year previously, and 'Bulletproof'. The lyrics from
the title song said it all:

> Watch as I go and bring myself back to life
> Nobody noticed we were ending the line
> I won't deny we had a hell of a time
> But it's time
> I'm inventing myself
> I'm inventing myself
> Not pretending to be someone else …

As part of the promotion for *Inventing Myself*, I did my second
tour of New Zealand. I called it the 'World Tour of New
Zealand', and through September and into early October
we did twenty-three concerts at venues up and down the
country, from Whangārei to Queenstown and pretty much
everywhere in between. In Christchurch, ticket sales were so
high that we shifted venue to the CBS Canterbury Arena,
and the same thing happened in Auckland where we moved
from the Town Hall to the ASB Theatre. I had my mate Troy
Kingi on backing vocals, along with Whenua Patuwai, who
just a couple of months before had been runner-up on *The
X Factor*. My best mate Fender Maeva was visual director,
doing choreography for me and the backing dancers.

About three weeks in, with fourteen concerts done and
nine to go, we got to Queenstown. We had a few hours to
kill so me and Fender and some of the boys got bikes and
took them for a ride. We always want to do the extreme
stuff, so we ended up at a skate bowl, doing jumps to see
who could get the highest. I was winning for a bit, then one

of the boys went up and beat me, so up I went again, flying over the top of the bowl on this bike, but as I was coming down I could see one of the others on his bike still in front of me. *Move, move, move* ... but he couldn't in time, and I crashed right into him. Yep, I was wearing jandals of course, and when I looked down, lying there in a mess of bikes, I saw that my jandal was now inside my toe. I ripped it out but my toe was wide open, and all the boys were laughing. I said, 'Ah, shut up! Look,' and they all went, 'Holy shit.' My toe was literally just hanging off by a thin piece of flesh. And, oh my gosh, we had a show to do and had to be at soundcheck in half an hour.

They rushed me to hospital; I was on the phone in the car trying to explain to my mum what had happened. 'Oh, had a little bit of an accident ...' Next thing, me and Fender were taking turns on the happy gas, and he was going, 'Suck it in, bro.'

We didn't really take in how serious it was. I said to the doctor, 'Can you just bandage it up, cos I've got a show.'

He looked at me like I was crazy. 'We're going to fly you to a bigger hospital,' he said.' It sunk in.

'No! I've got a show and then I've got nine other shows, so just stitch it up.' So they stitched it up, wrapped it in bandages and I found a boot that was big enough and got myself on stage for two and a half hours of singing and dancing, drugged to my eyeballs on painkillers.

I did those shows and never missed a beat. Every night the wound would open up and, as soon as the show was over, I'd be desperate with pain — 'Get my shoe off!' Out of all those shows, there was just one where I couldn't handle it anymore and I said to the audience, 'Whānau, I've got a really sore foot. Can I take my shoes off?' They were like, 'Yes!' So I performed the last four songs with no shoes on. But only once. The show must go on.

* * *

Being on tour is always such an awesome, supported experience for me, and I'm really lucky with that. I always have whānau as part of my team, and I make them work hard. They aren't allowed to forget I'm the boss, but we have so much fun.

A huge part of me being who I am is the band that I've had with me since the beginning. Three of my band members are brothers: Jacob, Ross and Junior Nansen. Jacob is music director and keyboardist. He's the big bro of the whole group. Ross is the drummer and Junior is bass player. These fallas are the best I've ever worked with. They've grown with me, the chemistry together is like nothing I've ever had. They've got my back on and off the stage. In every way, they click me into their family and them into mine. Lei and Tom are their mum and dad and have taken me in to live with them. I've been to their village in Sāmoa; they've been to my marae.

Then I've got Knox, my guitarist. He does all the production for my shows and he also produced my *Faith Hope Love* EP, the *Stan* EP, and a few of my singles. He's quiet as but so talented.

Then my back-up singers. I've had many, but right now I have Nate, Lilo and Ani. Incredible. My main horns are Tabhani on sax and Christian on trumpet, and also Forest on trumpet and Dan on sax as well. And my sound man is Nathan Collins.

And my family. I've done many gigs with my brothers and my sister-in-law.

All these people, everybody is a priceless asset to me, not just because of their skills but because of who they are. They are all extremely talented and good fallas. We have just the best time ever, and they are such hard workers. I tell my band the most crazy idea and in their heads, I'm sure they're like, *What the hell?*, but they always say, 'Yes,' and figure out a way to make it happen. I can't imagine being without them.

We've travelled everywhere together, shared so many experiences, all our ups and downs. And now, as October 2013 rolled on, we were about to share one of our most incredible highs.

* * *

Beyoncé, you're the only girl in the world … I love you. I love you. Beyoncé, I love you.

A highlight of highlights. Queen B. And me, the ultimate fan. I'd loved Beyoncé since I was seven years old and she was in Destiny's Child. And there I was, just turned 23, in my sequin jacket, her support act for eight of her concerts during her The Mrs. Carter Show World Tour, in Auckland, Sydney and Perth. In my final song of the night at the Sydney Super Dome, just before she came on, I did 'Waltzing Matilda', with a little freestyle in the middle — 'All I want to do is cook her a feed … I'm gonna cook her some eggs cos I love my eggs, I can cook them poached, fried, scrambled. If she wanted something flash like eggs benedict, I got you, B.' — my personal serenade, giggling to myself, having fun with the crowd as my backing vocals team cracked up behind me.

I was championed for the gig by the Sony big boss, the CEO of Sony Music Australia Denis Handlin, who made the recommendation to Beyoncé's manager and sent him my videos. I met Denis very soon after winning Idol, and from then till now he has been my musical chief. I've sometimes felt misunderstood as I've carved out my place in this industry, but his support has been rock solid right throughout. There's no doubt about his part in my musical journey.

My manager Champo rang me with the news. 'You might be opening for Beyoncé.'

'Just tell me if I am or not, please.' It was unbearable. He called me back and I went crazy, yelling and screaming. All my family and friends were so excited, so over the top, just loving it.

Beyoncé's manager later told me that at the time he got my videos, Beyoncé was in Brazil and he'd been having trouble getting communication from her. But when he sent her my videos she got back to him in five minutes with the message: 'He's the one.'

And I'm thinking, *She knows me! She knows me!*

I got my band together — my Nansen bros, Paul Toilalo on guitar, and three backing vocalists: Troy Kingi; my aunty, Ria Hall; and Erica Nansen, Jacob's wife.

I didn't want to just be an opening act. I wanted to be heard and I wanted to be seen. This was just around the time I was personally reconnecting with Aotearoa and I particularly wanted to represent that feeling of home, and our culture.

A friend suggested the Crowded House song 'Don't Dream It's Over', and we had the idea to sing it in Māori. We sent it to Erena Koopu, a kapa haka and reo expert from the Tauira Mai Tawhiti group, which Troy Kingi is also in, and she translated it. I've sung that song hundreds of times since, especially when I'm away from New Zealand — it always connects me to home.

So we got ready, and we did the first few concerts, but I still hadn't met Beyoncé. To tell the truth, I was scared. I didn't know if I'd cope being in the same room as her. But then, with no warning, on the third day, Beyoncé's publicist came to me and asked, 'Are you ready?'

'No, no, not now!'

But it was happening. Beyoncé's manager escorted me up to her room and, honestly, it passed in a blur. I knew I'd be nervous so I'd written down everything I wanted to say, and I never normally do that. We got up to her room and she was sitting there on a sofa; she told me I had one of the best voices she'd heard in a long time. And I said something like, 'Because of you, I am who I am.' Which was true — her intent, her strong work ethic, the fact she's a black woman in a white world; those things have always inspired me. And then she put her arms out to give me a hug, and it was the most awkward hug ever, because I had one arm stuck behind me. And yes, I smelled her hair — that's how close I got to my idol. And as I was leaving the room I clapped and jumped with excitement, which made her laugh. and she turned to someone and said, 'He's cute.'

Far out, man. I just met Beyoncé! It was the greatest day of my life. Better than Christmas. Thank you, Jesus.

CHAPTER TEN

Young boy I ain't no more

Nō tawhiti, nō tata
Nō te whenua o te Atua tātou
Ahakoa nō hea mai koe
Ka whawhai tonu mātou mōu
No matter if you're near or far
We come from the land of God
No matter where you belong
We'll fight for your freedom

— 'Aotearoa'

AOTEAROA. GENEROUS. INCLUSIVE. THAT'S HOW WE are. 'Oh, come in. Have a kaputī.'

It's like you don't have a choice. The cup of tea is going *on*. Get the cakes out. Open up the biscuits ... And after everything, 'No, no, no. You leave the dishes. It's all good.'

My great-grandmother at ninety-three, she will come with her guests to the door when they leave, even though it's hard for her, and she will stand there and wait until she can't see them anymore. That's such a normal thing, especially for our Māori and Pacific Islanders, but I'm sure this is the case in most cultures.

That's what my song 'Aotearoa' is about. When you come to our home, we welcome you. We are the tangata whenua and the tangata whenua take care of the manuhiri, the visitors. And then we take care of each other. That song, 'Aotearoa', arose out of the history of another popular anthem in te reo Māori, 'Poi E'.

'Poi E' was written by Ngoi Pēwhairangi with music by Dalvanius Prime, performed by the Pātea Māori Club in 1984. It was a sensation at the time, exploding onto the streets, onto the maraes and into the music charts. It spent four weeks at number one. Even though it came out before I was born, I grew up with that song. We all knew it, and the whole thing was very real to my whānau, as Dalvanius used to come up to Tamapahore all the time because a lot of my dad's cousins were from Pātea, although I didn't meet the big man myself.

'Poi E' is *so* Māori but it made it into the mainstream. That was a big thing for te ao Māori, very unusual at that time, a big thing for our people to have that representation.

Mātai Smith, the TV presenter who has been a part of revitalising te reo in the broadcasting world, approached me and said he'd love to see a new song that could do for our generation what 'Poi E' had done in that earlier time. He asked me to write a song for Māori Language Week 2014, thirty years since 'Poi E' came out.

So I wrote 'Aotearoa', in English, with Vince Harder. We've written multiple times together — any time I want to do stuff he's one of the first people I go to. Then Troy Kingi, who has been like a brother to me since we did *Mt Zion*, wrote the pre-chorus — 'Where we come from, we were made to be strong; Our legacy will carry on.' And then we sent our English lyrics to the translator Te Haumihiata Mason, one of the top dogs in te reo Māori. The translation process was amazing for me. I speak te reo, although I would never consider myself fluent, but here was a woman who wielded the language like poetry. Imagine the difference between the New Living Translation of the Bible and the old King James version. Or the difference between Stan Walker and Shakespeare. Straight up. With Te Haumihiata, everything had meaning that became beautiful. For instance, even that word we all know: reo. Yes, it means 'language', but it is also the fruit of the gods, the language of the heavens, the language that comes from the gods. Under her hand, every word revealed its intrinsic richness. Understanding this was a milestone for me, especially because of how wrong I'd often been made to feel for being Māori — too brown, a failure, just wrong. And now Te Haumihiata was showing me so much beauty and depth.

Also, just the magnificence of the project. I never thought I would be doing a song in my own language on a mainstream platform, with such a team of heavy hitters. As well as Vince producing the song, we recorded it with Troy, and also with Ria Hall and Maisey Rika. Aunty Ria is the lion, and Maisey is the princess, the whisperer, the ultimate tau person.

To me, the words in that song are so powerful. They say everything I feel about this place.

The song went to number two on the charts. You never really know how a song is going to land; initial chart success is only part of the story. 'Aotearoa' has grown in time, with huge numbers of ongoing sales and streaming, but to me its value is in the place it has as an anthem that unites us here in Aotearoa. More personally, I believe it shows that the truer I am to myself, the more my work resonates. When I sing it at concerts and festivals, the audience, even when they're predominantly Pākehā, know the words and sing them back to me — for me, that is the most incredible feeling ever. *You are us, I am you, we are all part of this earth.*

All countries need art that tells their own story, and 'Aotearoa' is a unique story about New Zealand. When I sang it at the concert in Christchurch, following the 2019 mosque attacks, it was the song that said: it doesn't matter where you come from, when you come here you are one of us. That's what I feel in my soul.

* * *

I was contracted with Sony to do five albums, and in 2015 they wanted my fifth one. At the time, I was working on original tracks but wasn't close to having material for an album. But it wouldn't have mattered anyway; Sony wanted me to do a collection of soul covers. I didn't want to do it. I felt, rightly or wrongly, like they were saying, 'You're not good enough to sing your own music.'

These were the chains of Idol that were hard to shake off. I had worked hard for years to shake off the image of myself as a crooner, a covers artist. And now here I was, bringing out an album as a covers artist. It wasn't my buzz.

Unfortunately, I didn't feel like I had a choice. I have learned to live with shit that goes wrong, so I knew that if I couldn't change it, I had to just find what I would love in this album. Over the years, I'd shared tracks on Facebook — old soul songs that I really loved, and they always got a strong response from people. I just had to treat the album as a self-indulgence, choose all the songs myself, songs I wish I'd written, songs I listened to my whole life. And I found the love in that.

I chose thirteen tracks, including 'Try a Little Tenderness', 'Endless love', 'Let's Get It On', and the Kate Bush song 'This Woman's Work'. Of course, there's nothing wrong with the music itself. And in many ways the album was a success.

From Sony's point of view, they were right. The album did well and they made their money from it. It went to number seven on the Australian album charts, and number three in New Zealand, got very good reviews and a lot of publicity. Even I, when listening to the tracks, thought, *Ooh, yo! Not bad*.

But in my heart and soul, it took a toll. I felt like I was going backwards, not progressing. My identity as an artist that I'd been trying so hard to get running on my own tracks, had been undermined, and it pushed me back towards the dark places again. Anger and uncertainty were like little chisels in my heart, and they just worked away at me.

That album came out in April and at the same time, between March and July, I was back in New Zealand for my second season of *The X Factor*. I had enjoyed the 2013 season, although it was definitely weird being on the other side of the judges' table so soon after I'd been a contestant. I got given the over-twenty-fives category and I was only twenty-two myself at the time, so it was strange to be giving advice to people older than me. But it made me realise how much I'd learned about the industry, and about performance in the years since.

But I felt like once was enough — if I've done something once, I don't want to do it again. It's a big commitment, and a lot of time away from my own career and goals.

However, when they announced the 2015 season, two years after the first season, my fellow judge from 2013, Melanie Blatt, from the British girl group All Saints, rung me up and said, 'I want to do it. You'd better do it, too. I'm only doing it if you do it.' I love Mel, and we got to be best mates doing *The X Factor* the first time. So, I relented: 'Okay then, we'll do it.'

We didn't know what we were getting ourselves into. Our fellow judges were Willy Moon and Natalia Kills, who'd been brought over from the UK, billed as international stars. They were recently married. Before the show began, Mel and I hung out with them and they seemed like lovely people, quite quiet, extremely into each other. But then, on the very first night of live TV, they laid into one of the contestants, like wolves rounding on a lamb, cruel and bullying. There's always good cop, bad cop on these reality shows, but they were just abusive.

The contestant, Joe Irvine, was wearing a suit and had his hair slicked, just like half the men in the world, but Kills chose to see him as copying Moon, who also had that look. She called the contestant a doppelgänger: 'I am disgusted at how much you have copied my husband,' she said. 'From the hair to the suit, do you not have any value or respect for originality?'

I got in a comment about how she'd borrowed her own look from Cleopatra, but she carried on, then Moon joined in, calling the contestant 'disgusting' and 'creepy'.

I've had a lot of time to learn when to open up my mouth and when to keep it shut. The tirade from Kills, then Moon, then back to Kills, went on and on; I realised that if I opened my mouth, not only could I not control them, but I wasn't sure I could control myself. You can't fight fire with fire, especially on live TV. It was not the time or the place.

But what I really thought was, they were idiots. Nasty bullies. I have rarely seen such a lack of compassion. And when we cut and finished the show they stormed off, and me and Mel looked at each other. *What the hell?*

They got fired that night. It was headline news all over the world. A lot of people were saying to me, is this a stunt?

They had all their theories. But I was like, 'Bro, they got fired. What do you think?'

I saw Kills only one more time, the following day, and there was no regret for the damage inflicted on either Joe Irvine or the show. The comments were designed to further her and Moon's own fame. 'I will just get 20,000 new followers,' she said. She will be who she will be. I just had to let that fool be a fool.

The big bosses were crying — what do we do, what do we do? I felt like always: the show must go on. These contestants had worked hard from the beginning; we couldn't pull the plug on them. It was time the focus went back on them. This is the thing about show business. You have so many unexpected twists and turns, but the show must go on.

And the show did go on. Those two were replaced by singer Natalie Bassingthwaighte and I Am Giant drummer Shelton Woolright. I wish they'd been there from the beginning.

* * *

2016. If you look at pictures of me from that year, it all looks really good. My social media feeds looked happy. I had a lot going on — I was acting in *The Stolen*, I went to the US to write songs, I did some big gigs, and in July I announced a November tour — the ten-date 'New Takeover' tour around New Zealand. It was to be my first concert tour since 2013.

In August, I went on the *Jono and Ben* TV show and sang a song written for me by some kids. They took my song 'Take It Easy' and rewrote it — 'You got to make it cheesy, cheesy ...' — and then I sang it back for them. It was actually one of the hardest performances I've ever done, because I almost laughed so much I couldn't sing. Such a crack-up.

I looked happy. Like life couldn't be better.

Don't believe what you see on social media. A performance is a performance.

Inside, my old feelings were eating me up. Self-love and self-respect power us to make good decisions for ourselves, but if that gets replaced by self-loathing then everything goes dark and our purpose gets lost in that darkness. I'm not a superhero, and even though Jesus is Superman, when I'm not feeling good I tend to walk away from Him and make my own choices. I stop doing the daily things that keep me connected to Him, and then I'm on my own. I'm accountable for every choice I make for myself and, with every choice I make, there's going to be a consequence — good or bad.

That was the year I really fell into a depression. I was blank inside, like I was nothing. I was having a lot of anxiety and sometimes felt like I was having a heart attack. Really bad insomnia. My girlfriend at the time, Lou, I said to her, 'Please bear with me and help me and love me because I don't know how to even love myself at the moment.' She knew I was struggling, although, to be fair, no one knew how bad it was getting, and that was on me because I never said.

I got together with Lou in 2013, the first love of my life as an adult. She was my everything and I planned to marry her. Stunning-as and very focused, we used to laugh a lot together. She was the first girlfriend who felt like a true companion, who I could talk to about anything — almost — including emotional trauma and how I really felt. She would write down her daily goals on an iCloud account that we shared, and at the top of her list was 'Remind Stan that he's amazing and I love him'. She really loved and cared for me, but I was so concerned about my problems and my goals that I forgot about her and she must have felt lonely at times.

I couldn't throw off the bad feelings of doing that covers album. My career was not where I wanted it to be and I was headbutting with everybody. Also, my health wasn't good. I was having a lot of pain in my stomach and for months, every time I had a shit there would be a puddle of blood. It got so bad I actually went to the doctor, on my own, didn't tell nobody, not even Lou, and they gave me an endoscopy and a colonoscopy, and said, 'You need to get your stomach out ASAP. There are polyps and your lining is eroding, that's why you're bleeding.'

But it wasn't cancer, not yet, so I just ignored them. I wasn't ready for that. Ignoring it meant it wasn't happening. I told nobody and just continued on. I'm good at that.

Increasingly, though, I was losing my mind.

It became usual for me to sit at home feeling depressed, crying, feeling like I had no control over anything. It wasn't like anyone was doing anything to me. These feelings were coming from inside — the same old shit, but everything was heightened now that I was an adult, facing into the world, feeling as though I was by myself.

I was wasting my money. I often went on spending sprees, and it was nothing for me to spend $10,000, $20,000 a pop on clothes in just an hour or two. Quality, quantity, everything. London is the place to shop — my favourite place for a binge. One time, I arrived with one suitcase and left with eleven, all full.

I bought shoes that cost $2000 and the only time I wore them was when I tried them on. I bought $800 shoes quite often, wore them once and chucked them. Same with most of my clothes — wear them once, if that, then chuck. I love the feel of new clothes, crisp and clean, and they weren't the same after I'd worn them.

Then I discovered dry-cleaning — someone, maybe it was Lou, must have told me about it. Wow! I'd never even heard of that before. I took some clothes there and when I got them back the first time I was shocked. They came back exactly how they were when they were new, all ironed. So then I didn't have to chuck my clothes away after just one wear. Dry-cleaning changed my life.

It wasn't just clothes. I don't even know what I spent it all on. Stuff. I didn't even keep it, and I don't even know where half of it is. It just meant nothing. When I think about it now, I feel ashamed to think of Nan, so content with nothing, while I stress about what I'm going to wear even though I have a million clothes.

I spent thousands of dollars on nothing because I just didn't care. Clothes. Food. I don't even know. As if I didn't have any care in the world. I watched my last $100,000 go down before my eyes, and I was like, *Whatever.*

I became overweight, and that is the one external sign that I can see in photos from that time. I was definitely getting to be a big boy.

My manager must've seen I was putting on weight because he suggested I see a dietician. He got me an appointment with this woman who'd been a dietician to Olympic athletes. She prodded at my lower abdomen, which was where I'd been experiencing pain, and I told her everything about how I thought I was going crazy, couldn't sleep, and she said, 'You're all right. It's actually all diet.' I was like, 'Surely not.' And she said, 'You are what you eat.' And she put me on a diet. Not what you think of when you hear the word 'diet'; it was a high-fat diet. I would make these Spanish omelettes — bacon, packed with normal cheese, cream cheese, onions, then I'd fold that over, and make me a feta and avocado mash and put it on top and eat that sucker.

Believe it or not, I lost ten kilos and my mind started changing, and I felt a bit better. But of course, I hadn't told her anything about our family history with cancer, or the fact that I'd been told my stomach was eroding, so she only knew part of the story.

So it was a different problem that she diagnosed. I found out later that the bit of me she prodded and which was sore was not even my stomach. That's higher up, and I wasn't yet having any real pain or sensation from there.

Out of our immediate whānau, it was just me and Mum who have the inherited cancer gene. I'd known since I was fifteen years old that I had it, and it had never meant much to me. I was the master at never worrying about that. But the biggest shock came in September that year, when we found out Mum had breast cancer. She'd found a lump, and it was found to be a large tumour.

It was the worst news ever. Far worse than anything happening to me. They were living in Melbourne at the time, so my little brother Noah could play in the AFL. I was there waiting for Mum to get home from her appointment, and when she walked in, she was crying. Now, our family is not normal. We still ain't. Normal would be, 'Oh my gosh, do you need anything? How can I help?' But Pāpā goes, 'Oh, let's go and play tennis!' I was so gobsmacked and confused, but I agreed to go with him. We got to the tennis court and I was sitting there, like, *Did that just happen? Has Mum got cancer?* I didn't know what to do. *What the hell are we doing here?* I realised this was all wrong. 'Let's go, Pāpā. Let's go home.' I couldn't even think straight.

I'm a mummy's boy. I cannot function in this life without my mum, who is also a part of my business. She's the biggest part of my life. My rock.

'Pāpā,' I said. 'You need to get over yourself. Look, your wife has cancer.'

'I can't deal with this.'

'Get over yourself now!'

I was trying to get our family to step up but I felt everyone was making it about themselves. My younger brother and sister kept on answering my mum back as if she wasn't sick. My older brothers were angry. 'It's your fault, it's your lifestyle.' Something to blame. That's how we deal with stuff. Just get angry, even after all these years.

Mum had the operation quite soon after she found out, got it done quick. She didn't have the breast removed, but just got the tumour cut out. She didn't do chemo — I don't think she could have handled that. She was really unhealthy at the time. Who am I to judge? Like mama, like son, as you will see.

At the end of each day, I had to wait for everyone to go to sleep, really asleep, and then I went into the toilet and I bawled my eyes out, threatening God: *Don't take my mum away from me. I'll turn away from you. I'll stop singing.*

I didn't want my mum to see me cry. I had to be her rock. If I had cried in front of her … actually, thinking about it now as I'm telling this story, I think she would have cried with me. I think she would probably have loved that. But at the time my thinking was I didn't want to be a burden and make it about me.

I cancelled my tour that I was supposed to do in November. My mum said, 'Do the tour.' I said, 'Hell, no.'

Some of my fans got angry with me for that, and I found that very sad. I think people have lost touch with being human beings. Where was the compassion and empathy? My mother had cancer.

For me, there was no question what came first — career, or my mum. My mum is always my number one.

Through that year I hadn't been feeling as connected to Lou. I was going through so much, I didn't have much to give, but I trusted her to support me and that I'd be better again soon. So at Christmas, even though Mum begged me to come home, because she was still recovering from her operation, I chose to spend it with my girlfriend, which is maybe the worst thing I've done. We had Christmas, and then we went down to Rūātoki with some friends, and that turned out to be a big healing time for me, like it always is down there. We stayed on my marae, Ōhutu, and I had the best sleep I'd had in years. There with my ancestors all around me, the love of my life and my best friends, I felt peaceful for the first time in months.

Me and Lou were at our best and we finally got back to being really close. My life was back on track.

But then my cousin came to me with tears in his eyes and asked me some questions I didn't understand, 'Has Lou ever given you reason to think she was unfaithful?' It turned out she had been having an affair for eight months. When I had said to her, 'Please bear with me and help me and love me', I didn't know she was already getting a little loving from someone else. I knew I was the cause that Lou cheated on me because I didn't give her much, and I didn't realise how bad I was as a boyfriend.

It just about killed me, especially knowing that the times I'd felt so close to her recently were like a lie. We'd been together for almost four years, but now my trust was broken and I was filled with disgust. A switch flipped in my head.

I'm a late reactor. I didn't cry to begin with, didn't feel the grief. I had gigs to do and I got through that — lucky I'm so good at putting on masks. But then I was sitting there having a drink with my friend Taran, one of my best friends who has helped me probably the most through all my hardships, when it all came out. I find I always turn to my girl mates. There's something about a female's perspective and in the way that they nurture and help. They're my sisters and I know they got me. My boys, sometimes, are just like, *Ooh, you all good, g?* And they don't know where else to take it.

So, that night, I let it all out, crying and going, 'I can't believe she did that to me!' And then I went on a rampage.

For the first few years of my career, I didn't drink alcohol at all. I lived a quiet life, coming home to my apartment at night, but then I realised I was missing out, bored and lonely. My friends would all go to clubs and have fun. So one day I grabbed a vodka and drank it down, drank a few more, couldn't handle it at all and blacked out. From then on I drank a little bit but not in a problem way, just social.

But now, after my break-up, I got naughty. Going out, being a little slut, sleeping around, which I'd never done before — the first time I did that, went home with someone, I felt so yuck and guilty, but then I got used to it. Taking drugs, being careless with my money. I was fast heading for zero, towards actual debt. Almost lost my house. I didn't care. I was in survival mode. Spend money. Make music. Have fun. Go hard or go home. It was like I lost my sanity.

I was not thinking about what was happening inside my stomach.

And strangely, despite everything, I was getting my mojo back. I did *Chasing Comets*, my first Aussie movie, and then in June 2017 I was back in New Zealand shooting the video for 'New Takeover' — a song and video that was like a confident brushstroke, a slash of paint on what had been an empty canvas. I had all this passion, all this heart inside me, and now, with that video, I knew exactly what I was going to do.

* * *

The high point for me in 2016 had been going to America to do writing sessions. I've done that lots of times, go for a month, work with different producers and writers every day. I go in there knowing what I want to write about, and so when I got together with this particular team in Los Angeles — Alexander Godwin, Mike Hunnid, Sidney Swift — I went in there with a strong vision and intention: *I was that young boy, but I'm not that young boy no more.* That intention became

'New Takeover', and that song was my anthem, my standing-up song, for me but also for my people. 'I got them scars like a soldier … We gonna get it, New takeover.' A declaration: we've been waiting for our moment and now we've got it. My passion and my heart has always been for my people.

My dream is to see my people set free. That means freedom in the mind, in the heart, in the soul, at home, in society, in the system, in their own country. My role in that is to be the voice for those who don't have a platform.

'New Takeover' is about that. *We gon get it.* All the forgotten, all the mistreated, all the left out, everything with a bad statistic attached to it, we gon get it. This is the new takeover. We're going to rise from the ashes. We're going to come back. That's what 'New Takeover' was and is.

From the minute I wrote the song, I knew what I wanted the video to be, and then I worked with Shae Sterling and Sammy Salsa to bring it to reality. It's a fusion of historic and modern Māori, an aesthetic of power. I channelled all my tūpuna who came before me, the lost land, the waterways. I'm riding a beautiful black stallion — a symbol of ultimate power. I've got my flag — the Tino Rangatiratanga, the Māori flag, designed by Hiraina Marsden, Jan Smith and Linda Munn in 1990, the year I was born.

Look out. We *on*.

It's very intentional — every element of that video has meaning. I would like to have filmed it in Tūhoe country, because our lives are the horses down there, and Tūhoe is all about strength and resistance, but we filmed at Muriwai and Bethells Beach in Auckland because of the black sand that is so distinctive to Aotearoa.

To come from where I've come from, to be so often told that I was too brown, that being Māori would never sell … then to produce a video that's visually so unapologetically indigenous Māori, that was probably one of the biggest moments of my career.

* * *

In 2017, I was invited to be part of the TV programme *DNA Detectives*. They tested me and discovered my DNA linked me right back to Rapa Nui, or Easter Island, where my ancestors must have set sail from hundreds of years ago. I was buzzing out. I'd always wanted to go to Rapa Nui, one of the most remote inhabited islands in the world, more than 7000 kilometres across the Pacific from New Zealand. The programme took me there and I met people I shared DNA with, who I had never known existed. And very early one morning, while it was still dark, I visited the Moai, the huge stone statues that scatter the landscape of that place.

Watching the sun unveil the Moai is one of the most incredible things I've ever experienced — a moment of powerful spiritual connection to whenua and tūpuna. I had tears in my eyes and goosebumps all over, and I felt like I knew exactly who they were. I felt that this was the same as the urupā back home, a tapu place. My cousin later told me they are indeed the headstones of the rangatira, and that their bones were buried below, because the ancients believed the bones contain your mana, your soul. He told me that later, but I already knew. I could feel all that, there in that place.

I experience feelings that come from the land itself, a sense of its spirit and the spirits of those buried there. I'm pretty on when it comes to stuff like that. Māori are very spiritual beings. To think of things as sacred is natural to us. It's part of the way we exist in the world.

Everything we do is sacred. Sex is sacred, touching the head is sacred. How we enter a marae, how we wash our hands, how we prepare food.

The three colours on the Tino Rangatiratanga flag — red, white and black — represent this aspect of our experience: red for Pāpātūānuku, the Earth mother; white for Te Ao Mārama, the realm of being and light, the physical world; and black for Te Kore, the unseen darkness, the void that's beyond human experience. We acknowledge that in our everyday lives — this world that's beyond what we see with our eyes, but we're actually living in it.

Māori have been drawn to the new religions, especially to Christianity, because for us it isn't strange to acknowledge the spiritual side of life. But for me, that wasn't enough to make me believe in God. For me, believing in God came from actual experience. Not just a feeling. I've felt stuff ever since I was a kid — spiritual stuff, feeling the land, feeling my connection to the whenua and to my tūpuna, my ancestors. But I reckon you actually have to have an experience of Jesus to know he is real. I know what's up now.

But that's for me. I don't care if you're Muslim, Buddhist, Christian or whatever. All I care about is the condition of your heart. Where's your heart at? It comes back to love for me. If God is love, and his grace surpasses all understanding, then who am I to judge anybody? Who am I to use the Bible as a weapon to condemn others? I feel like, if I'm judging, then I'm not acting out of love; if I'm judging, then I'm acting out of my own thing and I'm just as much a sinner as what I'm putting on others. So I don't really care who or what you are as long as your heart is good.

Sometimes I am the worst example of a Christian. But when I speak of Jesus, I'm speaking first-hand. It's a tangible thing for me, not just something I read or heard.

My faith is not always strong. But when I ask, *Where have you gone? Help me, God*, I'm saying that because I know He's real. I feel abandoned sometimes, forsaken, neglected. That's because I need answers right away. Sometimes I go, *Where the hell are you? I need you now!* I think he'll be like, *Oh, you need me now, do you? You didn't need me last night!* I'm sure he must laugh sometimes, eh!

Because we Māori are spiritual people, we feel it harder. I see this in my whānau — when they go from being whoever they were, drug addict, abuser, coming out of jail, to becoming a Christian, they go in so hard because they really understand it. It's not far-fetched to believe in the Holy Spirit or Jesus because they experience things spiritually, deeply anyway.

Whether it's the Moai of Rapa Nui, the land of Tamapahore or the love of Jesus, I am spiritually sensitive and that's fully my world.

CHAPTER ELEVEN

Help me in my weak times

Māmā, you the best in the world
You're more than diamonds or pearls
Help me in my weak times
You kept my head held high
You've always been my superwoman
You've always been the only woman
To ever have my heart

...

Oh, you pray for me, pray for me
Oh, I love it when you pray for me

— 'Thank You'

MUM, EVER MINDFUL OF THE TIME BOMB I CARRIED inside me, in the form of that mutated gene, pestered me all the time. 'Go and get some tests …' She didn't know I'd already had those tests done the year before when the doctor told me I had polyps and should get my stomach out straight away. But then, right after I'd done the 'New Takeover' shoot, she told me she'd met some amazing surgeons at the Peter MacCallum Cancer Centre in Melbourne. They knew about our family and they operated specifically on stomachs. They had the best facilities in the world.

Just at that time, I was back working in Sydney, songwriting in the studio there, and I had taken the opportunity to go to a Hillsong conference. I'd not been to church for ages, about a year, although I was always talking to God. *God, forgive me.*

The pastor that night was talking about blessings. He said, 'The trials you face seem big, but know that the blessing waiting for you further down the road is bigger. Just keep holding on.'

It's a miracle to me that the right message can come at the right time — this was just what I needed to hear. I felt so encouraged. *Thank you, Jesus.* I'm so up and down with my relationship but He's always there in the nick of time.

Most of the time, I turn away from Him because I feel guilty in myself. That old feeling that I don't love myself grabs hold of me. But He's just standing there, saying, *Son, I love you.*

I finally did it. Flew to Melbourne to meet these surgeons, just to shush Mum up. *It'll be all right …*

The day after my tests, I was back in Sydney in the studio and I wrote the first draft of my song 'Thank You' — it's for Mum, for everything she has gone through in her life, and for always being there for me. My favourite line is 'Oh, you pray for me …' because I'm the by-product of her prayers. I wrote it then, although I wouldn't sing it to her for many months down the track, by which time I had even more reason to thank her.

And the day after that, Mum called me and she was crying.

'Son, they think they've found some cancer.'

'They think? Yes or no? Don't ring up emotional and have no answer!'

She rang back an hour later. 'Stan, you've got cancer.'

It looked like it hadn't progressed beyond my stomach, but if we left it, it would spread. They were adamant about that. I had to get my stomach out as soon as possible. Once the cancer got hold, there would be a very poor prognosis. In fact, the doctors were certain I would die very quickly. When you think about it, I should always have known this was likely to happen. As soon as I was diagnosed with the mutated CDH1 gene, when I was fifteen, we all knew I had an eighty per cent chance of getting cancer. Back then, I was scared but then I got over it, blocked it out.

But now it had happened. I started cracking up. *Really? Wow. I've got cancer.* I didn't feel scared or threatened. Like I've said, I'm a slow reactor. I was just saying that word. *Cancer. I've got cancer.* And I went back into the studio like nothing had happened.

I didn't cry or feel sorry for myself. I'm so shallow, I was just like, *Oh, I'm going to be skinny.*

Every day after that our whole family, my siblings and Mum and Pāpā, got on the phone and did corporate prayer, which is where we all join together in prayer. We did it for Mum and now we did it for me. Mum would be like, 'Jesus, look after my baby.' And I could hear her crying, and that was the only time I cried, quietly, covering the mouthpiece up.

My brothers, of course, were angry at me. 'You got it cos of your lifestyle.'

That made me mad. 'I have no choice. Even if I was the healthiest person in the world, this is genetic.' I was happy it was me with the gene. It would be just awful if I had to watch my siblings get cancer. *I'm good, I'm strong, I've been through stuff.* This was just another curveball.

The first week after the diagnosis I ate healthy, and then I thought, *Stuff this, I'm not going to be able to eat any of this yummy food again.* I went on an eating binge and put on eighteen kilos in two months. At my heaviest, I was 102 kilos. Triple digits, had never done that before.

The doctors wanted to operate in August, but I was like, 'No, no, I've got to work. Push it back. I need to earn some money.' I still needed to have music coming out while I was in hospital, so the public wouldn't know there was anything wrong. I don't like admitting I'm sick. Stupid logic. I had my head stuck in the sand and I got the operation pushed to September.

I made the most of it with my family and friends, though. I would use it as a joke. I'd be like, 'Did you hear I've got cancer?' And I would use it against people to get them to do things for me, 'Oh, can you get that?' Why? 'Because I've got the cancer.' Or if I was being annoying and people asked me to shut up, I would act all weak and say, 'Sorry, you're being mean to me, my cancer's moving.' And the whole time I'm pointing down to my lower abdomen, not to my stomach at all. Until my operation, I didn't even know where my stomach actually was.

I did have pain lower down and that was because of all the food I was eating. But actually, for six months or more, I'd had a constant winded feeling in my actual stomach. Not hard-out pain but just always there, like a nagging toothache.

Meanwhile, I just carried on eating. Takeaways three times a day. Maccas, KFC and everything else. It felt all good. I loved eating and I loved eating fast. It was just towards the end I started losing my taste buds, and my breath.

A few days before my operation, my mate Jakiel came up with an idea. 'You should document it, do video diaries.' I could see it was a good idea.

I knew people at MediaWorks from my time doing *The X Factor*, so I had a meeting with Andrew Szusterman, MediaWorks' chief content officer at the time, and I laid it all out. 'It's a bit last minute, but I've got cancer and I'm having an op in a few days.' There were only two possible ends to this story — I live or I die — but regardless, I wanted to show the family going through the process. Us learning about everything. The before, during and after.

He said sweet and they started straight away, bringing the cameras out to my last gig in Palmerston North — the last time I sang with a stomach. Four days later, I was in Melbourne, at the Peter MacCallum Cancer Centre, and then into the Epworth Freemasons Hospital, taking my clothes off, putting on a hospital gown.

My whole stomach was going to get taken out. My oesophagus would be attached to my small intestine, which would begin operating as a small stomach. It would stretch over time, so that within six months I should be able to eat normally again. The doctors assured me there was no risk to my life — no one had died during this operation since my koko, twenty years before.

I knew I was going to beat the cancer, even though there were little moments when the opposite popped in my head: *Maybe I will die* … But what scared me far more than the idea of dying was disability — that maybe I wouldn't be able to sing anymore. The doctors didn't know, they had never operated on a singer before. My voice, my health, my life. The doctor talked to me about pros and cons but I wasn't really listening. *Yeah, yeah, all good. Get it over and done with.* I was excited and nervous. This was a place I'd been to before: facing a moment that was, literally, going to change my life.

I couldn't help but think back to the urupā at Tamapahore, all the graves, the whole history of everything that's gone wrong in our family since this gene entered our DNA. And now it was my turn.

In Wellington for a promotional screening of Taika Waititi's 2016 film *Hunt for the Wilderpeople*. I was so excited to get a part in this movie.

From left: Taika Waititi, Sam Neill, Troy Kingi, Julian Dennison, me, and Cohen Holloway. (Supplied by author)

'New Takeover' video shoot, 2017. The black stallion is the symbol of ultimate power. This song was for my people and it said: 'We gon get it. This is our moment.' (Supplied by author)

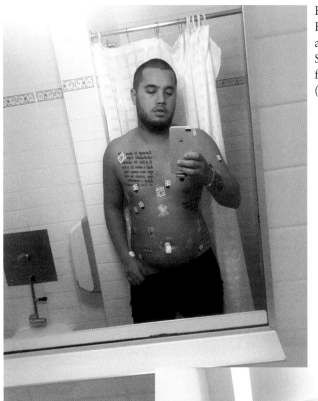

Epworth Freemasons Hospital in Melbourne, just after stomach surgery in September 2017. Cancer free, but a long road ahead. (Supplied by author)

My poor Māmā. Seeing me go through the operation to have my stomach removed — the same operation that killed her father — was one of the hardest things. The operation was the easy part. After that, I had setback after setback. (Supplied by author)

Taran, one of my all-time best mates, at One Love Festival in Tauranga, 2018. My New Zealand comeback show post stomach operation. Taran has always been there for me through all my hardships. (Supplied by author)

Me with Prime Minister Jacinda Ardern, at a youth dinner ceremony in Auckland early 2018. I was in a lot of pain, just getting out of hospital in Auckland where I'd almost gone into emergency surgery for my gallbladder, but I was so excited to meet Jacinda that I just swallowed a load of painkillers and antibiotics and carried on. (Supplied by author)

Waitangi Day, 2018.
I am descended from
Tūtahi and from
Nuka Taipari, two
chiefs who signed the
Treaty of Waitangi.
I've always felt a
strong connection
with Indigenous
Australians because
we share a similar
history of colonisation
and struggle. They are
us and we are them.
Ngā tangata whenua.
(Supplied by author)

Me and Māmā with
Jessica Mauboy in
2018. Jess is like a
sister to me. This
was my first time
seeing her since my
operation. We did a
concert together for
Mai FM in Auckland.
(Supplied by author)

On tour in New Zealand, 2018. Back home in Pāpāmoa, playing at the Pāpāmoa Beach Tavern with all my whānau there. (Supplied by author)

Ever since Idol, I've known singing was my calling. I want to use my gift to help people, to be a light for my whānau. (Supplied by author)

Hosting at the New Zealand Music Awards, 2018. I'm wearing my great-great-grandmother Ngapera Taahu's korowai, which is over 150 years old and made purely out of kiwi feathers. (Supplied by author)

Summer 2018 with my family in Mount Maunganui. When I think of my whānau now, I know that anything is possible. (Supplied by author)

Rūātoki, start of the new year in 2019, with Fender Maeva, my best mate. In Rūātoki I can breathe, I can be free from myself. (Supplied by author)

One Love Festival, 2019 — the whole crowd joined in singing the words to 'Aotearoa'. One of the greatest on-stage experiences ever. (Supplied by author)

In July 2019, me and other musicians went out to Ihumātao in South Auckland to perform for the people who had been occupying their stolen ancestral land. (Supplied by author)

2019 Springboard tour crew. We hit nine centres around Aotearoa — my celebration of being alive. (Supplied by author)

My Sony New Zealand family. I've been with Sony since the very beginning. This was taken at my Auckland show on my Springboard tour, 2019. They presented me with a plaque with all my musical achievements in New Zealand. (Supplied by Sony Music New Zealand)

Ōhotu Marae — my marae in Rūātoki. It's here that I had the most peaceful sleep of my whole life. (Supplied by author)

Tamapahore Marae — my home, my tūrangawaewae. (Supplied by author)

The love of my life, Lou Tyson. Back together again. (Supplied by author)

Me in 2020. Ready for the next chapter. (Photo by Damien Nikora)

What if I can't sing again? That was my bread and butter. My whole self.

Nevertheless, I trusted I would be all right. As I went in, I prayed: *God, I know that I'm going to live, there's no doubt in my mind. But God, if I need to go through the worst to show people what it's about, and to show that at the end of the day you are victorious in my life, then I'll do it.* Stupid! Why would I pray like I'm the big hero? I was basically saying to God: give me your worst. It was the dumbest thing I ever did.

Fourteenth of September 2017. Here we go. They started with the epidural — *Eh? I thought only pregnant women got that* — and oh my gosh, they had to try three or four times with the needles, up to that point the sorest thing ever.

Six hours later, I woke up and … I was sore. I had been thinking the operation was the hard part, but it wasn't. Everything was sore, my throat was sore. My uvula — that thing that hangs down at the back of your mouth — seemed to have swollen so much it was blocking my throat. I could hardly breathe, and when I fell asleep it was worse. It just seemed to fill up my airways. It was so severe. This is what so often happens to people who receive such intensive hospital treatment — they enter a whole new world of pain and recovery, and the old norms of being able to do whatever you want seem a long way away. This was going to become horribly familiar to me.

The surgery itself had gone perfectly. The surgeons, man, what they can do is amazing. They didn't even have to cut me open — they did keyhole surgery, and I literally had seven tiny holes. My whole stomach came out through my belly button. In the initial biopsy, they found one spot of

265

cancer; when they looked at my stomach after the operation, they discovered thirteen cancerous lesions.

'I can't breathe,' I told the nurses and doctors. It was normal, they said. Sore throat because of the tubes. I told them again, tears streaming down my face from frustration, from fear, from sadness at feeling like this. *I can't breathe.* To breathe — it's the most natural, basic thing. I'd never thought about it before. I'd just taken it for granted. But now, every breath was hard and I never felt like I got enough air. I've never been so scared in my whole life. For three days, they told me it was normal, and finally they did a chest x-ray and found one of my lungs had collapsed. I was so exhausted, I couldn't really be bothered being angry. They put me on oxygen and slowly, over the next few days, I began to breathe more easily, and my lung healed.

I recovered enough to go home, but then the first of the complications occurred. They told me that for six weeks I had to stay home, inside. In fact, I was only able to walk as far as the kitchen and it wasn't long before it was making me crazy. When you are lying in bed for that long, you are willing to risk everything just to feel the air in your lungs. Just to be out in the world. I became willing to risk it all for that one moment, so one day I convinced my brother Mike to let me come to the zoo with him and his family. They had me in a wheelchair, just getting pushed around. That's how desperate I was to be normal. I hadn't realised how fragile I was. Virtually no immune system. I started to get cold, and once I was home again, I got sick. So sick, so quickly, that I literally watched the blood draining away from my arms. My neck, my jaw and my whole body were paralysed with severe, uncontrollable shakes. I had no control of it whatsoever. I couldn't call for help. Luckily, I had my phone on my chest, I managed to press Mum's number and she came rushing in from the lounge. I saw her face when she saw me. She later told me I looked dead.

I was rushed back to hospital, this time with a terrible chest infection. I was just trying to breathe. It was all I could think. *Breathe, just breathe.* I also had the thought: *This is how I'm going to die.*

I could hear my dad crying, and he is the ugliest crier in the world. I could hear him, and I knew if I looked at him I would laugh, so I was like, *Don't look at him, don't look at him.* I was so scared I would laugh and miss my breath and die.

None of this was what I'd expected.

It was hard. I was fighting hard against the feeling that I wanted to give up. Thanking God I was alive but feeling worse than I knew it was possible to feel.

A month after the operation, I was feeling much better. I went back in to see my specialist, Dr Cuong, who had done the operation, and he told me I was all clear. I wouldn't have to worry about cancer anymore. Cancer-free. Around the same time, Mum got some test results back and she was cancer-free, too.

Hope. Hope came. Hope went. I knew I still wasn't right. Eating was getting harder and harder. I'd put the food in my mouth and chew it, but then I had to swallow. The food would go partway down and get stuck. Then I'd gag and spew it up. I just couldn't get food inside me, and I was getting more and more scared to swallow. Then, during a routine check-up, Dr Cuong found my oesophagus was narrowing. It wasn't my imagination — the food quite literally couldn't get down. Another complication. Again, I was back in hospital, struggling against a feeling of defeat. I could take nothing through my mouth and was being fed by intravenous fluids. Even the thought of how skinny I was getting didn't cheer me up no more.

They had to stretch my oesophagus but during the operation I heaved, and tore the oesophagus away from my small intestine. This was a disaster — the exact same thing that had ended up killing my koko. For my mum, I believe this was the hardest moment, reliving what had happened to Koko, remembering seeing him in hospital in a coma. For her, this was the nightmare she most dreaded. If I ate or drank anything, it would seep directly into my body and I could die. So they put me on a PICC line — an IV all the way through, straight to my heart and, although it was only supposed to be for a couple of days, I ended up being on that machine for two weeks, twenty-three hours a day. For my hour off, I'd shower, get wheeled out to the hospital garden and get some fresh air, then be brought back in to get hooked up again.

Man, I hate this. I wanted to be normal.

Then I had more pain, and had to have an emergency operation to remove my appendix. The operation took five and a half hours, and when they finally pulled it out they found there was nothing wrong with it. Another week in hospital. Setback after setback. Some of the setbacks were my fault. If I'd been healthier when I went in, if I hadn't been so impatient every time, if I'd just stayed home and rested —

but every time I felt a little bit better I was just so desperate to get outside of my four walls.

Finally, after longer in hospital than I ever anticipated, I was free to go. For a few days, I wandered around at home trying to recover. I felt like an eighty-year-old man — a sick eighty-year-old man. Weak and shuffling and filled with fear. When you're weak like that, you fear you'll never feel normal again. When you're as weak as I was, you fear you'll never have the energy or the ability to sing again. I needed something to make me feel I could step back into my old, normal world. I longed to be back in the studio, writing songs again. Mum rang Champo and even though Champo was dubious — he'd seen how weak I still was — he sought the advice of Denis Handlin, and Denis just made it all possible. He stood by me right through my illness and so, thanks to him, I flew to Sydney, stayed in a comfortable hotel, and managed at last to hobble into Sony and into the studio. Life was going to be possible again. And that's where I finished the song I'd written for Mum, 'Thank You'. By that time, I was almost overwhelmed by how much I had to thank her for. She'd saved my life yet again. *After all we've been through, You've never run out of love.*

* * *

A while after that, I went back home to Tauranga, to Tamapahore. I needed to reconnect with my marae after what I'd been through. It had been hard, but I knew — like, really knew now — what would have happened if I hadn't had the operation. They had found thirteen cancers in my stomach,

269

and it was an aggressive, fast-moving form of cancer. I would have been dead within a year. Maybe dead in six months. Dead at twenty-seven.

The big reason I went back to Tamapahore was because my mum was getting her moko kauae — the traditional marking Māori women wear on their chin. For us, it was about both our healings. After it was done, there in the wharenui of our marae, I sang her the song I had written all those months ago. *Māmā, you the best in the world, You're more than diamonds or pearls, Help me in my weak times, You kept my head held high.*

Now I need to convince others in my family with the mutant gene that they should get their stomachs out. 'Don't risk getting cancer.' It's a hard thing for people to hear, because they're of course afraid and they don't want to confront the truth — just like I was.

Time is precious to me now. There have been so many times in my life when I haven't wanted to be alive. So many times I've stood on the brink of suicide. Now that I've come so close to death, I know I want to live. Definitely.

For so long, in that period leading up to my cancer operation, I'd been winding down, losing everything — my passion, my joy in the industry, my money. Now, I had my creative mojo back. I was forward-looking, desperate to get well, desperate to get back to singing and creating and living my purpose. And I'd heard that message from the church — I may be facing an obstacle that is huge, but it's not as big as the blessing that's waiting for me.

God called my bluff. I'd been through the worst. We're good!

* * *

Soon after I had won Idol, I joined the Sony Foundation as an ambassador, raising the profile of its work to establish specialist cancer services for teenagers with cancer. I even became the face for some of the work and appeared in a campaign for You Can, alongside teenagers with cancer, not knowing that, not too far down the track, I myself was going to go through exactly what these other young people were going through. It was actually Denis Handlin, the head of Sony Music Australia and one of the founders of the Sony Foundation, who opened my eyes to realise there was a gap in care for young people with cancer in Australia, and that I could help make a difference. Up until quite recently, a teenager with cancer would either find themselves in a ward with really young kids, or with really old people — and there was a good chance there'd be no one else in their ward who fully got what they were going through, in terms of their identity. For a teenager to be so sick, to lose their hair, to be isolated from their friends and for their future to become uncertain, is a very particular situation, and also impacted their chance of survival. The Sony Foundation has raised millions of dollars for You Can over the years to establish special youth wards in hospitals, which support thousands of young people nationally. Even before I had my own experience of cancer, I could see how important the work was.

But after I'd had cancer myself, I was actually really surprised at how I felt when I met young people going through cancer treatment. I thought I'd left my own experience behind me. But instead I felt really emotional, I really understood what they were going through, so the work became even more meaningful. When the world got closed down because of the coronavirus in 2020, these young people suffered even more because their families and friends were no longer allowed to visit them in hospital or at home, so it was great to be able to do some livestreams with those kids wherever they were, just talking to them and playing music for an hour or so each time. I know what it's like lying in bed, being physically drained, feeling sick, and feeling that loneliness. Through the power of music, I feel like I can help take them away from all of that for a moment and give them some hope.

The royalties from my single 'Bigger' are going to support building You Can centres nationally throughout Australia. These youth cancer centres provide a home away from home where teenagers can chill, watch movies, play some music or PlayStation ... all the cool stuff to keep them in touch with the world outside.

I think we have to do things that are tangible, if we really want to help people. After the Australian bushfires of 2019–20, I visited one of the hardest hit areas, Batemans Bay. Man, I thought my life was hard. Those people had lost everything, sometimes even family members, and yet they were so resilient and compassionate towards others. I wanted to help, so I decided to donate part of the income I get from all my music streamed through the coming year to the Sony Foundation's Bushfire Appeal.

I love doing this work. At my own darkest hour, I got the support I needed, and I want to help others get the same.

* * *

Rarotonga, a summer evening in December 2017. It's a beautiful warmth. I love that if I stand outside, just quietly stand there, I can hear all the conversations going on between neighbours, the soft chattering in Cook Island Māori. I hear kids laughing as they all run through the hibiscus hedges from house to house, no fences anywhere. I hear the dogs and the chickens. I can smell the frangipani. I've missed this way of life. No care in the world.

They have stories in Rarotonga about all the waka that left to explore the oceans, and the great waka that made it all the way to Aotearoa. I sometimes wish my whānau had stayed behind where it's so warm but no, they had to choose the big, colder islands further south.

It's fourteen weeks since my operation, and I've chosen to do my come-back concert here in Avarua. I thought I'd be all good but as the evening closes in, I'm not even sure I can get through one song.

I've been focusing on getting my voice back ever since I recovered. I had to learn to sing again, as if I was singing out of a different body — which, at more than thirty kilos lighter, I am. It's been one of the most frustrating things ever. My mind was all the way there, way before my body was. My voice has been so tired and my notes haven't been coming out. It's taken many weeks to get back to a level where I think I can perform to an audience. But today, the soundcheck didn't go well. It was hard on my body, my lungs, my voice. My energy levels are uncertain.

Oh, have a little bit of grace for me. I got my stomach out. I could make excuses. Nah. I would never do that. I don't want them to even know that. I want them to look at me and go, *Faar, you're just the man.*

I haven't gone public about the cancer or the operation at all yet. There's been speculation in the media about my sudden weight loss, and some journalists decided I was on meth. That's frustrating, but I don't want to talk about it yet — I'm waiting for the documentary to come out in May 2018.

God will come through for me tonight. He always does. I get to the venue, nervous as. My stomach is sore. I don't know if it's nerves or something else. *Please, no.*

The band starts with 'Bulletproof'. *Here we go.* I open my mouth and out it comes. My voice! It's like a roar. One of the craziest things I've ever, ever experienced. I thought my voice was gone forever, but here it is, and it's back with a vengeance. The rain comes down. It's washing over me, soaking the audience. They don't care. I start to cry. The warm tropical rain masks my tears and I turn to the band and yell, 'Thank you, Jesus!'. I am alive. It feels like the first time in a long time. Back being me, doing what I do. My next phase has begun.

This is who I am. I'm not going to be held back.

Since then, I've done two tours around Aotearoa — the 'New Takeover' tour in 2018, and the 'Springboard' tour in 2019. I've appeared at countless festivals. I've got way more energy than I ever had. My focus — I feel like I'm on fire. But there's a difference. I can feel my limits a lot more than I used to, when I would just run on empty for months, or even go a whole year on empty. Now, I can't do that. When I get empty, I need to switch off to reboot, recharge. Part of that's about my body, but a big part is that my mindset's changed. I've been forced to learn to look after myself.

Before the operation, I just craved working, working, working. I was obsessed and addicted to work. I was always thinking about the next thing and never really completely present. Even in the time when I was losing my passion and not enjoying it, I was still obsessed. Any break and I'd be like, *I need to get back to work.*

Now, I've turned some of that craving into having breaks. I'll go and stay at my house in Ōhope, or visit my nannies at Tamapahore, or hang with my cousins in Rūātoki. Reset, settle in, rest. It takes a while, but then I'm just chill. That's weird for me, but I love that feeling. I don't get angry real quick. I don't get sad real quick. It's like putting my hands in the soil. It's real. This is who I am.

So, in some ways, everything's changed. I feel like I've matured and grown a lot, got me a bit more settled and slow. Still growing. This is life, I'm just going to be forever growing.

* * *

I escaped death. Yet death is always around me. As I was recovering, feeling my way back to my life just before Christmas 2017, I got some of the worst news possible.

I know the smell of death because I grew up smelling it — the smell of an embalmed body, a chemical smell. Cold. And I think it was when I was around eleven that I began to smell the smell of death sometimes, even when there wasn't a body.

The first time it happened, I became aware that I could smell something, but it took me a minute to recognise what it was. I sniffed and breathed it in, and then I realised: *Gee, it smells like death.*

I got home from school — I was at intermediate in Hamilton — to find my parents packing up the truck. 'Tiwi and Boz got killed. We're going straight home.' And we drove straight back to Tauranga to the funeral home. Tiwi and Boz were my cousins, older than me, but really close to my brothers, and they'd been killed in their car — they were coming back from work when their car went over the centre line and into the way of a truck. My poor Nanny Maybelle had to go and identify them.

It happened again when one of my uncles died. That smell. But when I first told my mum she told me not to be so stupid. 'Oh shush, don't say that.' The third time I smelt it I was scared. I rang my mum and told her, 'Mum, I smelled that smell again.' And she goes, 'Oh my gosh, boy, your aunty just died.'

But I didn't get the smell when my cousin Kaha killed himself, just before Christmas 2017, as I was getting over my operation and getting ready to start performing again, and I didn't smell it when my other cousin killed herself about a year later.

When Kaha killed himself, that was really hard. We grew up together. He was the same age as me. I remember when we were little kids, around the age of ten, we were having a lunch after church at someone's house. There was me, Kaha and two other boys. And for some reason they all started picking on me, running away from me. Usually me and

Kaha were best mates, but that time he went on their side. I grabbed this glass bottle and I chucked it at him. I didn't care about the other two, but him — he'd betrayed me. He chased me and we had this big fight, and afterwards my mum sat us both down and she's like, 'Say sorry to each other right now! You fallas, yous are blood. Boys, don't you ever forget, blood will always be thicker than water.'

I'll never forget that. That was the first and only big fight that Kaha and I ever had, and then we went outside. We were a bit shy for a minute, then we started running around this blow-up pool that was there on the grass, and next minute it was all normal again.

Later, it was him and his family, my Uncle Andrew and Aunty Denise, that I stayed with when I got kicked out by my parents. So, I'd grown up with him my whole life.

And then he killed himself. It was such a shock to me. These things are always a shock, even if you've seen the signs and have tried to help. It came out of the blue, and yet it didn't, if that makes any sense.

My other cousin, who was a year older than us, she told her mum: 'I understand what he's going through, Mum.' When she killed herself, too, it was such a tragedy, such a blow for us. Both of them had kids. And people get angry and say it's a selfish thing to do. But I understand how they must have felt — the isolation, the desperateness. I've been there many times myself, so many times I can't count, and I know that in that moment it doesn't feel selfish — it feels like the opposite: that the world will be better off without you.

It's so sad to think they felt that way, when of course it wasn't true. But that was the feeling they carried.

I can only speak for myself. It's a feeling of pressure that you can't get away from, failure, no sense of purpose. Feeling unloved, rejected, unwanted, hating yourself, disappointment — so many different things. But you just feel so low that it takes over your mind and you feel like it's better to just be done.

And all the people who are left behind, all they want is for that person to still be there.

I did not smell their deaths, but I still feel their deaths so deeply in my heart.

* * *

There was one more post-operative scare for me. Near the end of January 2018, three days before the One Love festival in Tauranga, the day before I was supposed to join Prime Minister Jacinda Ardern for dinner in support of her youth programme, my stomach started hurting. It had actually been sore for a couple of weeks, but suddenly it got worse. *No, this can't be happening.* Next minute, I'm in hospital again, and the doctors wanted to do an emergency operation for an infected gallbladder. No way. I couldn't miss my dinner with Jacinda. Couldn't miss One Love. Couldn't miss the ten more gigs over the next two months. 'Can I say no?'

'You can, but you shouldn't.'

'Give me all the drugs you've got because I need to get out of here.' I swallowed painkillers, antibiotics, and carried on. It turned out the butter and oil I'd been eating had inflamed my gallbladder, so I had to change my diet again.

But I kept my gallbladder. I felt like I'd lost enough bits of me already. Soon all that will be left is my heart.

And now I'm lucky enough to be enjoying life after cancer. I'm well. I can sing again, maybe better than ever. Looks-wise, not having a stomach is amazing. I love being skinny. I love the way I look now. I wish I had bigger legs — all my power used to be in my legs when I was solid, but I can still do sports days with my boys. Still do everything. I am not fragile. The only real reminder is that every three months, for the rest of my life, I have to have injections of vitamin B12. Without that I would die, because with my stomach gone, I can't absorb that vitamin in the normal way, and it's crucial for making my blood.

But I miss all the food I used to eat. Dairy was always my favourite thing. Cheese. I love it, but now too much and my new stomach gurgles. Ice cream, can't eat it. I miss it. A drink of milk, I'd have the runs. I used to have milk with everything, Weet-Bix, every day all day. I miss eating heaps because now I have to eat small. I miss takeaways, Maccas, KFC, cheeseburgers and Filet-o-Fish burgers. I can handle a flat white, which is weird.

But if I really want something, I'm prepared to pay the price — eat it, and then I'll spew or get the runs. But sometimes it's worth it.

What do I eat now? Air! Nah. I can eat most things but just not too much. I still eat hot chips. If I couldn't, oh my gosh, it would be atrocious.

* * *

My industry, the music industry, is also about fashion, and that's an aspect that I've always loved. And that was one of the things I decided, when I knew I was going to lose my stomach and lose so much weight: *When I get skinny, I want to go hard for fashion.* I'd always wanted to, but never thought I could carry off the look I wanted to. Sure enough, I'd lost thirty-six kilos, and so I was like a coat hanger. That's my payoff for nearly dying. I love it. Bro, chuck me in anything. I'm ready to make a stand.

Since my operation, I've evolved my look. I love to mix my culture with fashion. For me, that's normal. Why would I wear diamonds or pearls? They are not mine. A diamond that costs $50,000 is not as valuable to me as a piece of pounamu, or a bone carving that might cost just a couple of hundred dollars, or a precious korowai made of feathers. These things hold weight, hold meaning. They are from my land, from my people. And they look awesome. So dramatic, especially alongside high-end fashion.

Our jewellery is literally priceless, because you can't buy it for yourself. It must be gifted. Sometimes, I buy jewellery and wear it for a while, but I know that I will eventually give it away. That is my intention when I buy it.

When I hosted the Vodafone New Zealand Music Awards in 2018, I wore a Zambesi suit, and my great-great-grandmother's korowai, over 150 years old and one of only three existing korowai that are made completely of kiwi feathers. It is a taonga, so precious and fragile that it has to be kept in a special case. And I also wore a large bone around my neck, a giant heru, or comb. I got it in Hawai'i from a Māori carver working at the Polynesian Cultural Center — I gave it to my dad, but I still like to wear it.

In 2019, I was gifted a carved pig's tusk and dog's tooth by one of the Pacific's great waka carvers, Pāpā Mike Tavioni, from the island of Atiu in the Cook Islands. He gave them to me, and I wore them in my video for 'Choose', together with a Zambesi suit. For me, that's more precious than anything. There ain't no price on it.

On my first trip back to New Zealand after winning Idol, back in 2009, I performed at the Māori sports awards, and later this kuia came up to me and she put a beautiful whale bone around my neck. I didn't know her, but she probably just felt moved. I still have it, of course. That's never going anywhere. That's the very first one I was given.

Sometimes, of course, it's hard to give away the things I love. When my little brother got engaged, I gave him my favourite piece of pounamu. I looked at it, and I thought, *Oh, I don't want to give it.* But I also thought, *I want to give him my best.* I felt it, so I gave it. And this is the way we do things. With meaning and purpose.

One of my good friends, Sammy Salsa, is my stylist and he has helped me create my image over the years. I'll often have an idea, and then I pivot to him, and I'm like, 'Do your thing.' And he expands it, he makes it better, he brings it to life. We work together closely in that process. Sammy is the only one who can push me. He'll say, 'Just trust me,' and I will. For instance, we did an ad for Uber Eats and he put me in a pink suit. Then he went, wear this red hat. Put on all this bling. Add a pink fur coat. Why not. It's fashion!

I do enjoy the fashion world. I was on the catwalk at Fashion Week for New Zealand label Not For You in 2018, and have done shoots for Zambesi. I did a fashion spread in *Remix* magazine, heaps of shoots for this and that. I'm not a model but I know how to pose. Well, it's acting, isn't it. And I will always take my culture with me.

I went through all those operations because I had no choice. But here I am, skinny, and I'm loving it.

CHAPTER TWELVE

Moemoeā

Moe moe moemoeā
E kore rawa e riro
Maruāpō
He ārai e te ao
Ū mai, nau mai
He kaupare i a tāua
E kore angitu

— 'Moemoeā (Don't Dream It's Over)'

My mum and dad, they tried to put me in counselling back in the day, a couple of times, when I was little. The first time was while we were back living at Tamapahore, in my last year of primary school so I must have been about ten. I can't remember why they sent me then in particular, but they thought there was something wrong with me, and that that was how to fix it. It made me so angry. The counsellor kept asking, 'And how do you feel?' and talking to me in language I couldn't understand, using a tone I thought was not real. The whole experience, I felt I was being told there was something wrong with me, which I felt anyway. *Man, I want to kill you. How dare you do this to me? Why are you talking like that?*

Oh, I do need help.

I knew I did. But this wasn't right, and it wasn't right the next time they tried, a couple of years later, when I was at intermediate.

My thinking has always gone at a thousand miles an hour. My thinking goes way faster than what I do in real life, and I do things really fast, and I go so many places. But I can't keep up with my thinking. I dream up the biggest dreams and the biggest concepts. I think myself into destruction. I think myself into sadness. I think myself into ultimate joy.

My mind is this dangerous, super-creative, incredible, scary place. I've always wanted to be quiet and calm and just not have any worries, just chill. But counselling was not going to get me there.

Getting grounded into my whenua, into my whānau, is the only thing that truly calms me.

Rūātoki is the home I didn't grow up in. When I went there as a little kid with my parents, I always felt the connection, and after things changed at Mangatawa, after we lost our house and after the landscape changed with all the new highways and buildings, I turned strongly to my Tūhoe whānau.

Rūātoki is in Te Urewera, just over 100 kilometres from Tauranga. First there's tar seal, then there's gravel, then there's the Whakatāne River. The valley narrows and the hills and thick forests close in. Te Urewera is famous for its remoteness, and Tūhoe are famous for their independence and their adherence to Māori language and identity. The people of Tūhoe are known as Ngā Tamariki o te Kohu, the Children of the Mist. We were born from the union of the mist and the mountain, Maungapohatu; our land is part of us, and we are part of it.

When I get back home to the bush, to Rūātoki, I take my shoes off so I'm on the ground, and that really does something to me. Something good, something real, something right. I can be in the worst state of my life, fully depressed or just exhausted. I get back there and I just breathe. People are trying to fill us up with pills and ask us these silly questions that we don't know the answers to, when the answers are there: it's going back to our land, it's learning who we really are. Because, otherwise, we're all going to go crazy — and people have been going crazy for a long time because they're disconnected from their land. That's what I feel. I have always felt this, but I didn't always understand it. I didn't know how to articulate it.

My whānau down there all speak Māori most of the time. They live very simply. They don't have much, but they've got everything.

* * *

I ride horses with my cousins or nephews and nieces, and we take them across the river. The day is hot and the cold water rushes against me, but my horse is swimming easily and I feel the power of its legs. I hold on to its mane and let it go as it wants. Afterwards, we take the saddles off and we'll wade with them and let them have a swim by themselves.

The pure mountain air, the song of tūī, korimako and pīwakawaka, the laughing voices of my cousins. All the kids bombing into the river off their horses. The sunsets. It's the smallest things, the littlest things. The world that I live and breathe and exist and work in, that just don't matter to me. This is everything. This is my whole world right now. Here, I get to be free from myself. I'm no one, and it's mean.

* * *

My main connection in Rūātoki is my nan's marae, Ōhotu. Going inside of it, it's just this warm feeling. I feel still, and calm, and rested. I always have the best sleep of my life,

286

sleeping there in that wharenui. Mostly down there I stay at my Aunty Jocelyn's and Uncle Bussy's, who are a very integral part of my life in te ao Māori, and I visit with my nan across the road and we sit there with our cups of tea and we talk about everything. We talk about people and history, and it takes me further on my journey of whakapapa. All the learning comes from the people and the place. Going back to Rūātoki, I've learned more of who I am as a Māori. Our customs, our practices, our teachings, our stories, our history.

My nan lives in my great-great-grandmother's house, the homestead that we all come from — a big old house with a big kitchen. Every time you go into a Māori home, it feels warm. It always feels like a home whether it's big or small, flash or not. My nan's house is just so homely.

My Tūhoe connection has been a big part of shaping me into the man I am today — the way that I think, the way I use my reo. It's because of their history and their staunchness. There is no reason to apologise for being Māori or speaking Māori, because there was never any reason to think an apology was even needed. That is the Tūhoe way.

A few years ago, I took a group of my mates to Rūātoki for New Year's. They were all Māori, and they had all grown up ashamed of being Māori. They tried to cover up their identity by putting other words before it: Sāmoan Māori, Tongan Māori, even though Māori are the Tangata Whenua of the land they were brought up in and are living in. They watch 'Police Ten 7', they think that Māori are hori, dumb, thieves, aggressive, alcoholics.

They had never been to a marae before, or heard Māori spoken as a natural language.

We had adventures on the river and in the bush, we talked deeply in the peaceful nights, and they heard the sound of the reo. My family down there don't speak much English, so they heard us all speaking to each other in Māori, just as we went about our daily lives. My uncles, all tatted up, were bringing tents, tables, food. *This is the Tūhoe way. This is the Māori way. When you have manuhiri, we all chip in to welcome them.*

They saw our culture, rather than the things like abuse, alcoholism, drugs that have been attached to Māori. But those things are not our culture. Our culture is our reo, our tikanga, our whakapapa, our kai, our waiata, our everything.

My mates were like, 'I didn't know this was us. This is so beautiful.'

One of them said, 'Man, I've been trying to be something else, and I didn't know we were like this.'

Then I told them: 'This will always be your home. But now go back to your own marae. You have that, too. Don't just think this is it. This is over the whole country. You've just been caught up in city urbanised life, but we *all* have this.'

* * *

When I won Idol, I meant it when I said I did it for my family. We've had some tough times, in our generation but also before. Colonisation has continued to affect us down the generations, in all its different and unfolding manifestations. Not just the loss of land, which, as we can see in the example of the Mangatawa quarry, was even happening well within living memory, but the effects of that loss, of that massive social change, are being felt maybe even more strongly today.

This is just as great of a loss as losing your mother or your father. It's ultimately losing your identity. And for Māori it's worsened through the generations as people's lives got harder, as they moved to the cities, as jobs were lost, as intergenerational poverty kicked in.

What I do know from experience is that when you're disconnected from your land and your culture, from who you are, there's always going to be something going wrong. There's going to be a defect. There's going to be an emptiness that you will try to fill with something else until it turns into something ugly.

There have been troubled generations, but now is a hopeful time of awakening. Ka mua, ka muri. We walk backwards into the future. We look back so that we know where we're heading.

There is so much to be proud of, and I love finding out who I come from. My tūpuna. My DNA. I'm a nerd for whakapapa. There's always a few in every generation who are the whakapapa carriers. I'm one of them.

When you know where you come from and who you come from, man, it's like everything inside you awakens and you realise: *that's* why I'm like this. That's why I can do this. I carry their DNA. I carry their traits, I carry their mindsets, I carry their spirit.

When I speak my language, when I sing my language, when I wear my great-grandmother's korowai, when I wear my bone earrings and my bone taonga, I am fully who my ancestors have allowed me to be.

I want to learn more about myself through uncovering my past.

I'm sure people get annoyed at me because I just want to get into that whakapapa kōrero all the time, asking where you're from, who you come from, what are your connections, where's your marae, what are the names of your family. But for me it's the full meaning of who we are.

There are stereotypes of the drunk, drugged, violent Māori, and I myself have lived every one of those stereotypes. But now I have a responsibility. I have been given a gift, so many opportunities. Now I know: I have to be amazing because of who my ancestors were and what they did and the sacrifices they made. I have to be the man. I get to be outrageous and dream the biggest dreams because they have gone before me.

* * *

When I think about shame, it feels to me like the sticky, yellow-brown tar that's left after doing spots of dope. It's an ugly residue and it's fully potent. That tarry stuff, it hits you different. I don't like that feeling. It's paranoia.

Shame is one of the biggest killers of our people, the killer of dreams, the killer of potential, the killer of purpose. It fuels our addictions, our violence, our depression. It's another by-product of colonisation: shame to be proud of who we are.

It's a feeling that's soaked into our core. It has wrapped around us like a cloak. Our identity was taken from us; we came to believe we were wrong in our being. We felt ugly about ourselves.

Shame to know your worth. Shame to stand out. Shame to succeed. Shame to fail. It is a whakapapa of shame that has come down through the generations. It probably started as a way to protect ourselves — don't speak Māori, don't act Māori, Māori are dumb, Māori ain't allowed in here. Being Māori won't get you anywhere.

We have a word for shame that goes even deeper than the English word, and that is whakamā. It is about being inferior, inadequate, dishonoured, embarrassed. It's a feeling that seeks to hide itself behind certain behaviours.

For a long time, we weren't allowed to be proud. Our pride got beaten, killed, mocked out of generations. It was replaced by shame, and now it just is. I feel like we're coming into a stage now where we're allowed to be proud again.

There's this new generation, they're like, 'Yes, I am who I am.' And some people are like, 'Oh shush, this is weird.' It's because we're not used to it.

But many in the older generation love the pride they see in the young people. They've been waiting for that. They've been waiting for a revolution. They've been waiting for our kids to come back and fight for our whenua and fight for our people. I often ask the old people, 'What do you think about all this, about Ihumātao, about young people wearing moko, about the revitalisation of our language and culture?' And they say, 'Oh, we love it. We love what you're doing. You know, some stuff we don't get, but we love it. You're coming back to doing these things and fighting for the right things.'

A cousin of mine is one of four kids in her family. Her two sisters are light brown and have blue eyes; her little brother's hair is almost blonde; but she is dark, really dark, and she has dark eyes. One day we were walking home from school on a hot sunny day and she was jumping from shadow to shadow, and I said, 'What are you doing?' She went, 'I'm hiding from the sun.' She didn't want to get darker. She was shamed to be black. Even then, it shocked me. *Faar, that's such an out-of-it thing.* Shame of who you are.

Whenever I can, I take my nannies and aunties with me into my new world, like government dinners or music awards. They always go, 'No, no, no, we can't go in there. No, look at us. No, this is not our place.' Thinking they're not good enough. 'Don't make a fuss. We don't want to be seen. We don't want them to think, "Oh, these Māoris …".'

I used to be like that, too. I don't care anymore. If we're laughing too loud and people look at us like, 'Oh, look at these bloody Islanders laughing like that,' I'm like, 'What, don't you laugh this good?'

We are the worst judges of ourselves. My biggest critics are Māori people who think I should be more humble. I tell them, 'I can be proud and know my worth, but still have ultimate humility. Man, I'm thankful for everything, but I'm not going to sit here and not be happy for myself if I've just won something or if I've just done something awesome. That's so mean. When I win, you fallas win.' They often don't understand that you can be proud and humble at the same time. They think pride is shameful.

I back myself up. I believe in myself. I'm not going to feel that shame anymore.

My dad is the same. This is how far he's come. He talks to himself in the mirror every day and he goes, 'Ross, you're the man. Ross, you're a good husband. Ross, you're the best dad.

Ross, money comes to you.' He speaks this over his life every day and everything he says, he is.

We were a family that was soaked in shame.

But this is the miracle of our family.

* * *

There are a lot of Māori who say, 'We own the land.' We don't. We are the kaitiaki, just here to look after it. Thinking land is something to be owned is what's got everyone into the mess we're in today. Māori, other indigenous people throughout the Pacific, Pākehā — we all suffer when the land becomes a commodity to be sold and bought and plundered.

Even the Bible talks about healing the land. 'If my people ... turn from their wicked ways, then I will hear from heaven and will forgive their sin and heal their land ...' *If we change our ways, our land will heal.* When I read that, I feel like the Bible is speaking straight to us about climate change, and about the way we have failed to guard the health of our land and waters. The land is crying out for help. Essentially, we are the land and when the land is crying out, we're crying out. If it doesn't benefit the whenua, then it doesn't benefit the whānau: us.

We are the land. He tangata, he tangata.

'Not one more acre,' Dame Whina Cooper said when she led the hīkoi, the Māori land march, from Te Hāpua, in Northland, to Wellington in 1975. Over a thousand kilometres. One way or another, there have been many more acres lost since then, but also since her day there has been a revitalisation among our people, a growing pride in our role as guardians, and a determination to right the wrongs of history.

In July 2019, me and other musicians went out to Ihumātao in South Auckland to perform for the people who had been occupying their stolen ancestral land for four years. The land had been lived on and tended to by Māori since the fourteenth century but was brutally confiscated by the government in 1863, and given to a Scottish farming family who made their fortune off it. Then, in 2016, they sold it to Fletcher Building. Fletchers intended to build a housing development project there, but local mana whenua formed a group, Save Our Unique Landscape, and began occupying the land, claiming the original confiscation breached the Treaty of Waitangi. Those fallas, SOUL, are the example of standing up for what is right. They inspired people all around the country. The mana whenua of Ihumātao deserve to have the land returned to their care.

I was so privileged to be there at that beautiful display of kotahitanga, unity. I knew what they were doing was going to open a whole can of worms, and so it should. They were helping New Zealanders have a better understanding of our shared history, at the same time as making history. It's not about a name on a piece of paper, because even before that piece of paper was in existence, we were already here as kaitiaki.

It was a freezing night, midwinter, with spatters of rain at times, and lines of police standing shoulder to shoulder, like they were expecting trouble, eyeballing the hundreds of supporters who had come. Behind them flew heaps of Tino Rangatiratanga and He Whakaputanga flags, everyone bundled into warm clothes, all huddling together. So much tension, but so much good heart. *We are one race, we are the human race.* I was given a loud speaker and I spoke from my heart because, although I am a fighter, I am a man of peace, if that makes sense. What I felt there was the rightness of the kaupapa, the purpose, and the absolute need, on that day, in that place, for us to act always with grace and peace and harmony.

Creatively, strategically, our people are stepping up. We're coming. Making moves, making ground, revitalising. We need to find solutions so we can all win. No one wins until we all win.

One of the songs I sang that night was 'Moemoeā', my te reo version of the Crowded House song 'Don't Dream It's Over'. Since having it translated by Erena Koopu back in 2014, I've sung it all over the world, and I love it — I love the song, I love the melody. It's a song that's exactly about what's happening in our world today. For me, it's sad but it's got hope. There's always hope. Singing it in te reo Māori especially connects me always with home, and with the idea of home. So it was the perfect song for Ihumātao. It's the perfect song for now.

* * *

Dispossession is an ugly word. It's a heavy, dark, lonely word. It's a word that fills the voices of our kuia with sadness still, generations later. The hurt is there, generations later. Unfortunately, a lot of our people are broken and what the system tries to do is just lock them up, chuck them away, throw away the key.

We are mamae, in pain. Like me, I'm twenty-nine; I go home to Tamapahore and I feel sad like I want to cry. And I feel like that's what my tūpuna would have felt, too.

Obviously, Māori land's been taken all over the country. I come from two iwi that fought to keep our land. They were long, bitter fights and much was lost along the way, through battle, legislation, and legitimate sales born of poverty. I come from Ngāi Te Rangi, Ngāti Pūkenga, Ngā Pōtiki, and Tūhoe. Those fights were already fought for me.

I hear people say, 'Get over it. It happened more than a hundred years ago. You can't keep blaming colonisation for everything.'

I say to them, 'This is the situation: me and my people will come over to your patch of land. I'm going to tell you to get off. If you don't get off, we're going to steamroll your house, burn it down. We're going to kill a few of you, rape your wife and daughters. This is exactly what happened to my tūpuna. In Te Urewera, our fertile lands were confiscated, and all access to the sea and our kaimoana was cut off, our crops were burned, our homes destroyed, our stock killed or taken. Our people were killed, raped, imprisoned.'

That loss compounded over the following decades.

Our experience is the same as that of indigenous people all over the world, and the consequences are the same. I can see the weariness, how our people are weary and tired. The system has stuffed us up. And we become the statistics of everything that's bad.

We can't pretend these things didn't happen. We can't say that it doesn't matter. When I'm with my grandparents, they're like, 'Oh boy, this is where we grew up. This is our whenua. It got taken from us.' They're telling the real-life stories of what happened. Even though we can write everything down now, we still operate in the Māori way. They tell the stories to us and it is all done through talking and listening and learning. We still have to tell the stories and not all the stories are easy. A lot of our history, if you want to dive deep into everything, there's some dark stuff in there.

And we still have to fight these battles against those who want to fight fire with fire — these politicians who say, 'We need to come down on the gangs, we need to lock them up and throw away the key.' They'll spend millions and millions of dollars and it won't work to make things better for our people. We are by-products of all our history. We are by-products of a system that thinks, 'Oh, they're just a waste of time.'

We need to do things differently, cos it ain't working how we've been doing it.

* * *

My sense of self as a Māori comes from my whānau, from my reo, from my tikanga, from my tūpuna. But my sense of how the world sees me as a Māori comes from my daily experience in the world.

If I walk into an airport and I've got a hoodie on and I'm walking with people who are wearing similar clothes, I get stopped. I take my hoodie off, 'Oh, Stan! Sorry.' Why should it be 'oh, Stan' and why did you suspect me in the first place? The number of times I've heard: 'You're not one of those ones ... These bloody Māoris ... Oh no, you're not like them.'

What do you mean 'these bloody Māoris'? I *am* these bloody Māoris.

One day at primary school in Australia, my brother drew a tā moko on my face with a felt pen — a half-face moko. I thought I was so cool, but everyone at school looked at me weird, because they didn't know what it was. It was a little moment that made me aware of my difference to the mainstream — that things that were just so normal to me as a Māori were unknown to other people. Nowadays, you'd have to live in a cave to be ignorant of different cultures, but back then, there was no talk about it.

Mostly, I didn't even think about my difference, except that I was naturally drawn to other people who were like me. My best friend was Indigenous Australian. But other kids would make comments: 'Your lips are so big. Your nose is so flat.' And I was like, *Oh gosh, I've never even noticed.*

There's a lot said about Australian racism. People use terms like 'more racist' or 'less racist' but, to me, racism is racism. New Zealanders hide their racism but Australians are way more open and I kind of appreciate that, because you know exactly where you stand. In New Zealand, you could be in the same room with somebody, and they're smiling and saying, 'Hey, brother,' but when your back is turned they're like, 'You black bastard.'

Aussies are outright and don't bother with the politeness. *Bloody Kiwi.* I'm like, 'First of all, I ain't no bird. I'm a Māori.' *Bloody Māori. Bloody Abo.* Their culture tells them they are entitled, and that's wilful ignorance. Like everything, they are by-products of by-products — the result of what's gone before. We all are, but we all have the power to change.

Pākehā don't understand these things because they, Pākehā, are the norm. They just go out. They wear a hoodie, who cares? But for Māori, it's relentless. It doesn't matter if you're wearing a hoodie or looking regular, if you're big or small. I was once walking down the road with smartly dressed, good-looking, clean, tidy guys, me and my boys, just walking along, giggling about something — this is in broad daylight — and there was a Pākehā couple walking towards us. They looked at us then crossed the road, as if we were threatening. We started to raise our voices, even talking as if we were gay to try and be less threatening, and it was the first time I asked myself, *Why do we have to do that?* If we walk like this, let's just walk like this, let's laugh like this.

I've been in so many situations where boys think we're going to fight them, just because we're Māori. These are daily occurrences, so common we just expect it. If you're not Māori, can you imagine what that's like?

To be honest, some of our people actually do get into fights. But programmes like 'Police Ten 7', where you just see all our people being drunk, looking ugly, getting arrested — it forms a consensus, a certain view about us, that we're all like that. Even our own people believe, 'We are Māori, that's just how we are.' When a Pākehā does something wrong, does it reflect on all Pākehā?

Being rugged and hori and smoking dope and drinking and alcoholism and drugs and beating your missus up — these things do not have a colour.

If my people are losing, I'm losing. If my people don't win, all my winning doesn't count. Who am I to win if my people are losing? Who am I to be privileged when it's denied my people?

How do we actually decolonise our minds when all we've known is colonisation? We've been born into the world as it is now; we're generations deep. We live in a system that dehumanises people, so you could say it's not just Māori who need to be decolonised. We all have to be decolonised, in a way — like, be reminded of what it is to be simply human.

* * *

The outside world tells me one thing about being Māori, but if I know anything truthful about being Māori, I know it from being on marae. Happy times, sad times, the important thing is that we're all together.

Now that I'm not a kid anymore, I know my job when I go home for tangi. There's so much to be done, I'll be in the kitchen all day, getting ready for the manuhiri.

It's all planned, everyone's put into different teams. 'You get the beast, you get the seafood, us boys will go and get that from down the back …'

If we've got to go and kill a beast, we drive up to the paddock, hop off and run around, chasing the sheep till we've cornered it, grab it by its legs, tip it upside down, drag it to the ute. Then we put it on the back of the ute upside down with its head hanging over the back, and slice its neck, quick and clean. It bleeds out really quick, and then we take it back to be butchered.

All the men and the boys will be sitting there near where the hole for the hāngi has been dug — I might have helped dig that with my cousins. The men all have turns at cutting the meat up, and the boys sit there learning our traditions. The uncles all having a puff on their ciggies.

If you're in the seafood team, you all go down the back, down near where my nan used to live in her bach. Kids and adults. Everything's done with kids and adults, because the kids go along with their parents or their aunties and uncles, whatever, so they're learning, just like I did. Girls and boys, there's no difference. We get pipis, mussels, pāua, kina and all the good stuff.

Inside the kitchen, you got all the cooks doing the big cook-up, seafood, pots of everything. You have your head cook, who's the big boss of the kitchen, and they'll delegate. Everybody chips in. And there'll always be somebody eating and having a cup of tea while they're shelling. Tītīko are these tiny shellfish; you cook them in the pot, stick your needle inside the shell spiral and pull out a little snail thing. Get it out. Eat that. One for me, one for everybody.

Everybody's in the kitchen, men and women. You're laughing and talking. That's where you learn. That's where you learn your people skills, in the kitchen. It's where you get your connections.

Of course, any funeral is sad, but ours are so beautiful as well. There's just this constant busyness for three days. And then the last night before the funeral is the pō whakamutunga, the last goodbye, the last time we have with the tūpāpaku, the body. And that's when we celebrate. That's when we tell stories. We sing songs. We say speeches. We perform haka.

We do whatever we want to do to say our final goodbye to this person. And then, just before sunrise, the lid goes on and the body is ready to come outside.

I couldn't even count how many funerals I've been to in my life. I've been to funerals every single year, nearly always more than one a year. But no matter who it is, I end up in the kitchen. It's a natural thing for Māori who are brought up on the marae.

* * *

I love seeing photos of my tūpuna who carried moko. My great-great-grandmother Ngapera Black (Paraki) of Rūātoki appears in the late historian Michael King's book *Moko*, one of a group of three lovely old kuia photographed in 1970 by Marti Friedlander. Ngapera was aged eighty-seven at the time. One of the reasons they produced that book then was because traditional moko was passing out of Māori life. Most of the women photographed in that book had received their moko near the end of the nineteenth century. The traditional tattooists, the tohunga tā moko, were dying and not being replaced.

So by the time I came along, we didn't see much of it. Only on very old people.

But now there's a change. We're seeing it everywhere. To me, tā moko is the very opposite of the shame that's beaten us down for generations.

In regards to tā moko, for a long time even our people got captured by a colonised state of mind. Within the colonial belief systems of individualism and meritocracy, we began to believe that one had to earn the right to get a moko — had to be old, had to speak te reo, had to be extraordinary. That this person, through their own efforts, had earned the right. No. We don't have to earn the right. Tā moko is our blood right. We inherit that right through our blood, just by being who we are. It is our inheritance, ours from the moment we're born.

Our tā moko are our whakapapa kōrero — they tell the story of our whānau, hapū and iwi, the story we carry and are part of. Back in the day, we didn't have a written language. This was our written language. But not just our language, this was our history, literally written on our bodies. Every groove, every shape, every koru, every flick — it all means something.

The tattoos I've got on my body are the story of me. The glove that's on my right arm was done for me in Tauranga by my uncle, Gabe Te Huia, and it shows the mangōpare, the hammerhead shark, which is my kaitiaki, and then it shows my dad's mum, my nan, and my mum's dad, my koro, and the ocean where I come from, Tauranga Moana, and my marae, Tamapahore. I love this because when I sing, holding the microphone, I carry all these things right there with me.

On my neck is the word 'Ataahua', which means beautiful, and that was to be the name of the baby I lost when I was just eighteen.

On my chest, I have one of my favourite Bible verses, Jeremiah 33:3 — 'Karanga ki ahau, a ka whakahoki kupu ahau ki a koe, ka whakakitea hoki e ahau ki a koe nga mea nunui, nga mea pakeke, he mea kihai i mohiotia e koe' ('Call to me, and I will answer you, and show you the great and mighty things, which you do not know'). *There is always more.* That's what this reminds me, and what I hold on to, that even when I go through my bad stuff and get low, there is always more. I might not be able to see it yet, but it will be shown to me.

On one leg, I've got my brothers, my sister and my mum and dad.

On my other leg, I have Psalm 121:

He waiata; he pikitanga
Ka anga atu oku kanohi ki nga maunga
no reira nei te awhina moku
No Ihowa te awhina moku
no te kaihanga o te rangi, o te whenua
(I will lift up my eyes to the hills
From whence comes my help?
My help comes from the Lord
Who made heaven and earth)

My family has sung this psalm at every funeral that we've gone to. If we've got friends or family who are sick in hospital, we go in and we sing for them. We sing this, and other worship songs, to soothe their soul so they can be taken away from their pain for that time. We soothe them as they are dying or we help them to heal. Mum and Pāpā brought us up to do this; it's a good thing they have instilled in us.

For me, Psalm 121 is the song of peace. It probably means more to me than 'Whakaaria Mai' and 'Mā Te Mārie'. These songs all have the same strength and spirit, but Psalm 121 is our whānau waiata to bring peace to people. It is very much a part of my upbringing, my DNA, and now it's literally a part of me.

For me, my tattoos are the manifestation of who I am. I am a son, a grandson, I belong to the whenua. I am a man of God. I am Māori.

Our culture — man, I'm in love with it. I don't presume to know everything, and I'll always be on the path of learning. But being Māori makes me so happy and that's what I want to share with the world. My take on being Māori.

CHAPTER THIRTEEN

You shine so bright

Tryna be the best that we can be
There's more to us than what we can see
If faith is believing, it's knowing and it's seeing
That love will bring the healing to you and me
Break these chains, make a stand, walk together
hand in hand
When the sun rises tomorrow it's a new day again

— 'New Light'

FIFTEENTH OF MARCH 2019. TWO MOSQUES IN Christchurch were attacked by a hate-filled stranger, and many Muslim people were killed and injured.

I felt so helpless. I couldn't imagine or fathom what those people must have felt that day and in the weeks, months, years to come. As a Māori, I have been called many things, but I have never been called a terrorist, as Muslim people sometimes are. I have never seen my loved ones killed. I have always trusted that, when I pray, I am safe.

I wanted to respond in a way that would bring hope, love and healing. The best way I know how to do that is through singing. I'm more articulate in song than in talking, and I know that music is powerful. It speaks every single language.

I caught up with Vince Harder, one of my best mates and a big part of my career and life, my sanity. We wrote 'Bulletproof' together, and now, together, we wrote a new song, 'New Light'. Basically, it was my breakdown of the Bible verse that says, 'Love is the greatest thing of all.' It's very simple. Jesus did not condemn. He did not judge. He came to love. And God gave us one thing — he allowed us to have our choice. God allowed people to worship him in their own ways, and who are we to say they can't? It seemed simple to me. 'New light, praying for a new light, I'll be standing by your side … Got a long way to go, But I want you to know, You don't have to do it alone …'

Me and a lot of other artists got invited to perform at the You Are Us/Aroha Nui fundraising concert in Christchurch, raising money to help the victims of the mosque attacks. It was just one month after the shootings, and it was still very, very raw for everyone. More than 20,000 people crammed into the Christchurch Stadium, needing to get and give their love and support. I sang 'New Light', as well as 'Moemoeā' with Seth Haapu, and 'Aotearoa', and the crowd joined in and sang with me: 'No matter if you're near or far, we come from the land of God. No matter where you come from, we'll fight for your freedom.'

My songs that night said things I really wanted to say. I didn't want to do it just to do it. It was definitely emotional, and it was hard not to cry. All those people, with their hearts open, and their phones held high shining lights that looked like a flood of stars in the heavens. Yet at the end of the evening, my feeling of sadness was mixed with some kind of disgust.

We had been driven straight past the mosque that got shot up, Al Noor, without being taken in to meet the people whose mosque it was. And then there was so much being said about 'Christchurch', and this thing that had been done to Christchurch, but I kept feeling, *No, it was not an attack on Christchurch. It was the Muslim people who were attacked.* I looked around the park and I thought, where are they?

There was an after-party, and I got a bit tipsy and towards the end of the evening I knew what I had to do. I wasn't finished! I found an e-scooter and headed back through town to the mosque. Dumped the scooter right in the middle of the footpath in front of the gates. It was after midnight. There was an armed guard and I was wondering, *Am I even allowed to go in?* But a man came out from inside the mosque to greet me. I said, 'I'm so sorry. I'm a little bit intoxicated but I just wanted to come in …'

He welcomed me and invited me inside.

One of the most horrific aspects to the mass shooting was that the gunman filmed himself doing it, and the footage got spread around social media before anyone could stop it. It arrived on my Facebook newsfeed and I'd pressed play, thinking, *What's this?* I couldn't believe what I was seeing, and I'll never be able to wipe that scene from my memory.

By the time I went into it, the mosque itself had been repaired and cleaned. The people had been able to return for prayers after just one week. Now, walking through the doors of the mosque, I was filled with the thought: *This is where it happened. They were all in here. They were praying to God, and it happened right here.*

Just as they had said to the gunman, this falla was now saying to me: 'Come in, brother, come in.' And I sat in there and talked with them. *Your faith is so admirable. The fact that you will not be shaken.* By then it was about 2 a.m., and they were about to go pray and they asked if I wanted to come. What would Jesus do? So I went with them, even though I didn't know how to do the moves. And I just prayed my own prayers: *Thank you, Jesus. God is love. I want to be the example of love.* God is not judgmental. It's humans who are judgmental.

After our prayers, they were like, 'Brother, are you hungry? Do you want a drink?' And I sat with them till 7 a.m. I asked, 'What can we do for you?' They said, 'The fact that you are here supporting us, it's everything to us. We appreciate the concert, but the fact that you are here is what we care about.'

They asked how I got there, and I pointed outside and said, 'See that scooter right there in the middle of the gates …' They insisted that they would take me back to the hotel. They were so generous and welcoming to me, even in their grief. There are a lot of Christians I know who wouldn't have done that. We need to be better. We need to be the example of love. *Trying to be the best we can be, If faith is believing, it's knowing and it's seeing, That love will bring the healing …*

If love is the answer then our words ain't enough.

The month after that, I released my EP *Faith Hope Love*. It had four tracks: 'New Light', 'Moemoeā', 'Aotearoa' and my cover of the Kanye West song 'Ultralight Beam'. It was my ultimate response to the shootings, dedicated to the victims, and proceeds from sales went to Muslim families affected by this event.

* * *

Around that same time, I got together for a songwriting session with Matiu Walters from the band Six60, one of the bands that had made me realise New Zealand was an exciting place to do music. I knew Matiu already. He's a deep falla and so talented, one of the best songwriters, and I think my manager suggested we get together. So we went in to Neil

Finn's Roundhead Studios on Newton Road, Auckland, and sat on the couches in the bottom room, just jamming ideas. We were both feeling so thankful for what we had. This was very soon after the mosque attacks, and we were grateful we had our lives when so many had lost theirs so violently. Thankful for who we came from. We're just talking and talking, and the project went in that direction of being thankful.

We ended up writing 'Give', a song of hope, especially for me. In it, I'm talking to the people, my tūpuna, my kaumātua: 'Would've never ever made it this far without ya, Would've never made it through the night, But you shine so bright …' Acknowledging that I stand on their shoulders. On the shoulders of giants. Their love, their wairua, their faith, their example.

Making the video for that song was such a moving day for me. I brought us all together for it. I got my family: my mum, my dad, my brothers, my sis. I got my Aunty Leonie and Uncle Stan. I got my nephews and nieces. We held photos of the ones who had passed — the old people, but the young ones, too. My cousin who committed suicide, her photo held in love by my aunty and uncle, still a part of us.

'How you ever gonna change the world, if you can't change yourself?' There's my dad, wrapped in a korowai. A monster who changed into a gentle giant. How was that even possible? There's my mum, strong and loving.

There's me, once beaten and rejected, a stuffed-up kid with dreams but no hope. Look at me now — how happy I am, filled with love, not hate. How was that possible?

Living portraits. You take the photos, but it's what happens in between that's the real truth. It reminds me of the photos

I talked about at the beginning of this book — the photos of the rages, the happy nights drinking and singing, that never showed the beatings at the end of the night. The photos that told only half the truth. We've got a beautiful version of that now — something we can treasure forever, to remind us of how far we've come. We're calm now, tight, happy, so many good laughs.

My dad is the star of the 'Give' video, I think, because it is so unlikely that he's there at all. His healing has allowed us all to heal as a family.

He has gone from being my tormenter to being my protector. Of all the people in my family, he's the one who just knows when things aren't right for me. The times I've been suicidal, depressed, panicked, at the end of my tether, he just knows. He rings me up, 'Son? What's happening?'

I usually say, 'Nothing.'

'God woke me up at three in the morning. I had to wake up and start praying for you ...' And I'm sitting there with tears in my eyes, because he usually mentions the exact time I was feeling most in despair. Now, when I stuff up and my mum is angry with me, he's just concerned for me: 'Are you all right, son? Don't worry, son, we'll get through this.' Sometimes he'll say, 'You're the man, son. You're such a good son.'

How do I connect that man now, to how he was back then?

To me, this change in my dad and in all of us, is the grace of God. It's beyond understanding.

With Pāpā now, he fathers all the fatherless men. They're attracted to him. He'll be walking down the street and he'll see a big-as falla, and be, like, 'Bro,' and they turn around thinking that he wants a fight. He goes, 'Do you play rugby?' and they're like, 'Eh?'

Before you know it, Pāpā's in a conversation with him, found out he's got no dad, or has just had a punch-up with his dad, and honestly, next minute they're calling him Pāpā and coming to live with us, literally someone he's met on the side of the street.

I want to be a father one day. I want to be a husband. My prayer, every day, is like, 'God, help me to be a good husband, to be a good father, to be loving, to be a good man, to be a man of God. Help me to be who I'm supposed to be.' I want to be kind. I want to be loving. I want my children to always know they are loved. I don't want to react out of anger.

But I've got a lot to learn. A lot to *re*-learn. Through my whole life, relationships in general have pushed me to the edge. My relationship with my father almost killed me physically and made me want to kill myself. My relationship with my mother was shadowed by rejection and became part of why I wanted to kill myself because I didn't feel loved. My relationship with the guy who abused me made me so confused about who I was that I wanted to kill myself. Even my relationship with the music industry — I've felt at times that my soul was being destroyed, and I have found that very hard to deal with.

The path I've been on, and where I started out from, it's probably not surprising that I've struggled in my relationships with women. I've been terrible at relationships — I've chosen the wrong people for me, I've gone in too hard, I've been preoccupied with my own internal battles, and I've either wasted their time or they've hurt me. I've got a mouth on me and have caused hurt with words, too — but never with fists. I will never do that.

My relationships, even though they've all ended with hurt, are part of the journey and I don't have any malice against anyone.

While my relationship with Lou was emotionally empathetic, I didn't give her the love she needed. With my next one, I was everything I learnt I should have been with Lou, but she wasn't emotionally empathetic and so I felt rejected all the time. I would cry to her, 'Help me, you don't even love me the way I need you to,' and she didn't understand or relate at all. I felt like shit but I was hooked and stuck in a cycle that in some fucked-up way I thought was love.

I started drinking in that relationship, because when I drink I'm happy and if I stay drunk I don't get emotional. I never thought I could get addicted to alcohol, but it happened. I would get wasted, even by myself. So sad! Just to deal with it, to drink and get happy, and it became a habit. Even when I was with her, I'd take sneaky little drinks from the fridge, just to get by, and that would disgust her more. I couldn't handle it. I couldn't handle the way her rejection triggered all my shit feelings. But I am responsible for my own actions. And those actions and choices, I have to live with and learn from.

But the thing I did to make myself feel better only made me feel worse in the end.

My relationship with her was a creative partnership where we could dream dreams together and share our culture, which is such a beautiful thing and probably attracted me the most. The potential to have the best life with her didn't come about. But I never want to discount the positive things.

When we are modelled in certain ways, it is our normal to look for the same things in other relationships — not consciously, but because of what seems normal and familiar. But I see that I have unconsciously chosen partners who have, in their dynamic with me, played out aspects of earlier relationships. I have been lied to and cheated on, which is a major rejection. I have been verbally, emotionally and physically abused. I don't want to write about those things in detail, but will simply say that each relationship I have is a step along the way, and in the end helps me to learn more about how I was shaped by those earlier life experiences.

I never see it until it's too late. I hope that as I get older and learn more, I will avoid getting into toxic situations and that I will learn from my own stuff-ups.

In my childhood, it was the people I entrusted my heart to who were violent towards me. That's a hard thing to get over. Even years after those particular relationships have settled down, the patterns of emotion or psychology inside myself are still there. I can see it in my relationships: I give that person the most vulnerable part of me and when they take advantage of it I end up feeling so weak, rejected, unloved — and unfortunately in that pattern I have done that to people as well. I know that sounds crazy, when I write it down like that, but that's the way these feelings go. I know that's not what love is, but learning that is a work in progress. And that's another reason why I turn to Jesus, because that's a vision of perfect love.

'Love is patient, love is kind. It does not envy, it does not boast, it is not proud. It does not dishonour others, it is not self-seeking, it is not easily angered, it keeps no record of wrongs. Love does not delight in evil but rejoices with the truth. It always protects, always trusts, always hopes, always perseveres. Love never fails.' (1 Corinthians 13:4–8)

How have I coped with my relationship failures? Not very well. I have turned to drinking, drugs, sex, flushing money down the toilet like it's nothing, while digging myself into depression and anxiousness. I couldn't bear those feelings of being worthless and unloved and I tried to mask them with addictions.

It sounds like a sad story, but I know what's ahead of me, and I know I'll be good and happy one day. I'm so excited about that, about what's coming for me in the future. And in 2020 it happened. I found my way back to my best mate and the true love of my life, Lou Tyson. I'm wiser now, and I know more about how to love. Sometimes we have to go through the shit to get to the good place. I will never stop trying to be the best I can be for her.

* * *

For so many years I dragged around my hatred of my father. Pāpā was changing; he was on that long road, but I didn't understand. Now, he is my hero. Impossible made possible.

Even worse than my hatred of him was my hatred of myself, and those lingering feelings of self-hatred, that go-to place in my psyche, have been a factor in my relationships as well.

Nothing was going to change unless I changed. There's no magic wand. When I met Jesus, I was set on the road but, like my dad's, it was always going to be a long road. Probably it will be a life-long road. I hope so, because I always want to go on learning and changing. Sometimes, though, I get tired and wish I could just be all sorted, right now. I get sick of getting to hindsight, and wish I could be wise *before* I make mistakes.

Change takes years. It's not a straight road — like, it doesn't move smoothly forward, little by little. It's more like circles. To forgive others means I have to be open and empathetic to others; but being open-hearted means being open to the possibility of hurt and pain.

I still have my trust issues, a feeling that I need to guard myself. I guard my heart to protect my heart; I guard my heart out of old habits. I wonder about whether my trust issues contradict the forgiveness that I want to find in my heart. So that's what I mean when I say: the journey is long and the road is not straight.

I just try to have compassion, empathy and understanding — for other people, and for myself. I try; sometimes I fail. I ain't Jesus. I'm only human.

One thing I never say is: 'I'll forgive but I'll never forget.' That to me is bitter. It's like you're pretending to forgive but you're actually not. *Love keeps no record of wrongs.* So I forgive completely, and then something else happens, a new situation, and I have to battle within myself again, but maybe it's a little bit easier this time.

Forgiveness is the thing that has turned my life away from ugly. Forgiveness is my superpower.

* * *

Pāpā still gets emotional sometimes, and at random times he'll say, 'I'm sorry for ever being like that to you.' He will cry. He holds all that guilt. I don't have to live with beating my wife, I don't have to live with beating my children and being the monster in their lives. He has to live with that and there are times it haunts him. 'I'm sorry for ever doing that to you, my baby. Sorry for not being there for you.' He lives with not having protected me from getting sexually abused.

He feels all those feelings of self-disappointment. So I feel like he deserves my empathy. He fully deserves it. He's my hero, for an abused kid like he was to come out of that and to now be this amazing man.

I think back to how he used to apologise to me when he was beating me, or after he'd beaten me. I didn't trust those apologies then, because I knew it was going to happen again. And yet those apologies were real. He meant them. Those apologies were exactly the same as the apologies today. He was just fresh in it, hadn't learnt how to control himself. He used to beat people up and not feel anything about it. So for him to actually feel bad, and feel sorry and then actually come in and say sorry; now I look back and I'm like, *Yes, he meant it.*

I know what addictions are and I know what anger is. I know how hard it is to change yourself. I look at my own life and my struggle with relationships, with the industry, with my own self — it's a forever journey for me. I don't go through things easily, and everything's always hard out and intense. So I don't judge my dad's journey. And I separate the anger from the man, because the man has changed.

Never forget that the person who deserves the most blame also, maybe, deserves the most compassion.

* * *

I'm so proud of our family. My oldest brother Mike has started his own furniture company, making tables, chairs, everything out of pallets — recyclable, reusable. Russ is a professional singer and musician. He's so talented, and plays guitar, bass, drums. My little brother Noah is an assistant youth pastor, travelling the world as a vocalist in one of the biggest church music groups in Australia, Planetshakers, singing to thousands. They are all building amazing families, and they are all committed Christians. My little sister Mary-Grace finished school, the first of our whānau to do that ever. She's just eighteen so she's still finding her way. She is my best friend and the most loyal person I know. I am so proud of our baby.

My mother is a central part of my business. My father continues to work hard — he drives massive diggers at an industrial dump. He is the youngest-at-heart person I know. Now, he smothers me. He's like, 'Come here, my baby. Give me a kiss,' and I'm like, 'Yes, yes, that's enough.' He's the proudest dad, and there's so much love he can be sitting there and start crying, just from looking at us.

All credit to my mother and father. I remember once, when I was angry, yelling at them that they had taught me nothing. Now all I see coming from them is support.

In our family, we do everything hard. We play hard, we fight hard, we love hard. There's no in-between for us. Even though we would like to be calm and collected and just normal, that's not us. We're intense. When we fight, we fight to the death; when we love, we love to the death. When we forgive, we forgive forever.

* * *

Dark thoughts and feelings still randomly come to me, especially when I'm tired. If I'm not protecting myself, or watching myself properly, being onto it, then I'm opening myself up for those thoughts to come and play havoc in my mind and spirit: *Yo, you remember when this happened?* It could be sexual abuse, it could be a fight I had with someone, it could be me holding things against people. *Is this who you really are?* It could be my old self-hatred. *Ugh, you're never going to get there.*

And now I ask myself: how do I deal with the things in my life that feel like failures? How do I deal with memories that still revolt me? And my answer is: they're not going away. My past hasn't gone away. The past doesn't just vanish, no matter what you put on top of it. But here in the present I have a choice about how I deal with memories and feelings that still sometimes seem to come out of nowhere.

My youth pastor Sam goes, 'Bro, it's a daily choice that you have to make.' Every single day, I have to make choices — daily decisions that I'm not my past, I'm not who people said I was, I'm not what I believed myself to be. I have to make daily choices about who I am, what I'm going to do, what I need to do.

At the end of the day, even when your choice is taken away, you still have a choice. You have a choice to decide how you're going to feel, and how you're going to react, and how you're going to do whatever it is. Even with the worst things, I have a choice to put myself in the pit or bring myself out. I always try to take the high road; sometimes I fail because it's hard. *I'm dark. Don't come near me.* I wish I was one of those who it comes easy to.

I'm dramatic. I experience everything intensely. *Just relax, bro. Relax.* When the past haunts me I pray: *God, help me. Rescue me from my thoughts.*

In the time when I was drinking a lot, my friends and family were so shocked. *Man, you never used to drink like this* … And no one even knew how much, because I used different groups of friends at different times. Drunk mostly every day. Me and my mate, we got names for every day: Mad Mondays, Tragic Tuesdays, Wet Wednesdays, Thirsty Thursdays, Fry-yay, Sloppy Saturday, Sunday Sesh. I know those days like the back of my hand. I couldn't go on like that. It was ruining my body. I could feel I was starting to crack and get worn down. I had to ask myself: who am I? I had to somehow rise out of the ashes and be Stan again. I made my first choices not to drink, at least not every day. Get conscious of *not* drinking, rather than thinking, *When's the next drink?* Get back to focusing on my future, on my purpose, on my plans.

I don't want to be half-pie and I don't want to be drunk. I want to see what I can do if I'm conscious in every way — mentally, physically, spiritually. I want to be amazing.

On my side is the fact that I have the DNA of warriors in my blood: my mum who was always a fighter, who fought for her children like a lioness; all the chiefs who I come from, how they went to war for their land and their people. All the blood that flows in my veins is their legacy, and it gives me my strength and my attitude. When the dark thoughts come, I draw power from knowing who and what I come from.

I know I have my mental health issues, and old hurts that are not easy to overcome. But I keep trying, every day. Change takes time. Step by step by step.

And I'm overcoming. I'm overcoming these things. I am the impossible made possible; I am the example that proves change is possible. I can't change what happened in the past, but I am who I am today because of all that I have been through. I wouldn't have chosen the things in my past, but it's all part of my story.

People say things to me like, 'Oh, you're so brave and courageous.' I don't think that about myself, because I know the truth. But the only time I do think I was brave and courageous was when I first started talking about being sexually abused. I was so scared and afraid. It was the hardest thing ever, to speak those words out loud. But doing that has led me to the place I am now, where I feel actual compassion for myself, and understanding. Speaking those words put me on the path to not hating myself.

In 2017, I became an ambassador for Youthline/Coca-Cola's Good2Great programme. I get to travel around New Zealand talking to young Kiwis from all walks of life and different backgrounds, and help them to be the best version of themselves. I share my story, and it's really important these young kids know that even though I came from bad beginnings, and had all these things happen to me, they didn't last forever. The things I hated about myself are now the things that make me stand out. Those things have made me who I am today.

When I talk to young people, I tell them my story because I hope when they hear it and see what I've been through, they will start to believe that they, too, can be whatever they want be.

That's a big part of why I decided to tell my story in this book. To share my story, to say those words, to show that change is possible. Truth, love, forgiveness — these things break us out of jail.

Your past does not define your future.

How you ever gonna change the world, if you can't change yourself?

* * *

I've got a lot of scars on my body. Some of them, if you touch them a certain way, there's this pain even through the scar tissue, and a sting that comes from underneath. My arm that was broken in one of my dad's rages was never set properly and it's the same — I can still find a sore spot. But physical scars mean nothing to me. One scar inside is worse than any on my body. They're the ones that really damaged me and created a jail inside of me. My get-out-of-jail was letting go of secrets that were rotting me and ruining me, and forgiveness. Especially forgiveness.

I'm exposing my whole self in this book, and sometimes I think, *Faar, what will people think?* But this is my testimony. There will be some stuff that people won't get — maybe especially my belief in Jesus. But I'm just sharing my own experience, and I've been as honest as I can be. I hate seeing people in bondage and living in secrets and lies, like they don't know who they are. They're scared to *be*.

I feel like I've lived a part of my life in fear of being embarrassed, and being beaten down for being a weirdo, for there being something wrong with me. And now I'm all good with the way I am. I don't condemn myself no more — only for stupid decisions that I make these days. I want to encourage people: if you are a weirdo, just be a weirdo. There's no point trying to be different to what you are. I just hope that whoever reads this book will feel like they can do anything, be anybody, and that they can learn to love more, forgive more. Love themselves more.

At the beginning of this story, I was a stuffed-up little kid, beaten, abused, rejected. I was bruised but I had my dream, even though any dream back then was impossible.

Now, I've had a decade of incredible highs and done things I could barely even imagine when I was a kid, even with my big imagination. My career is already a long career. I'm in it for the long haul. I've travelled the world, I've sung in places I only dreamed of, I've grown heaps as a person, learned about life and different cultures and different beliefs.

I am proud of who I am and how far I've come. I am proud of my whānau, who have come on that long road with me. So many stories of childhood trauma end with separation, with escape. Not us. Our story is more extraordinary than that. We are closer than ever. We are the impossible made possible.

As I reach the end of this first chapter of my life, I am wrapped in the korowai of my tūpuna. I am adorned with the taonga of my people. My feet are solid on this whenua and my spirit sings because I'm home. I have my foundation. I'm ready for the next chapter.

GLOSSARY OF MĀORI TERMS

Aotearoa the Māori name for New Zealand
āpotoro apostle
ātaahua beautiful

haere mai welcome; hello
haka ceremonial dance or challenge
hākari communal feast
hāngi a traditional earth oven, and the food from it
hapū a group of related families
harirū part of the greeting process, coming from the
    English 'how d'y'do?'; colloquially pluralised to harirūs
hīkoi a communal walk or march
hīmene hymn
hīnaki eel pot

iwi the largest political grouping, comprising a number of
    hapū

kai to eat or drink; food
kaikaranga the woman who makes the ceremonial call to
    visitors on a marae
kaimoana food from the sea

kaitiaki guardian, usually of an environmental resource

kapa haka Māori performing arts

kaputī cup of tea

karanga a ritual call of welcome

kaumātua elderly

kaupapa policy; purpose

kōhanga reo literally, 'language nest'; an early childhood
  education system that promotes Māori language,
  knowledge and culture

koko the most important thing; a term of endearment for a
  special person

kōrero to speak; a conversation

koro/koroua an elderly man, especially a relative;
  colloquially pluralised to koros

korowai a traditional woven Māori cloak

kotahitanga unity

kuia an elderly woman; colloquially pluralised to kuias

kuia mau moko kuia who wear the traditional moko kauae
  — chin tattoo

mākutu a curse, sorcery, spiritual powers

mamae to be sad, in pain

mana whenua people who have a special right to manage a
  particular area of land

manuhiri guests

marae the home base of an iwi or hapū, comprising a
  complex of buildings and fenced grounds

moemoeā a dream, a vision

moko traditional tattoo, especially on the face

moko kauae chin tattoo

mokopuna grandchildren; colloquially abbreviated to
mokos

ngā mōrehu the survivors

pā historic Māori village or defensive settlement
paepae the bench on which orators sit at the front of the
wharenui
Pākehā New Zealander of European origin
pō whakamutunga the last night of a tangi; the final
goodbye
pōwhiri traditional welcoming ceremony

Rātana a Māori religious and political movement
reo language; specifically, the Māori language
rohe the territory of an iwi

tāhuna seaside, beach, sandy shore
taiaha a long-handled wooden weapon
tā moko traditional tattoo; also the practice of applying it
tangata whenua people of the land; indigenous people of
Aotearoa
tangi, short for **tangihanga** the communal ceremony for
mourning someone who has died
tau still, peaceful
te reo Māori the Māori language; sometimes abbreviated to
te reo
tikanga custom, correct procedure
tohunga tā moko traditional tattooists
tūpāpaku deceased person's body

tupuna ancestor, pluralised to tūpuna

tūrangawaewae place to stand, one's foundation in the
    world

urupā cemetery

whakamā shame, sadness

whakapapa genealogy, ancestry, bloodlines

whānau family group or extended family; also a common
    term for a number of people

whanaungatanga kinship, sense of family connection

whāngai customary practice in which a child is raised by
    someone other than his or her birth parents, though they
    are often part of the whānau

wharekai dining hall

wharenui the meeting house

whenua land

HELPLINES

Australia

Lifeline 13 11 14
Kids Helpline 1800 551 800
MensLine Australia 1300 789 978
Suicide Call Back Service 1300 659 467
Beyond Blue 1300 224 636
Headspace 1800 650 890
ReachOut au.reachout.com
You Can, Sony Foundation Australia sonyfoundation.org/
  what-we-do/you-can

New Zealand

Lifeline 0800 543 354 (0800 LIFELINE)
Suicide Crisis Helpline 0508 828 865 (0508 TAUTOKO)
Depression and Anxiety Helpline 0800 111 757
Kidsline 0800 54 37 54 (0800 KIDSLINE)
MusicHelps Wellbeing Service 0508 MUSICHELPS
Are You OK (family violence helpline) 0800 456 450
Rape Crisis 0800 883 300

ACKNOWLEDGMENTS

I would love to thank all who have been a part of my story. Every single one of you have played a part in my life, small or big. Nonetheless I am who I am because of all of you. A special thank you to my Māmā and Pāpā, my siblings and my best mates. All of my whānau and friends, I love you all.

Thank you to my Stan Walker team. My manager David Champion, my Grace Promoters whānau, my band, my Sony Music family, Denis, Kim, Taryn, Lizzie, Gareth, Jaden, Petrina, Mo, Olly and Shelley, Maree at Sony ATV, you are all incredible.

Thank you to HarperCollins for allowing me to share my story with the world. Margie Thomson for listening and interpreting my story while letting my voice shine through. My friend Jessica McMillan for helping me edit the book. My aunty Ria Hall for making sure our reo Māori is presented correctly and honoured.

To all my fans, I'm grateful to have you all. Thank you for your support and aroha throughout the years. The best is yet to come.

Thank you Jesus for an incredible journey thus far. Thank you for my life. Thank you for my gift. Thank you for all my blessings. Thank you for carrying me through it all. Thank you for what is to come.

Last but not least, thank you to the love of my life, Louise Maisie Tyson, soon to be Mrs Walker.

I hope this book has helped anyone and everyone that needs it. We all have a story. Just know that you are all important, loved and are born to have purpose in this world. If I have it, then so do you. Live passionately, love more, dream outrageously, forgive more.

Ngā mihi aroha kia koutou katoa.

CREDITS

'Aotearoa'

Words and music by Stan Walker, Vince Harder and Troy Kingi

Copyright © Native Tongue Music Publishing Ltd, EMI Music Publishing

Australia Pty Ltd and Vince Harder

Print rights for Native Tongue Music Publishing Ltd administered

in Australia and New Zealand by Hal Leonard Australia Pty Ltd

ABN 13 085 333 713

www.halleonard.com.au

International copyright secured. Used by permission. All rights reserved.

Unauthorised reproduction is illegal.

'Black Box'

Words and music by Jonas Jeberg, Wayne Hector, Lucas Secon And
Mich Hansen

Copyright © 2009 Cutfather Publishing Limited (PRS), BMG Bumblebee,

BMG Rights Management (UK) Limited [and Co-Publisher]

All rights on behalf of Cutfather Publishing Limited administered by

Warner-Tamerlane Publishing Corp

All rights for BMG Bumblebee and BMG Rights Management (UK)

administered by BMG Rights Management (US) LLC

Reprinted by permission of Hal Leonard LLC

All rights reserved. Used by permission.

Stan Walker

'He Kākano Āhua'
Written by Dr Hohepa Tamehana
Used by permission

'Find You'
Written by Stan Walker and Inoke Finau
Publishing by EMI Music Publishing Australia Pty Ltd
International copyright secured. All rights reserved. Used by permission.

'Missing You'
Written by Stan Walker
Publishing by EMI Music Publishing Australia Pty Ltd
International copyright secured. All rights reserved. Used by permission.

'I Surrender'
Written by Stan Walker
Publishing by EMI Music Publishing Australia Pty Ltd
International copyright secured. All rights reserved. Used by permission.

'Inside Out'
Written by Stan Walker, Audius Mtawarira and Leon Seenandan
Publishing by Sony/ATV Music Publishing (Australia) Pty Ltd/EMI Music
Publishing Australia Pty Ltd
International copyright secured. All rights reserved. Used by permission.

'Take it Easy'
Written by Stan Walker, Antonio Egizii and David Musumeci
Publishing by EMI Music Publishing Australia Pty Ltd
International copyright secured. All rights reserved. Used by permission.

Credits

'Bulletproof'

Written by Stan Walker, Lindsay Rimes and Vince Harder

Publishing by EMI Music Publishing Australia Pty Ltd

International copyright secured. All rights reserved. Used by permission.

'Inventing Myself'

Words and music by Andrew Macken and Thomas William Macken

Copyright © Native Tongue Music Publishing Ltd

Print rights for Native Tongue Music Publishing Ltd administered

in Australia and New Zealand by Hal Leonard Australia Pty Ltd

ABN 13 085 333 713

www.halleonard.com.au

Used by permission. All rights reserved. Unauthorised reproduction is Illegal.

'New Takeover'

Words and music by Stan Walker, Sidney Swift, Alexander Goodwin

and Michael McGregor

Copyright © 2017 EMI Music Publishing Australia Pty Ltd, Songs of

Swift Songs, Alexander Goodwin and Universal Music Publishing Pty Ltd

All rights for Songs Of Swift Songs administered worldwide by

Songs Of Kobalt Music Publishing

International copyright secured. All rights reserved. Used by permission.

Reprinted by permission of Hal Leonard LLC

'Thank You'

Written by Stan Walker, Michael Fatkin and Vince Harder

Copyright © EMI Music Publishing Australia Pty Ltd, Universal Music

Publishing Pty Ltd and Vince Harder

International copyright secured. All rights reserved. Used by permission.

Stan Walker